Voices
of the Renaissance
and Reformation

Edited by Robert G. Shearer, MA

Greenleaf Press
Lebanon, Tennessee

To my children

who have been patient with baba, lo these many years

Internet: www.greenleafpress.com
3761 Highway 109N, Unit D
Lebanon, Tennessee 37087
615-449-1617

GReenLeaf
P·R·E·S·S

Table of Contents

Author's Preface 1

Petrarch
Autobiography 3

Selected sonnets 12

Lorenzo Valla
On the Forgery of the Alleged Donation of Constantine 13

Lorenzo de' Medici
Letter to his son, Giovanni... 15

Savonarola
Excerpts from the Sermons of Advent 1493 and Lent 1494.. 19

Leonardo da Vinci
Excerpts from his notebooks 23

Michelangelo
Selected Poems 27

Machiavelli
Selections from the Prince 29

Erasmus
Preface to Sir Thomas More, from In Praise of Folly 31

John Wyclif

The Condemned Conclusions of John Wycliffe.................... 33

Reply of John Wycliffe to his Summons by the Pope to come to Rome, (1384) 34

Jan Hus

Final Declaration, July 1, 1415 37

Martin Luther

Luther's Account of the Reformation (written in 1545)
(from his Preface to the Complete Edition of Luther's Latin Works) 39

The 95 Theses (1517)............................ 49

Address to the Christian Nobility
of the German Nation (Aug 1520) 57

On the Babylonian Captivity of the Church (Oct 1520)......... 73

On the Freedom of a Christian (Nov 1520)............. 93

Preface to the Book of Romans (1522) 105

Ulrich Zwingli

The 67 Articles (1523)..........................117

Conrad Grebel

Letters to Thomas Müntzer (1524) 123

Michael Sattler

The Schleitheim Confession (1527)....................133

The Trial of Michael Sattler (1527)
(from The Martyr's Mirror) 137

A Letter Written by Michael Sattler, in Prison,
to the Church of God at Horb (1527) 141

William Tyndale

Excerpts from An Answer Unto
Sir Thomas More's Dialogue (1531) 145

Henry VIII (Thomas Cromwell)

Act in Restraint of Appeals (1533) 153
The Act of Supremacy (1534)...........................158

Thomas More

Last Letter to his daughter Margaret (1535) 159

John Calvin

Calvin's Account of his own life and conversion (written in 1557)
(from the preface to his Commentary on the Psalms) 161

The Geneva Confession (1536) 168

Reply to Cardinal Sadoleto (1539) 170

John Knox

The History of the Reformation of Scotland 183

Image Sources 188

Editor's Preface

I have long been frustrated with the available collections of primary source documents for the Renaissance and Reformation. Too often, the two movements have been seen as antithetical and studied separately. But in reading Valla's textual criticism of the Donation of Constantine and Tyndale's **Reply to Thomas More**, I was struck by how similar their methods were – and by their shared passion to seek out the truth by understanding the past on its own terms.

And so it should be for us. A short biography helps us to understand the significance of a historical figure, but if you really want to know them, you must read what they wrote. The best encounter would be to read the original text in the language it was composed in. For most of us, this is simply not practical. The texts of the period are in Latin, Italian, German, & French. Happily, for most purposes, there are good English translations. Perhaps a few of the students who read these passages in English will be intrigued enough to seek to understand them in their original language as well.

Many of the selections here are well-known and have long been part of the canon of assigned readings. But there are a few new additions here which are not typically found in other collections.

Not many will have read any of the sermons of Savonarola, but they communicate the passion of the Dominican orator in a striking fashion. One must imagine them being delivered in the cathedral of Florence in order to fully appreciate them.

Likewise, I have long been of the conviction that William Tyndale has been unjustly overlooked in the history of the English Reformation. I am very pleased to be able to include in this collection his own spirited defense of his translation work – which also shows how deeply he has read and been influenced by Martin Luther. Similar convictions led me to include readings by Michael Sattler and Conrad Grebel that are often (unjustly) overlooked.

Above all, these texts illustrate the historical truth that human nature has changed little, if at all, over the centuries. Thus, history remains, as Thucydides observed, "moral philosophy, teaching by examples."

- Rob Shearer
  April, 2009

From a copy by Mrs. Arthur Lemon of a portrait in the Laurentian Library, Florence

Petrarch

To Posterity

From James Harvey Robinson, ed. and trans. **Petrarch: The First Modern Scholar and Man of Letters** (New York: G.P. Putnam, 1898)

Greeting.---It is possible that some word of me may have come to you, though even this is doubtful, since an insignificant and obscure name will scarcely penetrate far in either time or space. If, however, you should have heard of me, you may desire to know what manner of man I was, or what was the outcome of my labors, especially those of which some description or, at any rate, the bare titles may have reached you.

To begin with myself, then, the utterances of men concerning me will differ widely, since in passing judgment almost everyone is influenced not so much by truth as by preference, and good and evil report alike know no bounds. I was, in truth, a poor mortal like yourself, neither very exalted in my origin, nor, on the other hand, of the most humble birth, but belonging, as Augustus Caesar says of himself, to an ancient family. As to my disposition, I was not naturally perverse or wanting in modesty, however the contagion of evil associations may have corrupted me. My youth was gone before I realized it; I was carried away by the strength of manhood; but a riper age brought me to my senses and taught me by experience the truth I had long before read in books, that youth and pleasure are vanity---nay, that the Author of all ages and times permits us miserable mortals, puffed up with emptiness, thus to wander about, until finally, coming to a tardy consciousness of our sins, we shall learn to know ourselves. In my prime I was blessed with a quick and active body, although not exceptionally strong; and while I do not lay claim to remarkable personal beauty, I was comely enough in my best days[1]. I was possessed of a clear complexion, between light and dark, lively eyes, and for long years a keen vision, which however deserted me, contrary to my hopes, after I reached my sixtieth birthday, and forced me, to my great annoyance, to resort to glasses.[2] Although I had previously enjoyed perfect health, old age brought with it the usual array of discomforts.

---

[1] None of the portraits of Petrarch, not even the well-known one in a codex of the Laurentian library, are authentic, unless it be the one reproduced at the beginning of this volume.

[2] Eye-glasses were a somewhat new invention when Petrarch resorted to them. Poggendorf cites the first reference to them (1299), which reads as follows: "I found myself so oppressed by age that without the so-called eye-glasses, which have recently been discovered as a godsend to poor old persons, I could neither read nor write." We know little of the construction of these first spectacles. An early German painting (15th century), in the National Gallery at London, shows a saint with a completely developed *pince-nez.*

My parents were honorable folk, Florentine in their origin, of medium fortune, or, I may as well admit it, in a condition verging upon poverty. They had been expelled from their native city,[3] and consequently I was born in exile, at Arezzo, in the year 1304 of this latter age which begins with Christ's birth, July the twentieth, on a Monday, at dawn. I have always possessed an extreme contempt for wealth; not that riches are not desirable in themselves, but because I hate the anxiety and care which are invariably associated with them. I certainly do not long to be able to give gorgeous banquets. I have, on the contrary, led a happier existence with plain living and ordinary fare than all the followers of Apicius, with their elaborate dainties. So-called *convivia,* which are but vulgar bouts, sinning against sobriety and good manners, have always been repugnant to me. I have ever felt that it was irksome and profitless to invite others to such affairs, and not less so to be bidden to them myself. On the other hand, the pleasure of dining with one's friends is so great that nothing has ever given me more delight than their unexpected arrival, nor have I ever willingly sat down to table without a companion. Nothing displeases me more than display, for not only is it bad in itself, and opposed to humility, but it is troublesome and distracting.

I struggled in my younger days with a keen but constant and pure attachment, and would have struggled with it longer had not the sinking flame been extinguished by death - premature and bitter, but salutary.[4] I should be glad to be able to say that I had always been entirely free from irregular desires, but I should lie if I did so. I can, however, conscientiously claim that, although I may have been carried away by the fire of youth or by my ardent temperament, I have always abhorred such sins from the depths of my soul. As I approached the age of forty, while my powers were unimpaired and my passions were still strong, I not only abruptly threw off my bad habits, but even the very recollection of them, as if I had never looked upon a woman. This I mention as among the greatest of my blessings, and I render thanks to God, who freed me, while still sound and vigorous, from a disgusting slavery which had always been hateful to me.[5]

---

[3] Petrarch's father and Dante were banished forever from Florence upon the same day, January 27, 1302.

[4] This is doubtless one of the two or three obscure references to Laura, in Petrarch's correspondences. His frigid statement of the case is characteristic of Petrarch the Humanist as contrasted with Petrarch the singer. Compare the fervor of the sonnets with the original of this passage:---Amore acerrimo, sed unico et honesto, in adolescentia laboravi, et diutius laborassem, nisi iam tepescentem ignem mors acerba, sed utilis, extinxisset.

[5] Petrarch, although a churchman, was the father of two illegitimate children, a son, Giovanni, born in 1337, and a daughter, Francesca, born, probably of the same mother, some six years later. The unfortunate mother was, according to Petrarch's own story, very harshly treated by him. The obscure *liaison* seems not to have afflicted him with the remorse which his purer attachment for Laura caused him. Only the latter is spoken of, and that at great length, in his imaginary confession to St. Augustine. The son proved an idle fellow who caused his father a world of trouble, even entering into collusion with a band of thievish servants to rob him. The plague cut short his unpromising career in his twenty-fourth

But let us turn to other matters. I have taken pride in others, never in myself, and however insignificant I may have been, I have always been still less important in my own judgment. My anger has very often injured myself, but never others. I have always been most desirous of honorable friendships, and have faithfully cherished them. I make this boast without fear, since I am confident that I speak truly. While I am very prone to take offence, I am equally quick to forget injuries, and have a memory tenacious of benefits. In my familiar associations with kings and princes, and in my friendship with noble personages, my good fortune has been such as to excite envy. But it is the cruel fate of those who are growing old that they can commonly only weep for friends who have passed away. The greatest kings of this age have loved and courted me. They may know why; I certainly do not. With some of them I was on such terms that they seemed in a certain sense my guests rather than I theirs; their lofty position in no way embarrassing me, but, on the contrary, bringing with it many advantages. I fled, however, from many of those to whom I was greatly attached; and such was my innate longing for liberty, that I studiously avoided those whose very name seemed incompatible with the freedom that I loved.

I possessed a well-balanced rather than a keen intellect, one prone to all kinds of good and wholesome study, but especially inclined to moral philosophy and the art of poetry. The latter, indeed, I neglected as time went on, and took delight in sacred literature. Finding in that a hidden sweetness which I had once esteemed but lightly, I came to regard the works of the poets as only amenities. Among the many subjects which interested me, I dwelt especially upon antiquity, for our own age has always repelled me, so that, had it not been for the love of those dear to me, I should have preferred to have been born in any other period than our own. In order to forget my own time, I have constantly striven to place myself in spirit in other ages, and consequently I delighted in history; not that the conflicting statements did not offend me, but when in doubt I accepted what appeared to me most probable, or yielded to the authority of the writer.

My style, as many claimed, was clear and forcible; but to me it seemed weak and obscure. In ordinary conversation with friends, or with those about me, I never gave any thought to my language, and I have always wondered that Augustus Caesar should have taken such pains in this respect. When, however, the subject itself, or the place or listener, seemed to demand it, I

---

year. Petrarch noted in his copy of Virgil, which he used as a family record: "Our Giovanni was born to be a trial and burden to me. While alive he tormented me with perpetual anxiety, and his death has wounded me deeply." The daughter was of a happier disposition. She married, and Petrarch rejoiced in two grandchildren. One of these, the little Francesco, was, when but a year old, a "perfect picture" of his illustrious grandfather, but the great hopes for the child's future were cut short by its early death. Petrarch comforts himself with the thought that the child "has gained eternal happiness with effort, and his departure has freed me from a continual source of solitude.

gave some attention to style, with what success I cannot pretend to say; let them judge in whose presence I spoke. If only I have lived well, it matters little to me how I talked. Mere elegance of language can produce at best but an empty renown.

My life up to the present has, either through fate or my own choice, fallen into the following divisions. A part only of my first year was spent at Arezzo, where I first saw the light. The six following years were, owing to the recall of my mother from exile, spent upon my father's estate at Ancisa, about fourteen miles above Florence. I passed my eighth year at Pisa[6], the ninth and following years in Farther Gaul, at Avignon, on the left bank of the Rhone, where the Roman Pontiff holds and has long held the Church of Christ in shameful exile. It seemed a few years ago as if Urban V. was on the point of restoring the Church to its ancient seat, but it is clear that nothing is coming of this effort, and, what is to me the worst of all, the Pope seems to have repented him of his good work, for failure came while he was still living. Had he lived but a little longer, he would certainly have learned how I regarded his retreat.[7] My pen was in my hand when he abruptly surrendered at once his exalted office and his life. Unhappy man, who might have died before the altar of Saint Peter and in his own habitation! Had his successors remained in their capital he would have been looked upon as the cause of this benign change, while, had they left Rome, his virtue would have been all the more conspicuous in contrast with their fault.

But such laments are somewhat remote from my subject. On the windy banks of the river Rhone I spent my boyhood, guided by my parents, and then, guided by my own fancies, the whole of my youth. Yet there were long intervals spent elsewhere, for I first passed four years at the little town of Carpentras, somewhat to the east of Avignon: in these two places I learned as much of grammar, logic, and rhetoric as my age permitted, or rather, as much as it is customary to teach in school: how little that is, dear reader, thou knowest. I then set out for Montpellier to study law, and spent four years there, then three at Bologna. I heard the whole body of the civil law, and would, as many thought, have distinguished myself later, had I but continued my studies. I gave up the subject altogether, however, so soon as it was no longer necessary to consult the wishes of my parents. My reason was that, although the dignity of the law, which is doubtless very great, and especially the numerous references it contains to Roman antiquity, did not fail to delight me, I felt it to be habitually degraded by those who practice it. It went against me painfully to acquire an art which I would not practice dishonestly, and could hardly hope to

---

[6] Petrarch's father, being still an exile, could not return with the family to Ancisa, in Florentine territory, but joined them when they moved to Pisa, which did not in those days belong to Florence.

[7] Urban V. (1362-1370) had transferred the papal court back to Rome after it remained for sixty years in France and Avignon, but after a year or two the disorder in Italy, as well as his own longing and that of his cardinals for their native land, overcame his good intentions and he returned to Avignon, where he died almost immediately, in December, 1370.

exercise otherwise. Had I made the latter attempt, my scrupulousness would doubtless have been ascribed to simplicity.

So at the age of two and twenty[8] I returned home. I call my place of exile home, Avignon, where I had been since childhood; for habit has almost the potency of nature itself. I had already begun to be known there, and my friendship was sought by prominent men; wherefore I cannot say. I confess this is now a source of surprise to me, although it seemed natural enough at an age when we are used to regard ourselves as worthy of the highest respect. I was courted first and foremost by that very distinguished and noble family, the Colonnesi, who, at that period, adorned the Roman Curia with their presence. However it might be now, I was at that time certainly quite unworthy of the esteem in which I was held by them. I was especially honored by the incomparable Giacomo Colonna, then Bishop of Lombez[9], whose peer I know not whether I have ever seen or ever shall see, and was taken by him to Gascony; there I spent such a divine summer among the foot-hills of the Pyrenees, in happy intercourse with my master and the members of our company, that I can never recall the experience without a sigh of regret.[10]

Returning thence, I passed many years in the house of Giacomo's brother, Cardinal Giovanni Colonna, not as if he were my lord and master, but rather my father, or better, a most affectionate brother - nay, it was as if I were in my own home.[11] About this time, a youthful desire impelled me to visit France and Germany. While I invented certain reasons to satisfy my elders of the propriety of the journey, the real explanation was a great inclination and longing to see new sights. I first visited Paris, as I was anxious to discover what was true and what fabulous in the accounts I had heard of that city.[12] On my return from this journey I went to Rome[13], which I had since my infancy ardently desired to visit. There I soon came to venerate Stephano, the noble head of the family of the Colonnesi, like some ancient hero, and was in turn treated by

---

[8] It seems strange that at twenty-two Petrarch should already have spent some seven years at the universities. It was not, however, unusual then. There were no entrance requirements, and the students were often mere boys. Rashdall places the age of freshmen at thirteen to sixteen years, but they might enter still younger. See *Universities of Europe in the Middle Ages*, vol. ii.,p. 604.

[9] Some thirty miles southwest of Toulouse.

[10] It was on this occasion that Petrarch formed his life-long friendship with "Socrates," who lived at Avignon, and with "Laelius," a Roman, who also resided at Avignon until the death of Cardinal Colonna, in 1348. To these two a great many of his letters are addressed.

[11] Petrarch was a commensal chaplain in the house of the Cardinal, as we learn from the Papal document granting him his first benefice, *apud* De Sade, *Memoires sur la Vie de petarque*, " Pieces justificatives, "vol. iii., No. 15.

[12] Petrarch's letters relating to Paris and Cologne are given below, Part IV.

[13] Probably some three years after the journey to the north.

him in every respect like a son. The love and good-will of this excellent man toward me remained constant to the end of his life, and lives in me still, nor will it cease until I myself pass away.

On my return, since I experienced a deep-seated and innate repugnance to town life, especially in that disgusting city of Avignon which I heartily abhorred, I sought some means of escape. I fortunately discovered, about fifteen miles from Avignon, a delightful valley, narrow and secluded, called Vaucluse, where the Sorgue, the prince of streams, takes its rise. Captivated by the charms of the place, I transferred thither myself and my books. Were I to describe what I did there during many years, it would prove a long story. Indeed, almost every bit of writing which I have put forth was either accomplished or begun, or at least conceived, there, and my undertakings have been so numerous that they still continue to vex and weary me. My mind, like my body, is characterized by a certain versatility and readiness, rather than by strength, so that many tasks that were easy of conception have been given up by reason of the difficulty of their execution. The character of my surroundings suggested the composition of a sylvan or bucolic song. I also dedicated a work in two books upon *The Life of Solitude*, to Philip, now exalted to the Cardinal-bishopric of Sabina. Although always a great man, he was, at the time of which I speak, only the humble Bishop of Cavaillon[14]. He is the only one of my old friends who is still left to me, and he has always loved and treated me not as a bishop (as Ambrose did Augustine), but as a brother.

While I was wandering in those mountains upon a Friday in Holy Week, the strong desire seized me to write an epic in an heroic strain, taking as my theme Scipio Africanus the Great, who had, strange to say, been dear to me from my childhood. But although I began the execution of this project with enthusiasm, I straightway abandoned it, owing to a variety of distractions. The poem was, however, christened *Africa*, from the name of its hero, and, whether from his fortunes or mine, it did not fail to arouse the interest of many before they had seen it.

While leading a leisurely existence in this region, I received, remarkable as it may seem, upon one and the same day[15], letters both from the Senate at Rome and the Chancellor of the University of Paris, pressing me to appear in Rome and Paris, respectively, to receive the poet's crown of laurel. In my youthful elation I convinced myself that I was quite worthy of this honor; the recognition came from eminent judges, and I accepted their verdict rather than that of my own better judgment. I hesitated for a time which I should give ear to, and sent a letter to Cardinal Giovanni Colonna, of whom I have already spoken, asking his opinion. He was so near

---

[14] The castle of Cavaillon is close by the valley of the Sorgue.
[15] September 1, 1340, when Petrarch was thirty-six years old.

that, although I wrote late in the day, I received his reply before the third hour on the morrow. I followed his advice, and recognized the claims of Rome as superior to all others. My acceptance of his counsel is shown by my twofold letter to him on that occasion, which I still keep. I set off accordingly; but although, after the fashion of youth, I was a most indulgent judge of my own work, I still blushed to accept in my own case the verdict even of such men as those who summoned me, despite the fact that they would certainly not have honored me in this way, had they not believed me worthy[16].

So I decided, first to visit Naples, and that celebrated king and philosopher, Robert, who was not more distinguished as a ruler than as a man of culture[17]. He was, indeed, the only monarch of our age who was the friend at once of learning and of virtue, and I trusted that he might correct such things as he found to criticize in my work. The way in which he received and welcomed me is a source of astonishment to me now, and, I doubt not, to the reader also, if he happens to know anything of the matter. Having learned the reason of my coming, the King seemed mightily pleased. He was gratified, doubtless, by my youthful faith in him, and felt, perhaps, that he shared in a way the glory of my coronation, since I had chosen him from all others as the only suitable critic. After talking over a great many things, I showed him my *Africa,* which so delighted him that he asked that it might be dedicated to him in consideration of a handsome reward[18]. This was a request that I could not well refuse, nor, indeed, would I have wished to refuse it, had it been in my power. He then fixed a day upon which we could consider the object of my visit. This occupied us from noon until evening, and the time proving too short, on account of the many matters which arose for discussion, we passed the two following days in the same manner. Having thus tested my poor attainments for three days, the King at last pronounced me worthy of the laurel. He offered to bestow that honor upon me at Naples, and urged me to consent to receive it there, but my veneration for Rome prevailed over the insistence of even so great a monarch as Robert. At length, seeing that I was inflexible in my purpose, he sent me on my way accompanied by royal messengers and letters to the Roman

---

[16] The invitations to Rome and Paris to receive the laurel crown have a history, as the reader will easily infer.

[17] Robert (who died in 1343) was the grandson of that Charles of Anjou (the brother of St. Louis) who had been called in by the popes to succeed the house of Hohenstaufen in the kingdom of Naples and Sicily. He was Petrarch's sovereign (*Fam.*,iv.,3) for Avignon belonged to him as Court of Provence, until sold to the popes by Robert's successor in 1348. Robert had resided at Avignon, 1318-1324. A letter from Petrarch to Robert, dated December 26, 1338, is preserved as well as a second one (Pisa, April 21, 1341), describing his coronation at Rome: *Fam.*,iv.,3, 7.

[18] The Latin--ut eam (scil. Africam) sibi inscribi magno pro munere posceret--may perhaps mean that the king asked that the book be dedicated to him as a *great favor*. If, however, Petrarch was rewarded for the attention, he was only one of the first to enjoy a source of revenue which was well known to later Humanists.

Senate, in which he gave enthusiastic expression to his flattering opinion of me. This royal estimate was, indeed, quite in accord with that of many others, and especially with my own, but to-day I cannot approve either his or my own verdict. In his case, affection and the natural partiality to youth were stronger than his devotion to truth.

On arriving at Rome, I continued, in spite of my unworthiness, to rely upon the judgment of so eminent a critic, and, to the great delight of the Romans who were present, I who had been hitherto a simple student received the laurel crown[19]. This occasion is described elsewhere in my letters, both in prose and verse. The laurel, however, in no way increased my wisdom, although it did arouse some jealousy - but this is too long a story to be told here.

On leaving Rome, I went to Parma, and spent some time with the members of the house of Correggio, who, while they were most kind and generous towards me, agreed but ill among themselves. They governed Parma, however, in a way unknown to that city within the memory of man, and the like of which it will hardly again enjoy in this present age.

I was conscious of the honor which I had but just received, and fearful lest it might seem to have been granted to one unworthy of the distinction; consequently, as I was walking one day in the mountains, and chanced to cross the river Enza to a place called Selva Piana, in the territory of Reggio, struck by the beauty of the spot, I began to write again upon the *Africa,* which I had laid aside. In my enthusiasm, which had seemed quite dead, I wrote some lines that very day, and some each day until I returned to Parma. Here I happened upon a quiet and retired house, which I afterwards bought, and which still belongs to me. I continued my task with such ardor, and completed the work in so short a space of time, that I cannot but marvel now at my dispatch[20]. I had already passed my thirty-fourth year when I returned thence to the Fountain of the Sorgue, and to my Transalpine solitude. I had made a long stay both in Parma and Verona[21], and everywhere I had, I am thankful to say, been treated with much greater esteem than I merited.

---

[19] Upon Easter Sunday, April 8, 1341.

[20] The great epic was never really finished (cf.*Fam.*,xiii.,II), and the Petrarch came in his old age to dislike even the mention of it. Cordini's edition is the best we have of the poem. An analysis of the *Africa* may be found in Korting, *op.cit.*,654 *sqq*.

[21] Petrarch returned to Vaucluse in 1342. When he was toward *thirty-eight* years old. There is an air of *Wahrheit und Dichtung* noticeable elsewhere in the letter. It was, for example, probably later, in 1344, on a second visit to Parma, that he bought his house, and then went to Verona, where he found letters of Cicero.

Some time after this, my growing reputation procured for me the good-will of a most excellent man, Giacomo the Younger, of Carrara, whose equal I do not know among the rulers of his time. For years he wearied me with messengers and letters when I was beyond the Alps, and with his petitions whenever I happened to be in Italy, urging me to accept his friendship. At last, although I anticipated little satisfaction from the venture, I determined to go to him and see what this insistence on the part of a person so eminent, and at the same time a stranger to me, might really mean. I appeared, though tardily, at Padua[22], where I was received by him of illustrious memory, not as a mortal, but as the blessed are greeted in heaven - with such delight and such unspeakable affection and esteem, that I cannot adequately describe my welcome in words, and must, therefore, be silent. Among other things, learning that I had led a clerical life from boyhood, he had me made a canon of Padua, in order to bind me the closer to himself and his city. In fine, had his life been spared, I should have found there an end to all my wanderings. But alas! nothing mortal is enduring, and there is nothing sweet which does not presently end in bitterness. Scarcely two years was he spared to me, to his country, and to the world. God, who had given him to us, took him again[23]. Without being blinded by my love for him, I feel that neither I, nor his country, nor the world was worthy of him. Although his son, who succeeded him, was in every way a prudent and distinguished man, who, following his father's example, always loved and honored me, I could not remain after the death of him with whom, by reason especially of the similarity of our ages, I had been much more closely united.

I returned to Gaul, not so much from a desire to see again what I had already beheld a thousand times, as from the hope, common to the afflicted, of coming to terms with my misfortunes by a change of scene[24].

---

[22] 1349.

[23] Giacomo was killed by his nephew, December, 1350.

[24] This autobiography breaks off abruptly here; we know not why.

Petrarch – two sonnets

Io son sì stanco sotto il fascio antico

I am so weary of the heavy load
Of all my sins and all my wicked ways
That I do fear to faint upon the road
And in my enemy's hands to end my days.
Lo! a true friend to rescue me draws nigh;
Unspeakable His courtesy and grace;
Then far beyond my sight He soars on high
So that in vain I strive to see His face.
But still His voice re-echoes with the strain,
'Ye who are heavy laden come to Me;
I am the way that others bar in vain.'
What grace, what mercy, what divine decree
Will clothe me with the pinions of the dove
To rise from earth and find my rest above?
    lxxxi

    1338 (?). Mascetta, p. 337.

Passa la nave mia colma d'oblio

My bark the raging surges overwhelm,
Tossing at midnight on the winter sea
'Twixt Scylla and Charybdis. At the helm
Sits Love, my master and my enemy.
At each oar stands some wicked thought and bold
That scoffs at death and shipwreck and the gale;
A driving blast, incessant, wet and cold
Of sighs and hopes and longings, strikes the sail;
Now tears rain hard in mists of wrath and scorn;
The weary sheets hang fluttering limp and drenched,
Twisted by ignorance, by error torn,
And my two beacon lights in gloom are quenched.
Amid these waves knowledge and skill are vain,
And I despair of reaching port again.
    clxxxix

    1338. See Mascetta, p. 325.

Translated by William Dudley Foulke in *Some Love Songs of Petrarch*, Oxford University Press, 1915

Lorenzo Valla

The Discourse of Lorenzo Valla on the Forgery of the Alleged Donation of Constantine
(excerpt)

English translation by Christopher B. Coleman (New Haven: Yale University Press, 1922)

"And first, I shall show that Constantine and Sylvester were not such men that the former would choose to give, would have the legal right to give, or would have it in his power to give those lands to another, or that the latter would be willing to accept them or could legally have done so. In the second place, if this were not so, though it is absolutely true and obvious, [I shall show that in fact] the latter did not receive nor the former give possession of what is said to have been granted, but that it always remained under the sway and empire of the Caesars. In the third place, [I shall show that] nothing was given to Sylvester by Constantine, but to an earlier Pope (and Constantine had received baptism even before that pontificate), and that the grants were inconsiderable, for the mere subsistence of the Pope. Fourth, that it is not true either that a copy of the Donation is found in the Decretum [of Gratian], or that it was taken from the History of Sylvester; for it is not found in it or in any history, and it is comprised of contradictions, impossibilities, stupidities, barbarisms and absurdities. Further I shall speak of the pretended or mock donation of certain other Caesars. Then by way of redundance I shall add that even had Sylvester taken possession, nevertheless, he or some other pontiff having been dispossessed, possession could not be resumed after such a long interval under either divine or human law. Last [I shall show] that the possessions which are now held by the supreme pontiff could not in any length of time, be validated by prescription."

Lorenzo de Medici

Lorenzo de Medici

Letter to his son, Giovanni, aged 16 after he was made a Cardinal in 1491 at age 14

Lorenzo de Medici (1449-1492) was the unofficial ruler of Florence from 1469 until his death. He was a humanist, arts patron - and a skillful politician. In 1489 he manages to have his son Giovanni made a cardinal, at the age of 14. Giovanni later ruled as Pope Leo X (reigned 1513-1521) and was also a patron of the arts. In the letter here Lorenzo warns his son to avoid vice and luxury.

You, and all of us who are interested in your welfare, ought to esteem ourselves highly favored by Providence, not only for the many honors and benefits bestowed upon our house, but more particularly for having conferred upon us, in your person, the greatest dignity we have ever enjoyed. This favor, in itself so important, is rendered still more so by the circumstances with which it is accompanied, and especially by the consideration of your youth and of our situation in the world. The first that I would therefore suggest to you is that you ought to be grateful to God, and continually to recollect that it is not through your merits, your prudence, or your solicitude, that this event has taken place, but through his favor, which you can only repay by a pious, chaste and exemplary life; and that your obligations to the performance of these duties are so much the greater, as in your early years you have given some reasonable expectations that your riper age may produce such fruits. It would indeed be highly disgraceful, and as contrary to your duty as to my hopes, if, at a time when others display a greater share of reason and adopt a better mode of life, you should forget the precepts of your youth, and forsake the path in which you have hitherto trodden. Endeavor, therefore, to alleviate the burden of your early dignity by the regularity of your life and by your perseverance in those studies which are suitable to your profession. It gave me great satisfaction to learn, that, in the course of the past year, you bad frequently, of your own accord, gone to communion and confession; nor do I conceive that there is any better way of obtaining the favor of heaven than by habituating yourself to a performance of these and similar duties. This appears to me to be the most suitable and useful advice which, in the first instance, I can possibly give you.

I well know, that as you are now to reside in Rome, that sink of all iniquity, the difficulty of conducting yourself by these admonitions will be increased. The influence of example is itself prevalent; but you will probably meet with those who will particularly endeavor to corrupt and incite you to vice; because, as you may yourself perceive, your early attainment to so great a dignity is not observed without envy, and those who could not prevent your receiving that honor will secretly endeavor to diminish it, by inducing you to forfeit the good estimation of the public; thereby precipitating you into that gulf into which they had themselves fallen; in which attempt, the consideration of your youth will give them a confidence of success. To these difficulties you ought to oppose yourself with the greater firmness, as there is at present less virtue amongst your brethren of the college. I acknowledge indeed that several of them are good and learned men, whose lives are exemplary, and whom I would recommend to you as patterns of your conduct. By emulating them you will be so much the more known and esteemed, in proportion as your age and the peculiarity of your situation will distinguish you from your colleagues. Avoid, however, as you would Scylla or Charybdis, the imputation of hypocrisy; guard against all ostentation, either in your conduct or your discourse; affect not austerity, nor ever appear too serious. This advice you will, I hope, in time understand and practice better than I can express it.

Yet you are not unacquainted with the great importance of the character which you have to sustain, for you well know that all the Christian world would prosper if the cardinals were what they ought to be; because in such a case there would always be a good pope, upon which the tranquility of Christendom so materially depends. Endeavor then to render yourself such, that if all the rest resembled you, we might expect this universal blessing. To give you particular directions as to your behavior and conversation would be a matter of no small difficulty. I shall, therefore, only recommend, that in your intercourse with the cardinals and other men of rank, your language be unassuming and respectful, guiding yourself, however, by your own reason, and not submitting to be impelled by the passions of others, who, actuated by improper motives, may pervert the use of their reasons. Let it satisfy your conscience that your conversation is without intentional offense; and if, through impetuosity of temper, any one should be offended, as his enmity is without just cause, so it will not be very lasting. On this your first visit to Rome, it will, however, be more advisable for you to listen to others than to speak much yourself.

You are now devoted to God and the church: on which account you ought to aim at being a good ecclesiastic, and to show that you prefer the honor and state of the church and of the apostolic see to every other consideration. Nor, while you keep this in view, will it be difficult for you to favor your family and your native place. On the contrary, you should be the link to bind this city closer to the church, and our family with the city; and although it be impossible to foresee what accidents may happen, yet I doubt not but this may be done with equal advantage to all: observing, however, that you are always to prefer the interests of the church.

You are not only the youngest cardinal in the college, but the youngest person that ever was raised to that rank; and you ought, therefore, to be the most vigilant and unassuming, not giving others occasion to wait for you, either in the chapel, the consistory or upon deputations. You will soon get a sufficient insight into the manners of your brethren. With those of less respectable character converse not with too much intimacy; not merely on account of the circumstance in itself, but for the sake of public opinion. Converse on general topics with all. On public occasions, let your equipage and address be rather below than above mediocrity. A handsome house and a well-ordered family will be preferable to a great retinue and a splendid residence. Endeavor to live with regularity, and gradually to bring your expenses within those bounds which in a new establishment cannot perhaps be expected. Silk and jewels are not suitable for persons in your station. Your taste will be better shown in the acquisition of a few elegant remains of antiquity, or in the collecting of handsome books, and by your attendants being learned and well-bred rather than numerous. Invite others to your house oftener than you receive invitations. Practise neither too frequently. Let your own food be plain, and take sufficient exercise, for those who wear your habit are soon liable, without great caution, to contract infirmities. The station of a cardinal is not less secure than elevated; on which account those who arrive at it too frequently become negligent; conceiving their object is attained and that they can preserve it with little trouble, This idea is often injurious to the life and character of those who entertain it. Be attentive, therefore, to your conduct, and confide in others too little rather than too much. There is one rule which I would recommend to your attention in preference to all others. Rise early in the morning. This will not only contribute to your health, but will enable you to arrange and expedite the business of the day; and as there are various duties incident to your station, such as the performance of divine service, studying, giving audience, and so forth, you will find the observance of this admonition productive of the greatest utility. Another very necessary precaution, particularly on your entrance into public life, is to deliberate every evening on what you may have to perform the following day, that you may not be unprepared for whatever may happen. With respect to your speaking in the consistory, it will be most becoming for you at present to refer the matters in debate to the judgment of his holiness2 alleging as a reason your own youth and inexperience. You will probably be desired to intercede for the favors of the pope on particular occasions. Be cautious, however, that you trouble him not too often; for his temper leads him to be most liberal to those who weary him least with their solicitations. This you must observe, lest you should give him offense, remembering also at times to converse with him on more agreeable topics; and if you should be obliged to request some kindness from him, let it be done with that modesty and humility which are so pleasing to his disposition. Farewell.

trans. by Merrick Whitcomb, **Source-Book of the Italian Renaissance**, revised ed. (Philadelphia: University of Pennsylvania Press, 1903), 82-86.

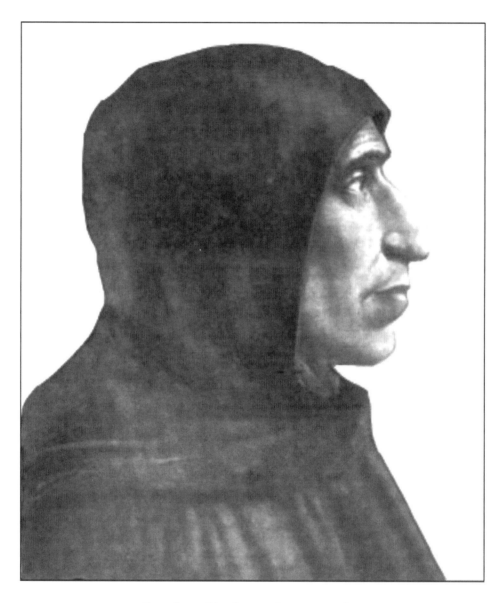

Brother Girolamo Savonarola
Dominican Friar & Preacher in Florence

Savonarola

Excerpts from the Sermons of Advent 1493 and Lent 1494

[The clergy] tickle men's ears with talk of Aristotle and Plato, Virgil and Petrarch, and take no concern in the salvation of souls. Why, instead of expounding so many books, do they not expound the one Book in which is the law and spirit of life! The Gospel, O Christians, you should ever have with you; not merely the letter, but the spirit of the Gospel. For if you lack the spirit of grace, what will it avail you to carry about the whole book? And again, still greater is the foolishness of those that load themselves with briefs and tracts and writings, so that they are like unto stalls at a fair. Charity does not consist in written papers! The true books of Christ are the Apostles and the Saints; the true reading of them is to imitate their lives. But in these days men are made books of the devil. They speak against pride and ambition, yet are plunged in both up to the eyes; they preach chastity, and maintain concubines; they prescribe fasting, and feast splendidly themselves. Those are useless books, false books, bad books, and books of the devil, for the devil has filled them with his malice.

These prelates exult in their dignities and despise others; these are they that would be feared and reverenced; these are they that seek the highest places in the synagogues, the chief pulpits of Italy. They seek to show themselves by day in the public squares, and be saluted, and called masters and rabbis, they make broad their phylacteries and enlarge the hems of their garments; they spit roundly; step gravely, and expect their slightest nod to be obeyed.

The princes of Italy are no better. These wicked princes are sent to chastise the sins of their subjects; they are truly a sad snare for souls; their courts and palaces are the refuge of all the beasts and monsters of the earth, for they give shelter to ribalds and malefactors. These wretches flock to their halls because it is there that they find ways and means to satisfy their evil passions and unbridled lusts. There are the false councilors, who continually devise new burdens and new taxes to drain the blood of the people. There are the flattering philosophers and poets, who, by force of a thousand lies and fables, trace the genealogy of those evil princes back to the gods; but, and worse than all, there are the priests who follow in the same course. This is the city of Babylon, O my brethren, the city of the foolish and the impious, the city that will be destroyed of the Lord!

See, how in these days prelates and preachers are chained to the earth by love of earthly things; the cure of souls is no longer their concern; they are content with the receipt of revenue; the preachers preach for the pleasure of princes, to be praised and magnified by them . . . And they have done worse than this, inasmuch as they have not only destroyed the Church of god, but built up another after their own fashion. This is the new Church, no longer built of living rock, namely, of Christians steadfast in the living faith, and in the mold of charity; but build of sticks, namely of Christians dry as tinder for the fires of hell. . . go thou to Rome and throughout Christendom; in the mansions of the great prelates and great lords, there is no concern save for poetry and the oratorical art. Go thither and see, thou shalt find them all with books of the humanities in their hands, and telling one another that they can guide men's souls by means of Virgil, Horace, and Cicero. Wouldst thou see how the Church is ruled by the hands of astrologers? And there is no prelate nor great lord that hath not intimate dealings with some astrologer, who fixeth the hour and the moment in which he is to ride out or undertake some piece of business. For these great lords venture not to stir a step save at their astrologer's bidding . . .

But in this temple of theirs there is one thing that delighteth us much. That is that all therein is painted and gilded. Thus our Church hath many fine outer ceremonies for the solemnization of ecclesiastical rites, grand vestments and numerous draperies, with gold and silver candlesticks, and so many chalices that it is a majestic sight to behold. There thou seest the great prelates with splendid mitres of gold and precious stones on their heads, and silver crosiers in hand; there they stand at the altar, decked with fine copes and stoles of brocade, chanting those beautiful vespers and masses, very slowly, and with so many grand ceremonies, so many organs and choristers, that thou art struck with amazement; and all these priests seem to thee grave and saintly men, thou canst not believe that they may be in error, but deem that all which they say and do should be obeyed even as the Gospel; and thus is our Church conducted. Men feed upon these vanities and rejoice in these pomps, and say that the Church of Christ was never so flourishing, nor divine worship so well conducted as at present, . . . likewise that the first prelates were inferior to these of our own times. . . The former, it is true, had fewer gold mitres and fewer chalices, for, indeed, what few they possessed were broken up to relieve the needs of the poor; whereas, our prelates, for the sake of obtaining chalices, will rob the poor of their sole means of support.

But dost thou know what I would tell the? In the primitive Church the chalices were of wood, the prelates of gold; in these days the Church hath chalices of gold and prelates of wood.

These have introduced devilish games among us; they have no belief in God, and jeer at the mysteries of our faith! What doest Thou, O Lord? Why dost Thou slumber? Arise, and come to deliver Thy Church from the hands of the devils, from the hand of tyrants, the hands of iniquitous prelates. Hast Thou forsaken Thy church? Dost Thou not love her? Is she not dear unto Thee? O Lord, we are become the despised of all nation; the Turks are masters of Constantinople; we have lost Asia, have lost Greece, we already pay tribute to the Infidel. O Lord

God, Thou hast dealt with us as a wrathful father, Thou hast cast us out from Thy presence! Hasten then the chastisement and the scourge, that it may be quickly granted us to return to Thee. Pour out your wrath upon the Gentiles! Be ye not scandalized, O my brethren by these words; rather, when ye see that the righteous desire chastisement, know that it is because they seek to banish evil, so that the kingdom of our Blessed Lord, Jesus Christ, may flourish in the world. The only hope that now remains to us, is that the sword of God may soon smite the earth.

From the **Life and Times of Girolamo Savonarola** by Professor Pasquale Villari, translated by Linda Villari London: T. Fisher Unwin, 1889

Leonardo da Vinci

Leonardo da Vinci

Preface to his Notebooks

I am fully conscious that not being a literary man certain presumptuous persons will think that they may reasonably blame me alleging that I am not a man of letters. Foolish folks do they not know that I might retort as Marius did to the Roman Patricians by saying that they who deck themselves out in the labors of others will not allow me my own. They will say that I, having no literary skill, cannot properly express that which I desire to treat of but they do not know that my subjects are to be dealt with by experience rather than by words and experience has been the mistress of those who wrote well. And so as mistress I will cite her in all cases.

Though I may not like them be able to quote other authors I shall rely on that which is much greater and more worthy -- on experience, the mistress of their Masters. They go about puffed up and pompous dressed and decorated with the fruits not of their own labors but of those of others. And they will not allow me my own. They will scorn me as an inventor but how much more might they -- who are not inventors but vaunters and declaimers of the works of others -- be blamed.

And those men who are inventors and interpreters between Nature and Man as compared with boasters and declaimers of the works of others must be regarded and not otherwise esteemed than as the object in front of a mirror when compared with its image seen in the mirror. For the first is something in itself and the other nothingness -- Folks little indebted to Nature since it is only by chance that they wear the human form and without it I might class them with the herds of beasts.

Many will think they may reasonably blame me by alleging that my proofs are opposed to the authority of certain men held in the highest reverence by their inexperienced judgments not considering that my works are the issue of pure and simple experience who is the one true mistress These rules are sufficient to enable you to know the true.

Among all the studies of natural causes and reasons Light chiefly delights the beholder; and among the great features of Mathematics the certainty of its demonstrations is what preeminently tends to elevate the mind of the investigator. Perspective therefore must be preferred to all the discourses and systems of human learning. In this branch of science the beam of light is explained on those methods of demonstration which form the glory not so much of Mathematics as of Physics and are graced with the flowers of both. But its axioms being laid down at great length, I shall abridge them to a conclusive brevity arranging them on the method both of their natural order and of mathematical demonstration sometimes by deduction of the effects from the causes, and sometimes arguing the causes from the effects adding also to my own conclusions some which though not included in them may nevertheless be inferred from them Thus if the Lord who is the light of all things vouchsafe to enlighten me I will treat of Light wherefore I will divide the present work into 3 Parts.

ON THE THREE BRANCHES OF PERSPECTIVE

There are three branches of perspective the first deals with the reasons of the apparent diminution of objects as they recede from the eye and is known as Diminishing Perspective. The second contains the way in which colors vary as they recede from the eye. The third and last is concerned with the explanation of how the objects in a picture ought to be less finished in proportion as they are remote (and the names are as follows):

> Linear Perspective
> The Perspective of Color
> The Perspective of Disappearance

[. . .]

THAT SCULPTURE IS LESS INTELLECTUAL THAN PAINTING AND LACKS MANY CHARACTERISTICS OF NATURE

I myself, having exercised myself no less in sculpture than in painting and doing both one and the other in the same degree, it seems to me that I can without invidiousness, pronounce an opinion as to which of the two is of the greatest merit and difficulty and perfection.

In the first place sculpture requires a certain light, that is from above -- a picture carries everywhere with it its own light and shade. Thus sculpture owes its importance to light and shade, and the sculptor is aided in this by nature, of the relief which is inherent in it, while the painter, whose art expresses the accidental aspects of nature, places his effects in the spots where nature must necessarily produce them. The sculptor cannot diversify his work by the various natural colors of objects; painting is not defective in any particular.

The sculptor, when he uses perspective, cannot make it in any way appear true; that of the painter can appear like a hundred miles beyond the picture itself. [The sculptor's] works have no aerial perspective whatever, they cannot represent transparent bodies, they cannot represent luminous bodies, nor reflected lights, nor lustrous bodies -- as mirrors and the like polished surfaces, nor mists, nor dark skies, nor an infinite number of things which need not be told for fear of tedium.

As regards the power of resisting time though, they have this resistance -- a picture painted on thick copper covered with white enamel on which it is painted with enamel colors and then put into the fire again and baked far exceeds sculpture in permanence.

It may be said that if a mistake is made it is not easy to remedy it. It is but a poor argument to try to prove that a work be the nobler because oversights are irremediable. I should rather say that it will be more difficult to improve the mind of the master who makes such mistakes than to repair the work he has spoilt. We know very well that a really experienced and good painter will not make such mistakes. On the contrary with sound rules he will remove so little at a time that he will bring his work to a good issue. Again the sculptor, if working in clay or wax, can add or reduce and when his model is finished it can easily be cast in bronze, and this is the last operation, and is the most permanent form of sculpture. Inasmuch as that which is merely of marble is liable to ruin, but not bronze.

Hence a painting done on copper, which as I said of painting may be added to or altered, resembles sculpture in bronze, which having first been made in wax could then be altered or added to; and if sculpture in bronze is durable, [the artist's] work in copper and enamel is absolutely imperishable.

Bronze is but dark and rough after all, but this latter is covered with various and lovely colors in infinite variety as has been said above or if you will have me only speak of painting on panel I am content to pronounce between it and sculpture saying that painting is the more beautiful and the more imaginative and the more copious while sculpture is the more durable but it has nothing else.

Sculpture shows with little labor what in painting appears a miraculous thing to do to make what is impalpable appear palpable flat objects appear in relief distant objects seem close. In fact painting is adorned with infinite possibilities which sculpture cannot command.

From **The Literary Works of Leonardo da Vinci** compiled and edited by Jean Paul Richter, London: Sampson Low Marston Searle & Rivington 1883

Michelangelo Buonarroti

Michelangelo

Selected Poems

XII

As when one, fair lady, carves away
The hard alpine stone
And a living figure
Grows as the marble disappears
So are our good works
In the trembling soul
Concealed by its flesh
Beneath a crude, hard crust
Only you, with my exhaustion
Can carve away from me
What I have neither strength nor will to do
-RS

XIV

To Vittoria Colonna [1550]

When divine Art conceives a form and face
She bids the craftsman for his first essay
To shape a simple model in mere clay
This is the earliest birth of Art's embrace
From the live marble in the second place
His mallet brings into the light of day
A thing so beautiful that who can say
When time shall conquer that immortal grace
Thus my own model I was born to be
The model of that nobler self whereto
Schooled by your pity lady I shall grow
Each surplus and each deficiency
You will make good
What penance then is due
For my fierce heat chastened and taught by you
- SYMONDS

Niccolò Machiavelli

Secretary to the second Chancery of the Republic of Florence

Machiavelli

Excerpts from The Prince

Chapter XIV: That Which Concerns a Prince on the Subject of the Art of War

The Prince ought to have no other aim or thought, nor select anything else for his study, than war and its rules and discipline; for this is the sole art that belongs to him who rules, and it is of such force that it not only upholds those who are born princes, but it often enables men to rise from a private station to that rank. And, on the contrary, it is seen that when princes have thought more of ease than of arms they have lost their states. And the first cause of your losing it is to neglect this art; and what enables you to acquire a state is to be master of the art. Francesco Sforza, though being martial, from a private person became Duke of Milan; and the sons, through avoiding the hardships and troubles of arms, from dukes became private persons. For among other evils which being unarmed brings you, it causes you to be despised, and this is one of those ignominies against which a prince ought to guard himself, as is shown later on.

Chapter XV: Concerning Things for Which Men, and Especially Princes, are Blamed

It remains now to see what ought to be the rules of conduct for a prince toward subject and friends. And as I know that many have written on this point, I expect I shall be considered presumptuous in mentioning it again, especially as in discussing it I shall depart from the methods of other people. But it being my intention to write a thing which shall be useful to him to apprehends it, it appears to me more appropriate to follow up the real truth of a matter than the imagination of it; for many have pictured republics and principalities which in fact have never been known or seen, because how one lives is so far distant from how one ought to live, that he who neglects what is done for what ought to be done, sooner effects his ruin than his preservation; for a man who wishes to act entirely up to his professions of virtue soon meets with what destroys him among so much that is evil.

Hence, it is necessary for a prince wishing to hold his own to know how to do wrong, and to make use of it or not according to necessity. Therefore, putting on one side imaginary things concerning a prince, and discussing those which are real, I say that all men when they are spoken of, and chiefly princes for being more highly placed, are remarkable for some of those qualities which bring them either blame or praise; and thus it is that one is reputed liberal, another miserly...; one is reputed generous, one rapacious; one cruel, one compassionate; one faithless, another faithful.... And I know that every one will confess that it would be most praiseworthy in a prince to exhibit all the above qualities that are considered good; but because they can neither be entirely possessed nor observed, for human conditions do not permit it, it is necessary for him to be sufficiently prudent that he may know how to avoid the reproach of those vices which would lose him his state...

Chapter XVII: Concerning Cruelty and Clemency, and Whether it is Better to be Loved than Feared

Upon this a question arises: whether it is better to be loved than feared or feared than loved? It may be answered that one should wish to be both, but, because it is difficult to unite them in one person, it is much safer to be feared than loved, when, of the two, either must be dispensed with. Because this is to be asserted in general of men, that they are ungrateful, fickle, false, cowardly, covetous, and as long as you succeed they are yours entirely; they will offer you their blood, property, life, and children, as is said above, when the need is far distant; but when it approaches they turn against you. And that prince who, relying entirely on their promises, has neglected other precautions, is ruined; because friendships that are obtained by payments, and not by nobility or greatness of mind, may indeed be earned, but they are not secured, and in time of need cannot be relied upon; and men have less scruple in offending one who is beloved than one who is feared, for love is preserved by the link of obligation which, owing to the baseness of men, is broken at every opportunity for their advantage; but fear preserved you by a dread of punishment which never fails.

Nevertheless a prince ought to inspire fear in such a way that, if he does not win love, he avoids hatred; because he can endure very well being feared whilst he is not hated, which will always be as long as he abstains from the property of his citizens and subjects and from their women.

Niccolo Machiavelli, **The Prince**, ed. W. K. Marriott. London: J. M. Dent and Sons, 1908

Erasmus of Rotterdam
Preface to In Praise of Folly

to his friend, THOMAS MORE, health:

As I was coming awhile since out of Italy for England, that I might not waste all that time I was to sit on horseback in foolish and illiterate fables, I chose rather one while to revolve with myself something of our common studies, and other while to enjoy the remembrance of my friends, of whom I left here some no less learned than pleasant.

Among these you, my More, came first in my mind, whose memory, though absent yourself, gives me such delight in my absence, as when present with you I ever found in your company; than which, let me perish if in all my life I ever met with anything more delectable.

And therefore, being satisfied that something was to be done, and that that time was no wise proper for any serious matter, I resolved to make some sport with the praise of folly. But who the devil put that in your head? you'll say. The first thing was your surname of More, which comes so near the word Moriae (folly) as you are far from the thing. And that you are so, all the world will cleat you.

In the next place, I conceived this exercise of wit would not be least approved by you; inasmuch as you are wont to be delighted with such kind of mirth, that is to say, neither unlearned, if I am not mistaken, not altogether insipid, and in the whole course of your life have played the part of a Democtitus. And though such is the excellence of your judgment that it was even contrary to that of the people's, yet such is your incredible ability and sweetness of temper that you both can and delight to carry yourself to all men a man of all hours. Wherefore you will not only with good will accept this small declamation, but take upon you the defense of it, for as much as being dedicated to you, it is now no longer mine but yours.

But perhaps there will not be wanting some wranglers that may cavil and charge me, partly that these toys are lighter than may become a divine, and partly more biting than may beseem the modesty of a Christian, and consequently exclaim that I resemble the ancient comedy, or another Lucian, and snarl at everything. But I would have them whom the lightness or foolery of the argument may offend to consider that mine is not the first of this kind, but the same thing that has been often practiced even by great authors: when Homer, so many ages since, did the like with the battle of frogs and mice; Virgil, with the gnat and puddings; Ovid, with the nut; when Polycrates and his corrector Isocrates extolled tyranny; Glauco, injustice; Favorinus, deformity and the quartan ague; Synescius, baldness; Lucian, the fly and flattery; when Seneca made such sport with Claudius' canonizations; Plutarch, with his dialogue between Ulysses and Gryllus; Lucian and Apuleius, with the ass; and some other, I know not who, with the hog that made his last will and testament, of which also even St. Jerome makes mention.

And therefore if they please, let them suppose I played at tables for my diversion, or if they had rather have it so, that I rode on a hobbyhorse. For what injustice is it that when we allow every course of life its recreation, that study only should have none? Especially when such toys are not without their serious matter, and foolery is so handled that the reader that is not altogether thick-skulled may reap more benefit from it than from some men's crabbish and specious arguments.

As when one, with long study and great pains, patches many pieces together on the praise of rhetoric or philosophy; another makes a panegyric to a prince; another encourages him to a war against the Turks; another tells you what will become of the world after himself is dead; and another finds out some new device for the better ordering of goat's wool: for as nothing is more trifling than to treat of serious matters triflingly, so nothing carries a better grace than so to discourse of trifles as a man may seem to have intended them least.

For my own part, let other men judge of what I have written; though yet, unless an overweening opinion of myself may have made me blind in my own cause, I have praised folly, but not altogether foolishly.

And now to say somewhat to that other cavil, of biting. This liberty was ever permitted to all men's wits, to make their smart, witty reflections on the common errors of mankind, and that too without offense, as long as this liberty does not run into licentiousness; which makes me the more admire the tender ears of the men of this age, that can away with solemn titles. No, you'll meet with some so preposterously religious that they will Sooner endure the broadest scoffs even against Christ himself than hear the Pope or a prince be touched in the least, especially if it be anything that concerns their profit; whereas he that so taxes the lives of men, without naming anyone in particular, whither, I pray, may he be said to bite, or rather to teach and admonish? Or otherwise, I beseech you, under how many notions do I tax myself? Besides, he that spares no sort of men cannot be said to be angry with anyone in particular, but the vices of all.

And therefore, if there shall happen to be anyone that shall say he is hit, he will but discover either his guilt or fear. Saint Jerome sported in this kind with more freedom and greater sharpness, not sparing sometimes men's very name. But I, besides that I have wholly avoided it, I have so moderated my style that the understanding reader will easily perceive my endeavors herein were rather to make mirth than bite. Nor have I, after the example of Juvenal, raked up that forgotten sink of filth and ribaldry, but laid before you things rather ridiculous than dishonest.

And now, if there be anyone that is yet dissatisfied, let him at least remember that it is no dishonor to be discommended by Folly; and having brought her in speaking, it was but fit that I kept up the character of the person. But why do I run over these things to you, a person so excellent an advocate that no man better defends his client, though the cause many times be none of the best? Farewell, my best disputant More, and stoutly defend your Moria

John Wyclif

The Condemned Conclusions of John Wycliffe (from the Bull of Pope Gregory XI, Against John Wycliffe)

1. That the material substance of bread and of wine remains, after the consecration, in the sacrament of the altar.

2. That the accidents do not remain without the subject, after the consecration, in the same sacrament.

3. That Christ is not in the sacrament of the altar identically, truly and really in his proper corporeal presence.

4. That if a bishop or priest lives in mortal sin he does not ordain, or consecrate, or baptize.

5. That if a man has been truly repentant, all external confession is superfluous to him or useless.

6. That it is not founded in the gospel that Christ instituted the mass.

7. That God ought to be obedient to the devil.

8. That if the pope is fore-ordained to destruction and a wicked man, and therefore a member of the devil, no power has been given to him over the faithful of Christ by any one, unless perhaps by the Emperor.

9. That since Urban VI, no one is to be acknowledged as pope; but all are to live, in the way of the Greeks, under their own laws.

10. To assert that it is against sacred scripture that men of the Church should have temporal possessions.

11. That no prelate ought to excommunicate any one unless he first knows that the man is excommunicated by God.

12. That a prelate thus excommunicating is thereby a heretic or excommunicate.

13. That a prelate excommunicating a clerk who has appealed to the king, or to a council of the kingdom, on that very account is a traitor to God, the king and the kingdom.

14. That those who neglect to preach, or to hear the word of God, or the gospel that is preached, because of the excommunication of men, are excommunicate, and in the day of judgment will be considered as traitors to God.

15. To assert that it is allowed to any one, whether a deacon or a priest, to preach the word of God, without the authority of the apostolic see, or of a Catholic bishop, or of some other which is sufficiently acknowledged.

16. To assert that no one is a civil lord, no one is a bishop, no one is a prelate, so long as he is in mortal sin.

17. That temporal lords may, at their own judgment, take away temporal goods from churchmen who are habitually delinquent; or that the people may, at their own judgment, correct delinquent lords.

18. That tithes are purely charity, and that parishoners may, on account of the sins of their curates, detain these and confer them on others at their will.

19. That special prayers applied to one person by prelates or religious persons, are of no more value to the same person than general prayers for others in a like position are to him.

20. That the very fact that any one enters upon any private religion whatever, renders him more unfitted and more incapable of observing the commandments of God.

21. That saints who have instituted any private religions whatever, as well of those having possessions as of mendicants, have sinned in thus instituting them.

22. That religious persons living in private religions are not of the Christian religion.

23. That friars should be required to gain their living by the labor of their hands and not by mendicancy.

24. That a person giving alms to friars, or to a preaching friar, is excommunicate; also the one receiving.

Reply of John Wycliffe to his Summons by the Pope to come to Rome, 1384

I have joyfully to tell to all true men that believe what I hold, and legates to the pope; for I suppose that if my faith be rightful and given of God, the pope will gladly confirm it; and if my faith be error, the Pope will wisely amend it.

I suppose over this that the gospel of Christ be [the] heart of the corpus of God's law; for I believe that Jesus Christ, that gave in His own person this gospel, is very God and very man, and by this heart passes all other laws.

I suppose over this that the pope be most obliged to the keeping of the gospel among all men that live here; for the pope is highest vicar that Christ has here in earth. For moreness of Christ's vicar is not measured by worldly moreness, but by this, that this vicar sues more Christ by virtuous living; for thus teacheth the gospel, that this is the sentence of Christ.

And of this gospel I take as believe, that Christ for [the] time that He walked here, was [the] most poor man of all, both in spirit and in having; for Christ says that He had nought for to rest His head on. And Paul says that He was made needy for our love. And more poor might no man be, neither bodily nor in spirit. And thus Christ put from Him all manner of worldly lordship. For the gospel of John telleth that when they would have made Christ king, He fled and hid Him from them, for He would none such worldly highness.

And over this I take it as believe, that no man should sue the pope, nor no saint that now is in heaven, but in as much as he sues Christ. For John and James erred when they coveted worldly highness; and Peter and Paul sinned also when they denied and blasphemed in Christ; but men should not sue them in this, for then they went from Jesus Christ. And this I take as wholesome counsel, that the pope leave his worldly lordship to worldly lords, as Christ gave them,---and move speedily all his clerks to do so. For thus did Christ, and taught thus his disciples, till the fiend had blinded this world. And it seems to some men that clerks that dwell lastingly in this error against God's law, and flee to sue Christ in this, been open heretics, and their fautors been partners.

And if I err in this sentence, I will meekly be amended, yea, by the death, if it be skilful, for that I hope were good to me. And if I might travel in mine own person, I would with good will go to the pope. But God has needed me to the contrary, and taught me more obedience to God than to men. And I suppose of our pope that he will not be Antichrist, and reverse Christ in this working, to the contrary of Christ's will; for if he summon against reason, by him or by any of his, and pursue this unskilful summoning, he is an open Antichrist. And merciful intent excused not Peter, that Christ should name him Satan; so blind intent and wicked counsel excuses not the pope here; but if he ask of true priests that they travel more than they may, he is not excused by reason of God, that he should not be Antichrist. For our belief teaches us that our blessed God suffers us not to be tempted more than we may; how should a man ask such service? And therefore pray we to God for our Pope Urban the Sixth, that his old holy intent be not quenched by his enemies. And Christ, that may not lie, says that the enemies of a man been especially his home family; and this is sooth of men and fiends.

From: Oliver J. Thatcher, ed., **The Library of Original Sources** (Milwaukee: University Research Extension Co., 1907), Vol. V: The Early Medieval World, pp. 378-382.

Jan Hus
Rector, University of Prague

Jan Hus
Final Declaration, July 1, 1415

I, Jan Hus, in hope a priest of Jesus Christ, fearing to offend God, and fearing to fall into perjury, do hereby profess my unwillingness to abjure all or any of the articles produced against me by false witnesses. For God is my witness that I neither preached, affirmed, nor defended them, though they say that I did. Moreover, concerning the articles that they have extracted from my books, I say that I detest any false interpretation which any of them bears. But inasmuch as I fear to offend against the truth, or to gainsay the opinion of the doctors of the Church, I cannot abjure any one of them. And if it were possible that my voice could now reach the whole world, as at the Day of Judgment every lie and every sin that I have committed will be made manifest, then would I gladly abjure before all the world every falsehood and error which I either had thought of saying or actually said!

I say I write this of my own free will and choice.

Written with my own hand, on the first day of July.

From: Herbert B. Workman and R. Martin Pope, eds., **The Letters of John Hus**, (London: Hodder and Stoughton, 1904), pp. 275-276

Martin Luther by Lucas Cranach 1520

Martin Luther
Preface to the Complete Edition of Luther's Latin Works (1545)

Translated by Bro. Andrew Thornton, OSB from the "Vorrede zu Band I der Opera Latina der Wittenberger Ausgabe. 1545" in vol. 4 of _Luthers Werke in Auswahl_, ed. Otto Clemen, 6th ed., (Berlin: de Gruyter. 1967). pp. 421-428.

> **Translator's Note**: The material between square brackets is explanatory in nature and is not part of Luther's preface. The terms "just, justice, justify" in the following reading are synonymous with the terms "righteous, righteousness, make righteous." Both sets of English words are common translations of the Latin "justus" and related words. A similar situation exists with the word "faith"; it is synonymous with "belief." Both words can be used to translate Latin "fides." Thus, "We are justified by faith" translates the same original Latin sentence as does "We are made righteous by belief."

Dear Reader,

I have steadfastly resisted those who wanted my books published, or perhaps I had better call them the confused products of my nighttime study. First, I did not want the labors of the ancient authors to be buried under my new works and the reader to be hindered from reading them. Second, there now exists, thanks to the grace of God, a good number of systematically arranged books, especially the "Loci communes" of **Philip**, [**Philip Melanchthon**, scholar of Greek and associate of Luther at Wittenberg] from which a theologian or bishop can get a thorough foundation [cf Titus 1:9], so that he might be strong in preaching the doctrine of virtue. Third, and most importantly, the Bible itself is now available in almost every language. The disordered train of events, however, has seen to it that my works resemble a wild, disorganized chaos, which now even I cannot easily put into order.

For these reasons I wanted all my books to be buried in perpetual oblivion, that thus there might be room for better books. But other people, by their bold and unrelenting arguments, badgered me into publishing mine. They maintained that, if I did not permit them to be published while I was alive, people would publish them after I was dead anyway, people ignorant of the sequence of events and of the causes behind them. Thus instead of one confusion, there would be many. I also had to take into account the wish and command of our most illustrious **Prince Elector Johann Frederick**, who ordered or rather forced the printers not only to print this edition but also to get it done quickly.

Above all I beg the reader, for the sake of our Lord Jesus Christ, to read these works with discernment, or perhaps I should say with compassion. The reader should know that I was once a monk, the most rabid of papists, when I took up this whole affair. I was so drunk, so submerged in the pope's doctrines, that I was ready, if I could, to kill or help kill those who would have advocated by so much as a single syllable withdrawing obedience to the pope. That's how much of a Saul I was [i.e., St. Paul, who, before his conversion, was called Saul and who was zealous in his persecution of Christians], as many still are. I wasn't so icy cold in defending the papacy as was **Eck** and those like him, who seemed to me to defend the pope more for the sake of their bellies than through serious commitment. To this day they seem to me to be laughing at the pope like Epicureans. I took the matter seriously because I had a horrible fear of the Last Day, yet still wished from the depths of my heart to be saved.

Consequently you will find that, in my earlier writings, I most humbly conceded many important things to the pope, things which I later detested and now detest as being the greatest blasphemy and abomination. Therefore, dear reader, kindly ascribe this error or, as my calumniators call it, this contradiction to the time and to my inexperience. At first I was alone and surely much too inept and unlearned to be dealing with such matters. For, as God is my witness, it was by accident and not by my own will or desire that I got involved in all this turmoil.

When in 1517 indulgences were sold (I wanted to say promulgated) in these regions for disgraceful profit, I was a preacher, a young Doctor of Theology, as they say. I began to dissuade the people from lending an ear to the shouts of the indulgence-sellers. I told them that they had better things to do and that I was sure that in these matters I had the pope on my side. I was relying greatly on his trustworthiness, since in his decrees he had very clearly condemned the excesses of the quaestors [name of a treasury official in ancient Rome] as he called the indulgence preachers.

Shortly thereafter I wrote two letters, one to **Albert, the archbishop of Mainz**, who was getting half the money from the indulgences (the other half was going to the pope, a fact of which I was at the time ignorant),the other to the ordinary of the place, **Jerome, bishop of Brandenburg**. I begged them to put a stop to the shameless blasphemy of the quaestors, but they despised this poor little brother. Therefore, finding myself despised, I published a list of theses and, at the same time, a sermon in German on indulgences. A little later I published the "Explanations," in which, in deference to the pope, I maintained that indulgences should not be condemned but that the works of charity should be preferred to them.

What I did toppled heaven and consumed earth by fire. I am denounced to the pope, commanded to go to Rome, and the entire papacy rises up against me alone. These things happened in 1518 when **Maximilian** was holding the Diet at Augsburg, at which **Cardinal Cajetan** was the legate of the pope. The most illustrious **Duke Frederick of Saxony**, Prince Elector, took up my cause with the Cardinal and asked that I not be forced to go to Rome but that he, **Cajetan**, should summon me to a hearing and take care of the matter. Shortly thereafter the Diet was adjourned.

Meanwhile the Germans were getting tired of putting up with the plunderings, the buying and selling, and the endless frauds of the Roman rascals. They were waiting with bated breath for the outcome of so important a matter, which neither bishop nor theologian had ever before dared to touch. This mood of the populace encouraged me, because those crafty "Romanations" with which they had filled and fatigued the whole world were now hateful to everyone.

Poor and on foot I came to Augsburg, my expenses paid by **Prince Frederick**. I had from him letters commending me to the senate and to certain good men. I was there for three days before I approached the Cardinal, because those good men strongly advised me not to go to the Cardinal until I had a safe conduct pass from the Emperor. The Cardinal had been summoning me every day through a certain spokesman. This latter pestered me greatly, saying that if I'd only recant, then everything would be all right. But long the injury, long the detour back.

Finally, on the third day, the spokesman came and demanded to know why I hadn't yet approached the Cardinal, who was waiting to receive me most kindly. I answered that I was complying with the advice of good men to whom I had been commended by **Prince Frederick** and that they had advised me not to go to see the Cardinal unless I had a safe conduct pass from the Emperor. I said that they were requesting one from the imperial senate and that I would come as soon as it had been obtained. He got very angry and said: "Do you think **Prince Frederick** is going to take up arms for your sake?" I said, "I don't want him to." He asked, "Where will you stay?" I replied, "Under heaven." He then asked, "If you had the pope and the cardinals in your power, what would you do?" I said. "I'd show them every reverence and honor." Then He moved his finger in an Italian gesture and said, "Hem." Then he went away and never came back.

The same day the imperial senate informed the Cardinal that I had been given a safe conduct; they warned him that he should not plan to have anything too severe in store for me. It is said that he answered, "Fine, but I shall act according to my duty." These events were the beginning of this whole commotion; the rest can be learned from what follows.

That same year, 1518, **Prince Frederick** had called **Philip Melanchthon** here to Wittenberg to teach Greek, doubtless so that I might have a colleague in my labors of teaching theology. His works testify to what the Lord has accomplished through **Melanchthon**, his instrument, not only in literature but also in theology, despite the fact that Satan and all his brood are infuriated.

The following year, in February of 1519, **Emperor Maximilian** died, and by the law of the Empire **Duke Frederick** became vicar. Then the fury of the tempest abated a little, and gradually excommunication, the papal thunderbolt, came to be held in contempt. **Eck** and **Caraccioli** brought from Rome a bull [a papal decree] condemning me. The former conveyed it to Wittenberg, the latter to **Duke Frederick**, who was at the time in Cologne, where he and the other princes were to receive **Charles**, the newly elected Emperor. **Duke Frederick** got very indignant at that papal rascal and courageously told him off in no uncertain terms because in his absence he and **Eck** had disturbed his dominions and those of his brother. He gave them such a magnificent tongue lashing that they went away from him shamed and disgraced. The prince, endowed as he was with unbelievable natural ability, knew all about the crafty ways of the Roman curia [the administrative apparatus of the Roman Church]; he knew exactly how to treat them. He was a man with a good clear nose, and he could smell more and farther than the Romanists could either hope or fear.

Thereafter they stopped testing **Frederick**. Furthermore, he paid no honor to the rose that they call "golden" [a special mark of papal esteem] which **Leo X** sent him that same year; on the contrary, he ridiculed it. Thus the Romanists were forced to give up any hope of duping such a prince. The Gospel advanced successfully under the protection of this prince and was propagated far and wide. His authority influenced many; since he was a most wise and keen-sighted prince, he could incur no suspicion, except among the hateful, that he was out to encourage and support heresy. This did the papacy great harm.

In the same year, 1519, there was held at Leipzig the debate to which **Eck** had challenged **Karlstadt** and me. But by no letter of mine could I secure a safe conduct from **Duke George**, and so I entered Leipzig not as a debater but as a spectator under the safe conduct which had been given to **Karlstadt**. I don't know who was blocking my way, since I was sure that, up to that time, **Duke George** had not been hostile to me.

In Leipzig **Eck** came to me in my lodgings. He said he had learned that I had refused to debate. I answered, "How can I debate if I can't secure a safe conduct from **Duke George**?" He answered, "I came here to debate with you, and if I can't, then I don't want to debate with **Karlstadt** either. What if I get a safe conduct for you? Will you debate with me then?" I said, "Get it and I will." He left, and shortly thereafter I too got a safe conduct and so had the opportunity of debating.

Eck did this because he thought he would cover himself with glory in debating my proposition in which I denied that the pope was the head of the church by divine right. In this proposition **Eck** had a golden opportunity of flattering the pope and of meriting his thanks and of overwhelming me with hatred and ill-will. That is exactly what he did throughout the whole debate, but he neither proved his position nor refuted mine. Even **Duke George** said to **Eck** and me at breakfast, "Whether it's by divine right or by human right, still he's the pope." If he hadn't been influenced by the arguments, he would never have said such a thing but would have approved of **Eck** alone.

From my case you can see how hard it is to struggle free from errors which become fixed by universal standard and changed by time-honored custom into nature. How true the proverb is: "It's hard to abandon customs" and "Custom is a second nature." How right Augustine was when he said, "Custom, if it is not resisted, becomes necessity." I had been reading and teaching the Sacred Scriptures diligently in private and in public now for seven years, so that I knew almost all of them by heart. Then too, I had imbibed the beginnings of the knowledge of Christ and of faith in him, i.e., that it is faith in Christ and not works that justifies and saves us. Finally, I was now defending publicly that proposition of which I'm speaking, namely, that the pope was not the head of the church by divine right. But I still didn't see the necessary conclusion, i.e., that the pope must be from the devil, for what is not from God must be from the devil.

I was so absorbed, as I have said, by the example and title of the Holy Church as well as by my own customary way of thinking, that I conceded that the pope was head of the church by human right. However, if that right is not supported by divine authority, then it is a lie and comes from the devil. After all, we obey our parents and the civil authorities, not because they themselves command it, but because God wants us to (cf. 1 Peter). That is why I can, with a little less hatred, put up with those who cling so tenaciously to the papacy, especially those who haven't read the sacred Scriptures or even the secular writings, since I myself had read the sacred Scriptures diligently for so many years and still clung tenaciously to the papacy.

In 1519, as I've already said, **Leo X** sent the Golden Rose through **Karl von Miltitz**; with many arguments he urged me to be reconciled to the pope. **Miltitz** had seventy apostolic briefs, and if **Prince Frederick** would hand me over, as the pope was asking by sending the Rose, he would post one of the briefs in each town and so conduct me safely to Rome. But **Miltitz** betrayed to me what was really in his heart when he said, "**Martin**, I thought you were some aged theologian who used to sit next to the stove and debate with himself, but now I see that you're still a strong young man. If I had twenty-five thousand armed men, I don't think I could convey you to Rome. I've been sounding out the opinions of people along the way to see what they thought of you. For every one for the pope there are three for you against the pope." That's ridiculous! He had asked the women and serving girls in the inns what they thought of the Roman See [the Latin "sedes" = "seat"]. They didn't know what the word meant and, thinking of a household chair, they answered, "How are we supposed to know what kind of chairs you have at Rome? We don't know whether they're made out of wood or stone.

Miltitz begged me, therefore, to do everything I could to make peace, and he would do his best to see that the pope did the same. I promised that I would most promptly do anything that I could in good conscience do. I said that I too wanted peace and that I had been drawn by force into these squabbles and had been forced by circumstances to do everything I did; I was not to blame. **Miltitz** had summoned the Dominican friar, **Johann Tetzel**, the originator of this tragedy. With threatening words from the pope he so broke the man, who up to that time had been the terror of all and a fearless crier of indulgences, that he wasted away and was finally consumed by a mental illness. When I found this out, I wrote him, before he died, a kindly letter in which I comforted him and told him to take heart and not to fear my memory. But perhaps his conscience and the wrath of the pope sent him to the grave. People thought **Miltitz** and his line of action were useless, but it seems to me that if the man at Mainz [i.e., **Archbishop Albrecht** of Mainz] had followed **Miltitz**'s course from the beginning when I had reprimanded him, and if the pope had followed it before he condemned me without a hearing and raged with his bulls, and if they had suppressed **Tetzel**'s fury, the affair wouldn't have resulted in such an uproar. It's all the fault of the man at Mainz, who was tricked by his own cleverness with which he wanted to suppress my doctrine and to save his money which he'd sought through indulgences. Now they seek counsel in vain; now they make efforts in vain. The Lord has awakened and stands to judge the peoples [cf. Psalm 76:9 and Daniel 9:14]. Even if they were able to kill us, they still wouldn't have what they want; in fact, they'd have even less than they have now while we are alive and well. Some among them, whose nose is not completely inactive, can smell this well enough.

Meanwhile in that same year, 1519, I had begun interpreting the Psalms once again. I felt confident that I was now more experienced, since I had dealt in university courses with St. Paul's Letters to the Romans, to the Galatians, and the Letter to the Hebrews. I had conceived a burning desire to understand what Paul meant in his Letter to the Romans, but thus far there had stood in my way, not the cold blood around my heart, but that one word which is in chapter one: "The justice of God is revealed in it." I hated that word, "justice of God," which, by the use and custom of all my teachers, I had been taught to understand philosophically as referring to formal or active justice, as they call it, i.e., that justice by which God is just and by which he punishes sinners and the unjust.

But I, blameless monk that I was, felt that before God I was a sinner with an extremely troubled conscience. I couldn't be sure that God was appeased by my satisfaction. I did not love, no, rather I hated the just God who punishes sinners. In silence, if I did not blaspheme, then certainly I grumbled vehemently and got angry at God. I said, "Isn't it enough that we miserable sinners, lost for all eternity because of original sin, are oppressed by every kind of calamity through the Ten Commandments? Why does God heap sorrow upon sorrow through the Gospel and through the Gospel threaten us with his justice and his wrath?" This was how I was raging with wild and disturbed conscience. I constantly badgered St. Paul about that spot in Romans 1 and anxiously wanted to know what he meant.

I meditated night and day on those words until at last, by the mercy of God, I paid attention to their context: "The justice of God is revealed in it, as it is written: 'The just person lives by faith.'" I began to understand that in this verse the justice of God is that by which the just person lives by a gift of God, that is by faith. I began to understand that this verse means that the justice of God is revealed through the Gospel, but it is a passive justice, i.e. that by which the merciful God justifies us by faith, as it is written: "The just person lives by faith." All at once I felt that I had been born again and entered into paradise itself through open gates. Immediately I saw the whole of Scripture in a different light. I ran through the Scriptures from memory and found that other terms had analogous meanings, e.g., the work of God, that is, what God works in us; the power of God, by which he makes us powerful; the wisdom of God, by which he makes us wise; the strength of God, the salvation of God, the glory of God.

I exalted this sweetest word of mine, "the justice of God," with as much love as before I had hated it with hate. This phrase of Paul was for me the very gate of paradise. Afterward I read **Augustine**'s "On the Spirit and the Letter," in which I found what I had not dared hope for. I discovered that he too interpreted "the justice of God" in a similar way, namely, as that with which God clothes us when he justifies us. Although **Augustine** had said it imperfectly and did not explain in detail how God imputes justice to us, still it pleased me that he taught the justice of God by which we are justified.

Better armed now with these thoughts, I began for the second time to interpret the Psalms. The work would have grown into a large commentary, but I was summoned the following year to Worms for the Diet convened by **Emperor Charles V** and so had once again to leave the work I had begun.

I am telling you all this, dear reader, so that, if you are going to read my little works, you should remember that I am one of those, as I said above, who, as **Augustine** writes of himself, makes progress by writing and teaching. I am not one of those who out of nothing suddenly become perfect (although in fact they are nothing), who don't work, who aren't tempted, who have no experience, but who, with one look into the Scriptures, exhaust their whole spirit.

Up to that point, 1520-21, the indulgence affair was still going on. There followed the affairs dealing with the sacraments and with the Anabaptists, about which I will write prefaces in other volumes, if I live to do so.

Good-bye in the Lord, dear reader, and pray that the word may increase against Satan, because he is powerful and evil. And now he has become extremely vicious and savage because he knows that he has only a short time and that the kingdom of his pope is endangered. May God strengthen in us what he has accomplished. May he prosper his work which he has begun in us for his glory [cf. Phillipians 1:6 and Psalm 68:29]. Amen.

This translation was made by Bro. Andrew Thornton, OSB, for the Saint Anselm College Humanities Program. It is distributed on the internet by Project Wittenberg with the permission of the author.

Letter of indulgence for the benefit of building St. Peter's Church at Rome made out for the widow Katharina von Trebra at Gehofen and her sons, Hans and Konrad in the name of the archbishop of Mainz on the third day of March, 1517, signed by the notary public Heinricus Kappe. With seal attached.

Martin Luther

The 95 Theses on the Power and Efficacy of Indulgences (1517)

Published in: **Works of Martin Luther,** Adolph Spaeth, L.D. Reed, Henry Eyster Jacobs, et Al., Trans. & Eds.(Philadelphia: A. J. Holman Company, 1915), Vol.1, pp. 29-38

Out of love for the truth and the desire to bring it to light, the following propositions will be discussed at Wittenberg, under the presidency of the Reverend Father Martin Luther, Master of Arts and of Sacred Theology, and Lecturer in Ordinary on the same at that place. Wherefore he requests that those who are unable to be present and debate orally with us, may do so by letter.

In the Name our Lord Jesus Christ. Amen.

1. Our Lord and Master Jesus Christ, when He said *Poenitentiam agite*, willed that the whole life of believers should be repentance.

2. This word cannot be understood to mean sacramental penance, i.e., confession and satisfaction, which is administered by the priests.

3. Yet it means not inward repentance only; nay, there is no inward repentance which does not outwardly work divers mortifications of the flesh.

4. The penalty [of sin], therefore, continues so long as hatred of self continues; for this is the true inward repentance, and continues until our entrance into the kingdom of heaven.

5. The pope does not intend to remit, and cannot remit any penalties other than those which he has imposed either by his own authority or by that of the Canons.

6. The pope cannot remit any guilt, except by declaring that it has been remitted by God and by assenting to God's remission; though, to be sure, he may grant remission in cases reserved to his judgment. If his right to grant remission in such cases were despised, the guilt would remain entirely unforgiven.

7. God remits guilt to no one whom He does not, at the same time, humble in all things and bring into subjection to His vicar, the priest.

8. The penitential canons are imposed only on the living, and, according to them, nothing should be imposed on the dying.

9. Therefore the Holy Spirit in the pope is kind to us, because in his decrees he always makes exception of the article of death and of necessity.

10. Ignorant and wicked are the doings of those priests who, in the case of the dying, reserve canonical penances for purgatory.

11. This changing of the canonical penalty to the penalty of purgatory is quite evidently one of the tares that were sown while the bishops slept.

12. In former times the canonical penalties were imposed not after, but before absolution, as tests of true contrition.

13. The dying are freed by death from all penalties; they are already dead to canonical rules, and have a right to be released from them.

14. The imperfect health [of soul], that is to say, the imperfect love, of the dying brings with it, of necessity, great fear; and the smaller the love, the greater is the fear.

15. This fear and horror is sufficient of itself alone (to say nothing of other things) to constitute the penalty of purgatory, since it is very near to the horror of despair.

16. Hell, purgatory, and heaven seem to differ as do despair, almost-despair, and the assurance of safety.

17. With souls in purgatory it seems necessary that horror should grow less and love increase.

18. It seems unproved, either by reason or Scripture, that they are outside the state of merit, that is to say, of increasing love.

19. Again, it seems unproved that they, or at least that all of them, are certain or assured of their own blessedness, though we may be quite certain of it.

20. Therefore by "full remission of all penalties" the pope means not actually "of all," but only of those imposed by himself.

21. Therefore those preachers of indulgences are in error, who say that by the pope's indulgences a man is freed from every penalty, and saved;

22. Whereas he remits to souls in purgatory no penalty which, according to the canons, they would have had to pay in this life.

23. If it is at all possible to grant to any one the remission of all penalties whatsoever, it is certain that this remission can be granted only to the most perfect, that is, to the very fewest.

24. It must needs be, therefore, that the greater part of the people are deceived by that indiscriminate and high-sounding promise of release from penalty.

25. The power which the pope has, in a general way, over purgatory, is just like the power which any bishop or curate has, in a special way, within his own diocese or parish.

26. The pope does well when he grants remission to souls [in purgatory], not by the power of the keys (which he does not possess), but by way of intercession.

27. They preach man who say that so soon as the penny jingles into the money-box, the soul flies out [of purgatory].

28. It is certain that when the penny jingles into the money-box, gain and avarice can be increased, but the result of the intercession of the Church is in the power of God alone.

29. Who knows whether all the souls in purgatory wish to be bought out of it, as in the legend of Sts. Severinus and Paschal.

30. No one is sure that his own contrition is sincere; much less that he has attained full remission.

31. Rare as is the man that is truly penitent, so rare is also the man who truly buys indulgences, i.e., such men are most rare.

32. They will be condemned eternally, together with their teachers, who believe themselves sure of their salvation because they have letters of pardon.

33. Men must be on their guard against those who say that the pope's pardons are that inestimable gift of God by which man is reconciled to Him;

34. For these "graces of pardon" concern only the penalties of sacramental satisfaction, and these are appointed by man.

35. They preach no Christian doctrine who teach that contrition is not necessary in those who intend to buy souls out of purgatory or to buy confessionalia.

36. Every truly repentant Christian has a right to full remission of penalty and guilt, even without letters of pardon.

37. Every true Christian, whether living or dead, has part in all the blessings of Christ and the Church; and this is granted him by God, even without letters of pardon.

38. Nevertheless, the remission and participation [in the blessings of the Church] which are granted by the pope are in no way to be despised, for they are, as I have said, the declaration of divine remission.

39. It is most difficult, even for the very keenest theologians, at one and the same time to commend to the people the abundance of pardons and [the need of] true contrition.

40. True contrition seeks and loves penalties, but liberal pardons only relax penalties and cause them to be hated, or at least, furnish an occasion [for hating them].

41. Apostolic pardons are to be preached with caution, lest the people may falsely think them preferable to other good works of love.

42. Christians are to be taught that the pope does not intend the buying of pardons to be compared in any way to works of mercy.

43. Christians are to be taught that he who gives to the poor or lends to the needy does a better work than buying pardons;

44. Because love grows by works of love, and man becomes better; but by pardons man does not grow better, only more free from penalty.

45. 45. Christians are to be taught that he who sees a man in need, and passes him by, and gives [his money] for pardons, purchases not the indulgences of the pope, but the indignation of God.

46. Christians are to be taught that unless they have more than they need, they are bound to keep back what is necessary for their own families, and by no means to squander it on pardons.

47. Christians are to be taught that the buying of pardons is a matter of free will, and not of commandment.

48. Christians are to be taught that the pope, in granting pardons, needs, and therefore desires, their devout prayer for him more than the money they bring.

49. Christians are to be taught that the pope's pardons are useful, if they do not put their trust in them; but altogether harmful, if through them they lose their fear of God.

50. Christians are to be taught that if the pope knew the exactions of the pardon-preachers, he would rather that St. Peter's church should go to ashes, than that it should be built up with the skin, flesh and bones of his sheep.

51. Christians are to be taught that it would be the pope's wish, as it is his duty, to give of his own money to very many of those from whom certain hawkers of pardons cajole money, even though the church of St. Peter might have to be sold.

52. The assurance of salvation by letters of pardon is vain, even though the commissary, nay, even though the pope himself, were to stake his soul upon it.

53. They are enemies of Christ and of the pope, who bid the Word of God be altogether silent in some Churches, in order that pardons may be preached in others.

54. Injury is done the Word of God when, in the same sermon, an equal or a longer time is spent on pardons than on this Word.

55. It must be the intention of the pope that if pardons, which are a very small thing, are celebrated with one bell, with single processions and ceremonies, then the Gospel, which is the very greatest thing, should be preached with a hundred bells, a hundred processions, a hundred ceremonies.

56. The "treasures of the Church," out of which the pope. grants indulgences, are not sufficiently named or known among the people of Christ.

57. That they are not temporal treasures is certainly evident, for many of the vendors do not pour out such treasures so easily, but only gather them.

58. Nor are they the merits of Christ and the Saints, for even without the pope, these always work grace for the inner man, and the cross, death, and hell for the outward man.

59. St. Lawrence said that the treasures of the Church were the Church's poor, but he spoke according to the usage of the word in his own time.

60. Without rashness we say that the keys of the Church, given by Christ's merit, are that treasure;

61. For it is clear that for the remission of penalties and of reserved cases, the power of the pope is of itself sufficient.

62. The true treasure of the Church is the Most Holy Gospel of the glory and the grace of God.

63. But this treasure is naturally most odious, for it makes the first to be last.

64. On the other hand, the treasure of indulgences is naturally most acceptable, for it makes the last to be first.

65. Therefore the treasures of the Gospel are nets with which they formerly were wont to fish for men of riches.

66. The treasures of the indulgences are nets with which they now fish for the riches of men.

67. The indulgences which the preachers cry as the "greatest graces" are known to be truly such, in so far as they promote gain.

68. Yet they are in truth the very smallest graces compared with the grace of God and the piety of the Cross.

69. Bishops and curates are bound to admit the commissaries of apostolic pardons, with all reverence.

70. But still more are they bound to strain all their eyes and attend with all their ears, lest these men preach their own dreams instead of the commission of the pope.

71. He who speaks against the truth of apostolic pardons, let him be anathema and accursed!

72. But he who guards against the lust and license of the pardon-preachers, let him be blessed!

73. The pope justly thunders against those who, by any art, contrive the injury of the traffic in pardons.

74. But much more does he intend to thunder against those who use the pretext of pardons to contrive the injury of holy love and truth.

75. To think the papal pardons so great that they could absolve a man even if he had committed an impossible sin and violated the Mother of God -- this is madness.

76. We say, on the contrary, that the papal pardons are not able to remove the very least of venial sins, so far as its guilt is concerned.

77. It is said that even St. Peter, if he were now Pope, could not bestow greater graces; this is blasphemy against St. Peter and against the pope.

78. We say, on the contrary, that even the present pope, and any pope at all, has greater graces at his disposal; to wit, the Gospel, powers, gifts of healing, etc., as it is written in I. Corinthians xii.

79. To say that the cross, emblazoned with the papal arms, which is set up [by the preachers of indulgences], is of equal worth with the Cross of Christ, is blasphemy.

80. The bishops, curates and theologians who allow such talk to be spread among the people, will have an account to render.

81. This unbridled preaching of pardons makes it no easy matter, even for learned men, to rescue the reverence due to the pope from slander, or even from the shrewd questionings of the laity.

82. To wit: -- "Why does not the pope empty purgatory, for the sake of holy love and of the dire need of the souls that are there, if he redeems an infinite number of souls for the sake of miserable money with which to build a Church? The former reasons would be most just; the latter is most trivial."

83. Again: -- "Why are mortuary and anniversary masses for the dead continued, and why does he not return or permit the withdrawal of the endowments founded on their behalf, since it is wrong to pray for the redeemed?"

84. Again: -- "What is this new piety of God and the pope, that for money they allow a man who is impious and their enemy to buy out of purgatory the pious soul of a friend of God, and do not rather, because of that pious and beloved soul's own need, free it for pure love's sake?"

85. Again: -- "Why are the penitential canons long since in actual fact and through disuse abrogated and dead, now satisfied by the granting of indulgences, as though they were still alive and in force?"

86. Again: -- "Why does not the pope, whose wealth is to-day greater than the riches of the richest, build just this one church of St. Peter with his own money, rather than with the money of poor believers?"

87. Again: -- "What is it that the pope remits, and what participation does he grant to those who, by perfect contrition, have a right to full remission and participation?"

88. Again: -- "What greater blessing could come to the Church than if the pope were to do a hundred times a day what he now does once, and bestow on every believer these remissions and participations?"

89. "Since the pope, by his pardons, seeks the salvation of souls rather than money, why does he suspend the indulgences and pardons granted heretofore, since these have equal efficacy?"

90. To repress these arguments and scruples of the laity by force alone, and not to resolve them by giving reasons, is to expose the Church and the pope to the ridicule of their enemies, and to make Christians unhappy.

91. If, therefore, pardons were preached according to the spirit and mind of the pope, all these doubts would be readily resolved; nay, they would not exist.

92. Away, then, with all those prophets who say to the people of Christ, "Peace, peace," and there is no peace!

93. Blessed be all those prophets who say to the people of Christ, "Cross, cross," and there is no cross!

94. Christians are to be exhorted that they be diligent in following Christ, their Head, through penalties, deaths, and hell;

95. And thus be confident of entering into heaven rather through many tribulations, than through the assurance of peace.

Elector Frederick the Wise
by Lucas Cranach

Martin Luther
Address To The Nobility of the German Nation, 1520

Introduction

To his most Serene and Mighty Imperial Majesty and to the Christian Nobility of the German Nation. Dr. Martinus Luther.

The grace and might of God be with you, Most Serene Majesty, most gracious, well-beloved gentlemen!

It is not out of mere arrogance and perversity that I, an individual poor man, have taken upon me to address your lordships. The distress and misery that oppress all the Christian estates, more especially in Germany, have led not only myself, but everyone else, to cry aloud and to ask for help, and have now forced me too to cry out and to ask if God would give His Spirit to anyone to reach a hand to His wretched people. Councils have often put forward some remedy, but it has adroitly been frustrated, and the evils have become worse, through the cunning of certain men. Their malice and wickedness I will now, by the help of God, expose, so that, being known, they may henceforth cease to be so obstructive and injurious. God has given us a young and noble sovereign, and by this has roused great hopes in many hearts; now it is right that we too should do what we can, and make good use of time and grace.

The first thing that we must do is to consider the matter with great earnestness, and, whatever we attempt, not to trust in our own strength and wisdom alone, even if the power of all the world were ours; for God will not endure that a good work should be begun trusting to our own strength and wisdom. He destroys it; it is all useless, as we read in Psalm xxxiii., "There is no king saved by the multitude of a host; a mighty man is not delivered by much strength." And I fear it is for that reason that those beloved princes the Emperors Frederick, the First and the Second, and many other German emperors were, in former times, so piteously spurned and oppressed by the popes, though they were feared by all the world. Perchance they trusted rather in their own strength than in God; therefore they could not but fall; and how would the sanguinary tyrant Julius II have risen so high in our own days but that, I fear, France, Germany, and Venice trusted to themselves? The children of Benjamin slew forty-two thousand Israelites, for this reason: that these trusted to their own strength (Judges xx., etc.).

That such a thing may not happen to us and to our noble Emperor Charles, we must remember that in this matter we wrestle not against flesh and blood, but against the rulers of the darkness of this world (Eph. vi. 12), who may fill the world with war and bloodshed, but cannot themselves be overcome thereby. We must renounce all confidence in our natural strength, and take the matter in hand with humble trust in God; we must seek God's help with earnest prayer, and have nothing before our eyes but the misery and wretchedness of Christendom, irrespective of what punishment the wicked may deserve. If we do not act thus, we may begin the game with great pomp; but when we are well in it, the spirits of evil will make such confusion that the whole world will be immersed in blood, and yet nothing be done. Therefore let us act in the fear of God and prudently. The greater the might of the foe, the greater is the misfortune, if we do not act in the fear of God and with humility. If popes and Romanists have hitherto, with the devil's help, thrown kings into confusion, they may still do so, if we attempt things with our own strength and skill, without God's help.

The Three Walls Of The Romanists

The Romanists have, with great adroitness, drawn three walls round themselves, with which they have hitherto protected themselves, so that no one could reform them, whereby all Christendom has fallen terribly.

Firstly, if pressed by the temporal power, they have affirmed and maintained that the temporal power has no jurisdiction over them, but, on the contrary, that the spiritual power is above the temporal.

Secondly, if it were proposed to admonish them with the Scriptures, they objected that no one may interpret the Scriptures but the Pope.

Thirdly, if they are threatened with a council, they pretend that no one may call a council but the Pope.

Thus they have secretly stolen our three rods, so that they may be unpunished, and intrenched themselves behind these three walls, to act with all the wickedness and malice, which we now witness. And whenever they have been compelled to call a council, they have made it of no avail by binding the princes beforehand with an oath to leave them as they were, and to give moreover to the Pope full power over the procedure of the council, so that it is all one whether we have many councils or no councils, in addition to which they deceive us with false pretences and tricks. So grievously do they tremble for their skin before a true, free council; and thus they have overawed kings and princes, that these believe they would be offending God, if they were not to obey them in all such knavish, deceitful artifices.

Now may God help us, and give us one of those trumpets that overthrew the walls of Jericho, so that we may blow down these walls of straw and paper, and that we may set free our Christian rods for the chastisement of sin, and expose the craft and deceit of the devil, so that we may amend ourselves by punishment and again obtain God's favour.

(a) The First Wall

That the Temporal Power has no Jurisdiction over the Spirituality

Let us, in the first place, attack the first wall.

It has been devised that the Pope, bishops, priests, and monks are called the spiritual estate, princes, lords, artificers, and peasants are the temporal estate. This is an artful lie and hypocritical device, but let no one be made afraid by it, and that for this reason: that all Christians are truly of the spiritual estate, and there is no difference among them, save of office alone. As St. Paul says (1 Cor. xii.), we are all one body, though each member does its own work, to serve the others. This is because we have one baptism, one Gospel, one faith, and are all Christians alike; for baptism, Gospel, and faith, these alone make spiritual and Christian people.

As for the unction by a pope or a bishop, tonsure, ordination, consecration, and clothes differing from those of laymen-all this may make a hypocrite or an anointed puppet, but never a Christian or a spiritual man. Thus we are all consecrated as priests by baptism, as St. Peter says: "Ye are a royal priesthood, a holy nation" (1 Peter ii. 9); and in the book of Revelations: "and hast made us unto our God (by Thy blood) kings and priests" (Rev. v. 10). For, if we had not a higher consecration in us than pope or bishop can give, no priest could ever be made by the consecration of pope or bishop, nor could he say the mass, or preach, or absolve. Therefore the bishop's consecration is just as if in the name of the whole congregation he took one person out of the community, each member of which has equal power, and commanded him to exercise this power for the rest; in the same way as if ten brothers, co-heirs as king's sons, were to choose one from among them to rule over their inheritance, they would all of them still remain kings and have equal power, although one is ordered to govern.

And to put the matter even more plainly, if a little company of pious Christian laymen were taken prisoners and carried away to a desert, and had not among them a priest consecrated by a bishop, and were there to agree to elect one of them, born in wedlock or not, and were to order him to baptise, to celebrate the mass, to absolve, and to preach, this man would as truly be a priest, as if all the bishops and all the Popes had consecrated him. That is why in cases of necessity every man can baptise and absolve, which would not be possible if we were not all priests. This great grace and virtue of baptism and of the Christian estate they have quite destroyed and made us forget by their ecclesiastical law. In this way the Christians used to choose their bishops and priests out of the community; these being afterwards confirmed by other bishops, without the pomp that now prevails. So was it that St. Augustine, Ambrose, Cyprian, were bishops.

Since, then, the temporal power is baptised as we are, and has the same faith and Gospel, we must allow it to be priest and bishop, and account its office an office that is proper and useful to the Christian community. For whatever issues from baptism may boast that it has been consecrated priest, bishop, and pope, although it does not beseem everyone to exercise these offices. For, since we are all priests alike, no man may put himself forward or take upon himself, without our consent and election, to do that which we have all alike power to do. For, if a thing is common to all, no man may take it to himself without the wish and command of the community. And if it should happen that a man were appointed to one of these offices and deposed for abuses, he would be just what he was before. Therefore a priest should be nothing in Christendom but a functionary; as long as he holds his office, he has precedence of others; if he is deprived of it, he is a peasant or a citizen like the rest. Therefore a priest is verily no longer a priest after deposition. But now they have invented *characteres indelebiles*, and pretend that a priest after deprivation still differs from a simple layman. They even imagine that a priest can never be anything but a priest-that is, that he can never become a layman. All this is nothing but mere talk and ordinance of human invention.

It follows, then, that between laymen and priests, princes and bishops, or, as they call it, between spiritual and temporal persons, the only real difference is one of office and function, and not of estate; for they are all of the same spiritual estate, true priests, bishops, and popes, though their functions are not the same-just as among priests and monks every man has not the same functions. And this, as I said above, St. Paul says (Rom. xii.; 1 Cor. xii.), and St. Peter (1 Peter ii.): "We, being many, are one body in Christ, and severally members one of another." Christ's body is not double or twofold, one temporal, the other spiritual. He is one Head, and He has one body.

We see, then, that just as those that we call spiritual, or priests, bishops, or popes, do not differ from other Christians in any other or higher degree but in that they are to be concerned with the word of God and the sacraments-that being their work and office-in the same way the temporal authorities hold the sword and the rod in their hands to punish the wicked and to protect the good. A cobbler, a smith, a peasant, every man, has the office and function of his calling, and yet all alike are consecrated priests and bishops, and every man should by his office or function be useful and beneficial to the rest, so that various kinds of work may all be united for the furtherance of body and soul, just as the members of the body all serve one another.

Now see what a Christian doctrine is this: that the temporal authority is not above the clergy, and may not punish it. This is as if one were to say the hand may not help, though the eye is in grievous suffering. Is it not unnatural, not to say unchristian, that one member may not help another, or guard it against harm? Nay, the nobler the member, the more the rest are bound to help it. Therefore I say, Forasmuch as the temporal power has been ordained by God for the punishment of the bad and the protection of the good, therefore we must let it do its duty throughout the whole Christian body, without respect of persons, whether it strikes popes, bishops, priests, monks, nuns, or whoever it may be. If it were sufficient reason for fettering the temporal power that it is inferior among the offices of Christianity to the offices of priest or confessor, or to the spiritual estate-if this were so, then we ought to restrain tailors, cobblers, masons, carpenters, cooks, cellarmen, peasants, and all secular workmen, from providing the Pope or bishops, priests and monks, with shoes, clothes, houses or victuals, or from paying them tithes. But if these laymen are allowed to do their work without restraint, what do the Romanist scribes mean by their laws? They mean that they withdraw themselves from the operation of temporal Christian power, simply in order that they may be free to do evil, and thus fulfill what St. Peter said: "There shall be false teachers among you, . . . and in covetousness shall they with feigned words make merchandise of you" (2 Peter ii. 1, etc.).

Therefore the temporal Christian power must exercise its office without let or hindrance, without considering whom it may strike, whether pope, or bishop, or priest: whoever is guilty, let him suffer for it.

Whatever the ecclesiastical law has said in opposition to this is merely the invention of Romanist arrogance. For this is what St. Paul says to all Christians: "Let every soul" (I presume including the popes) "be subject unto the higher powers; for they bear not the sword in vain: they serve the Lord therewith, for vengeance on evildoers and for praise to them that do well" (Rom. xiii. 1-4). Also St. Peter: "Submit yourselves to every ordinance of man for the Lord's sake, . . . for so is the will of God" (1 Peter ii. 13, 15). He has also foretold that men would come who should despise government (2 Peter ii.), as has come to pass through ecclesiastical law.

Now, I imagine, the first paper wall is overthrown, inasmuch as the temporal power has become a member of the Christian body; although its work relates to the body, yet does it belong to the spiritual estate. Therefore, it must do its duty without let or hindrance upon all members of the whole body, to punish or urge, as guilt may deserve, or need may require, without respect of pope, bishops, or priests, let them threaten or excommunicate as they will. That is why a guilty priest is deprived of his priesthood before being given over to the secular arm; whereas this would not be right, if the secular sword had not authority over him already by Divine ordinance.

It is, indeed, past bearing that the spiritual law should esteem so highly the liberty, life, and property of the clergy, as if laymen were not as good spiritual Christians, or not equally members of the Church. Why should your body, life, goods, and honour be free, and not mine, seeing that we are equal as Christians, and have received alike baptism, faith, spirit, and all things? If a priest is killed, the country is laid under an interdict: why not also if a peasant is killed? Whence comes this great difference among equal Christians? Simply from human laws and inventions.

It can have been no good spirit, either, that devised these evasions and made sin to go unpunished. For if, as Christ and the Apostles bid us, it is our duty to oppose the evil one and all his works and words, and to drive him away as well as may be, how then should we remain quiet and be silent when the Pope and his followers are guilty of devilish works and words? Are we for the sake of men to allow the commandments and the truth of God to be defeated, which at our baptism we vowed to support with body and soul? Truly we should have to answer for all souls that would thus be abandoned and led astray.

Therefore it must have been the arch-devil himself who said, as we read in the ecclesiastical law, If the Pope were so perniciously wicked, as to be dragging souls in crowds to the devil, yet he could not be deposed. This is the accursed and devilish foundation on which they build at Rome, and think that the whole world is to be allowed to go to the devil rather than they should be opposed in their knavery. If a man were to escape punishment simply because he is above the rest, then no Christian might punish another, since Christ has commanded each of us to esteem himself the lowest and the humblest (Matt. xviii. 4; Luke ix. 48).

Where there is sin, there remains no avoiding the punishment, as St. Gregory says, We are all equal, but guilt makes one subject to another. Now let us see how they deal with Christendom. They arrogate to themselves immunities without any warrant from the Scriptures, out of their own wickedness, whereas God and the Apostles made them subject to the secular sword; so that we must fear that it is the work of antichrist, or a sign of his near approach.

(b) The Second Wall

That no one may interpret the Scriptures but the Pope

The second wall is even more tottering and weak: that they alone pretend to be considered masters of the Scriptures; although they learn nothing of them all their life. They assume authority, and juggle before us with impudent words, saying that the Pope cannot err in matters of faith, whether he be evil or good, albeit they cannot prove it by a single letter. That is why the canon law contains so many heretical and unchristian, nay unnatural, laws; but of these we need not speak now. For whereas they imagine the Holy Ghost never leaves them, however unlearned and wicked they may be, they grow bold enough to decree whatever they like. But were this true, where were the need and use of the Holy Scriptures? Let us burn them, and content ourselves with the unlearned gentlemen at Rome, in whom the Holy Ghost dwells, who, however, can dwell in pious souls only. If I had not read it, I could never have believed that the devil should have put forth such follies at Rome and find a following.

But not to fight them with our own words, we will quote the Scriptures. St. Paul says, "If anything be revealed to another that sitteth by, let the first hold his peace" (1 Cor. xiv. 30). What would be the use of this commandment, if we were to believe him alone that teaches or has the highest seat? Christ Himself says, "And they shall be all taught of God." (St. John vi. 45). Thus it may come to pass that the Pope and his followers are wicked and not true Christians, and not being taught by God, have no true understanding, whereas a common man may have true understanding. Why should we then not follow him? Has not the Pope often erred? Who could help Christianity, in case the Pope errs, if we do not rather believe another who has the Scriptures for him?

Therefore it is a wickedly devised fable-and they cannot quote a single letter to confirm it-that it is for the Pope alone to interpret the Scriptures or to confirm the interpretation of them. They have assumed the authority of their own selves. And though they say that this authority was given to St. Peter when the keys were given to him, it is plain enough that the keys were not given to St. Peter alone, but to the whole community. Besides, the keys were not ordained for doctrine or authority, but for sin, to bind or loose, and what they claim besides this from the keys is mere invention. But what Christ said to St. Peter: "I have prayed for thee that thy faith fail not" (St. Luke xxii. 32), cannot relate to the Pope, inasmuch as the greater part of the Popes have been without faith, as they are themselves forced to acknowledge; nor did Christ pray for Peter alone, but for all the Apostles and all Christians, as He says, "Neither pray I for these alone, but for them also which shall believe on Me through their word" (St. John xvii.). Is not this plain enough?

Only consider the matter. They must needs acknowledge that there are pious Christians among us that have the true faith, spirit, understanding, word, and mind of Christ: why then should we reject their word and understanding, and follow a pope who has neither understanding nor spirit? Surely this were to deny our whole faith and the Christian Church. Moreover, if the article of our faith is right, "I believe in the holy Christian Church," the Pope cannot alone be right; else we must say, "I believe in the Pope of Rome," and reduce the Christian Church to one man, which is a devilish and damnable heresy. Besides that, we are all priests, as I have said, and have all one faith, one Gospel, one Sacrament; how then should we not have the power of discerning and judging what is right or wrong in matters of faith? What becomes of St. Paul's words, "But he that is spiritual judgeth all things, yet he himself is judged of no man" (1 Cor. ii. 15), and also, "we having the same spirit of faith"? (2 Cor. iv. 13). Why then should we not perceive as well as an unbelieving pope what agrees or disagrees with our faith?

By these and many other texts we should gain courage and freedom, and should not let the spirit of liberty (as St. Paul has it) be frightened away by the inventions of the popes; we should boldly judge what they do and what they leave undone by our own believing understanding of the Scriptures, and force them to follow the better understanding, and not their own. Did not Abraham in old days have to obey his Sarah, who was in stricter bondage to him than we are to any one on earth? Thus, too, Balaam's ass was wiser than the prophet. If God spoke by an ass against a prophet, why should He not speak by a pious man against the Pope? Besides, St. Paul withstood St. Peter as being in error (Gal. ii.). Therefore it behoves every Christian to aid the faith by understanding and defending it and by condemning all errors.

(c) The Third Wall

That no one may call a council but the Pope

The third wall falls of itself, as soon as the first two have fallen; for if the Pope acts contrary to the Scriptures, we are bound to stand by the Scriptures, to punish and to constrain him, according to Christ's commandment, "Moreover, if thy brother shall trespass against thee, go and tell him his fault between thee and him alone; if he shall hear thee, thou hast gained thy brother. But if he will not hear thee, then take with thee one or two more, that in the mouth of two or three witnesses every word may be established. And if he shall neglect to hear them, tell it unto the Church; but if he neglect to hear the Church, let him be unto thee as a heathen man and a publican" (St. Matt. xviii. 15-17). Here each member is commanded to take care for the other; much more then should we do this, if it is a ruling member of the community that does evil, which by its evil-doing causes great harm and offence to the others. If then I am to accuse him before the Church, I must collect the Church together. Moreover, they can show nothing in the Scriptures giving the Pope sole power to call and confirm councils; they have nothing but their own laws; but these hold good only so long as they are not injurious to Christianity and the laws of God. Therefore, if the Pope deserves punishment, these laws cease to bind us, since Christendom would suffer, if he were not punished by a council. Thus we read (Acts xv.) that the council of the Apostles was not called by St. Peter, but by all the Apostles and the elders. But if the right to call it had lain with St. Peter alone, it would not have been a Christian council, but a heretical conciliabulum. Moreover, the most celebrated council of all-that of Nicaea-was neither called nor confirmed by the Bishop of Rome, but by the Emperor Constantine; and after him many other emperors have done the same, and yet the councils called by them were accounted most Christian. But if the Pope alone had the power, they must all have been heretical. Moreover, if I consider the councils that the Pope has called, I do not find that they produced any notable results.

Therefore when need requires, and the Pope is a cause of offence to Christendom, in these cases whoever can best do so, as a faithful member of the whole body, must do what he can to procure a true free council. This no one can do so well as the temporal authorities, especially since they are fellow-Christians, fellow-priests, sharing one spirit and one power in all things, and since they should exercise the office that they have received from God without hindrance, whenever it is necessary and useful that it should be exercised. Would it not be most unnatural, if a fire were to break out in a city, and every one were to keep still and let it burn on and on, whatever might be burnt, simply because they had not the mayor's authority, or because the fire perchance broke out at the mayor's house? Is not every citizen bound in this case to rouse and call in the rest? How much more should this be done in the spiritual city of Christ, if a fire of offence breaks out, either at the Pope's government or wherever it may! The like happens if an enemy attacks a town. The first to rouse up the rest earns glory and thanks. Why then should not he earn glory that descries the coming of our enemies from hell and rouses and summons all Christians?

But as for their boasts of their authority, that no one must oppose it, this is idle talk. No one in Christendom has any authority to do harm, or to forbid others to prevent harm being done. There is no authority in the Church but for reformation. Therefore if the Pope wished to use his power to prevent the calling of a free council, so as to prevent the reformation of the Church, we must not respect him or his power; and if he should begin to excommunicate and fulminate, we must despise this as the doings of a madman, and, trusting in God, excommunicate and repel him as best we may. For this his usurped power is nothing; he does not possess it, and he is at once overthrown by a text from the Scriptures. For St. Paul says to the Corinthians "that God has given us authority for edification, and not for destruction (2 Cor. x. 8). Who will set this text at nought? It is the power of the devil and of antichrist that prevents what would serve for the reformation of Christendom. Therefore we must not follow it, but oppose it with our body, our goods, and all that we have. And even if a miracle were to happen in favour of the Pope against the temporal power, or if some were to be stricken by a plague, as they sometimes boast has happened, all this is to be held as having been done by the devil in order to injure our faith in God, as was foretold by Christ: "There shall arise false Christs and false prophets, and shall show great sings and wonders, insomuch that, if it were possible, they shall deceive the very elect" (Matt. xxiv. 23); and St. Paul tells the Thessalonians that the coming of antichrist shall be "after the working of Satan with all power and signs and lying wonders" (2 Thess. ii. 9).

Therefore let us hold fast to this: that Christian power can do nothing against Christ, as St. Paul says, "For we can do nothing against Christ, but for Christ" (2 Cor. xiii. 8). But, if it does anything against Christ, it is the power of antichrist and the devil, even if it rained and hailed wonders and plagues. Wonders and plagues prove nothing, especially in these latter evil days, of which false wonders are foretold in all the Scriptures. Therefore we must hold fast to the words of God with an assured faith; then the devil will soon cease his wonders.

And now I hope the false, lying spectre will be laid with which the Romanists have long terrified and stupefied our consciences. And it will be seen that, like all the rest of us, they are subject to the temporal sword; that they have no authority to interpret the Scriptures by force without skill; and that they have no power to prevent a council, or to pledge it in accordance with their pleasure, or to bind it beforehand, and deprive it of its freedom; and that if they do this, they are verily of the fellowship of antichrist and the devil, and having nothing of Christ but the name.

Of The Matters To Be Considered In The Councils

Let us now consider the matters which should be treated in the councils, and with which popes, cardinals, bishops, and all learned men should occupy themselves day and night, if they love Christ and His Church. [. . .]

1. . . .pomp is a stumbling-block, and the Pope, for the very salvation of his soul, ought to put if off . . .

2. . . . I advise, however, that there be made fewer cardinals, or that the Pope should have to support them out of his own purse. It would be amply sufficient if there were twelve, and if each of them had an annual income of one thousand guilders. . .

3. If we took away ninety-nine parts of the Pope's Court and only left one hundredth, it would still be large enough to answer questions on matters of belief. [. . .]

. . . If the Pope can make a law on the day after his election by which he takes our benefices and livings to which he has no right, the Emperor Charles should so much the more have a right to issue a law for all Germany on the day after his coronation that in future no livings and benefices are to fall to Rome by virtue of the Pope's month, but that those that have so fallen are to be freed and taken from the Romish robbers. This right he possesses authoritatively by virtue of his temporal sword.

Twenty-Seven Articles Respecting The Reformation Of The Christian Estate

Now though I am too lowly to submit articles that could serve for the reformation of these fearful evils, I will yet sing out my fool's song, and will show, as well as my wit will allow, what might and should be done by the temporal authorities or by a general council.

1. Princes, nobles, and cities should promptly forbid their subjects to pay the annates to Rome and should even abolish them altogether. [. . .]

2. . . . . They should ordain, order, and decree that henceforth no benefice shall be drawn away to Rome, and that no benefice shall be claimed there in any fashion whatsoever; and after having once got these benefices out of the hands of Romish tyranny, they must be kept from them, and their lawful incumbents must be reinstated in them to administer them as best they may within the German nation. [. . .]

3. It should be decreed by an imperial law that no episcopal cloak and no confirmation of any appointment shall for the future be obtained from Rome. The order of the most holy and

renowned Nicene Council must again be restored, namely that a bishop must be confirmed by the two nearest bishops or by the archbishop. [. . .]

4. Let it be decreed that no temporal matter shall be submitted to Rome, but all shall be left to the jurisdiction of the temporal authorities. [. . .]

5. Henceforth no reservations shall be valid, and no benefices shall be appropriated by Rome, whether the incumbent die there, or there be a dispute, or the incumbent be a servant of the Pope or of a cardinal; and all courtiers shall be strictly prohibited and prevented from causing a dispute about any benefice, so as to cite the pious priests, to trouble them, and to drive them to pay compensation. [. . .]

6. [. . .] Now all priests ought to know, or rather it should be a public ordinance, that no secret sin constitutes a reserved case, if there be no public accusation; and that every priest has power to absolve from all sin, whatever its name, if it be secret, and that no abbot, bishop, or pope has power to reserve any such case; and, lastly, that if they do this, it is null and void, and they should, moreover, be punished as interfering without authority in God's judgment and confusing and troubling without cause our poor witless consciences. But in respect to any great open sin, directly contrary to God's commandments, there is some reason for a "reserved case"; but there should not be too many, nor should they be reserved arbitrarily without due cause. For God has not ordained tyrants, but shepherds, in His Church, as St. Peter says (1 Peter v. 2).

7. The Roman See must abolish the papal offices, and diminish that crowd of crawling vermin at Rome, so that the Pope's servants may be supported out of the Pope's own pocket, and that his court may cease to surpass all royal courts in its pomp and extravagance; [. . .]

8. The terrible oaths must be abolished which bishops are forced, without any right, to swear to the Pope, by which they are bound like servants, and which are arbitrarily and foolishly decreed in the absurd and shallow chapter *Significasti*. [. . .]

9. The Pope should have no power over the Emperor, except to anoint and crown him at the altar, as a bishop crowns a king; nor should that devilish pomp be allowed that the Emperor should kiss the Pope's feet or sit at his feet, or, as it is said, hold his stirrup or the reins of his mule, when he mounts to ride; much less should he pay homage to the Pope, or swear allegiance, as is impudently demanded by the popes, as if they had a right to it. The chapter *Solite*, in which the papal authority is exalted above the imperial, is not worth a farthing, and so of all those that depend on it or fear it; for it does nothing but pervert God's holy words from their true meaning, according to their own imaginations, as I have proved in a Latin treatise. [. . .]

10. The Pope must withdraw his hand from the dish, and on no pretence assume royal authority over Naples and Sicily. He has no more right to them than I, and yet claims to be the lord-their

liege lord. They have been taken by force and robbery, like almost all his other possessions. [. . .] The same should be done with Bologna, Imola, Vicenza, Ravenna, and whatever the Pope has taken by force and holds without right in the Ancontine territory, in the Romagna, and other parts of Italy, interfering in their affairs against all the commandments of Christ and St. Paul. [. . .]

11. The custom of kissing the Pope's feet must cease. It is an unchristian, or rather an anti-Christian, example that a poor sinful man should suffer his feet to be kissed by one who is a hundred times better than he. [. . .]

12. Pilgrimages to Rome must be abolished, or at least no one must be allowed to go from his own wish or his own piety, unless his priest, his town magistrate, or his lord has found that there is sufficient reason for his pilgrimage. This I say, not because pilgrimages are bad in themselves, but because at the present time they lead to mischief; for at Rome a pilgrim sees no good examples, but only offence. They themselves have made a proverb, "The nearer to Rome, the farther from Christ," and accordingly men bring home contempt of God and of God's commandments. It is said, "The first time one goes to Rome, he goes to seek a rogue; the second time he finds him; the third time he brings him home with him." But now they have become so skilful that they can do their three journeys in one, and they have, in fact, brought home from Rome this saying: "It were better never to have seen or heard of Rome." [. . .]

13. . . . Let no more mendicant monasteries be built! God help us! there are too many as it is. Would to God they were all abolished, or at least made over to two or three orders! It has never done good, it will never do good, to go wandering about over the country. [. . .]

14. . . . Therefore we learn from the Apostle clearly, that every town should elect a pious learned citizen from the congregation and charge him with the office of minister; the congregation should support him, and he should be left at liberty to marry or not. He should have as assistants several priests and deacons, married or not, as they please, who should help him to govern the people and the congregation with sermons and the ministration of the sacraments, as is still the case in the Greek Church. [. . .]

15. . . . If your superiors will not allow you to confess your secret sins to whomsoever you will, then take them yourself, and confess them to your brother or sister, to whomsoever you will; be absolved and comforted, and then go or do what your wish or duty commands; only believe firmly that you have been absolved, and nothing more is necessary. [. . .]

16. It were also right to abolish annual festivals, processions, and masses for the dead, or at least to diminish their number; for we evidently see that they have become no better than a mockery, exciting the anger of God and having no object but money-getting, gluttony, and carousals. [. . .]

17. One should also abolish certain punishments inflicted by the canon law, especially the interdict, which is doubtless the invention of the evil one. [. . .]

Excommunication should not be used except where the Scriptures command it, that is, against those that have not the right faith, or that live in open sin, and not in matters of temporal goods. [. . .]

18. One should abolish all saints' days, keeping only Sunday. [. . .]

19. The degrees of relationship in which marriage is forbidden must be altered, such as so-called spiritual relations in the third and fourth degrees; and where the Pope at Rome can dispense in such matters for money, and make shameful bargains, every priest should have the power of granting the same dispensations freely for the salvation of souls. [. . .]

Besides this, fasts must be made optional, and every kind of food made free, as is commanded in the Gospels (Matt. xv.II). [. . .]

20. The country chapels and churches must be destroyed, such as those to which the new pilgrimages have been set on foot: Wilsnack, Sternberg, Treves, the Grimmenthal, and now Ratisbon, and many others. [. . .]

21. It is one of the most urgent necessities to abolish all begging in Christendom. No one should go about begging among Christians. It would not be hard to do this, if we attempted it with good heart and courage: each town should support its own poor and should not allow strange beggars to come in, whatever they may call themselves, pilgrims or mendicant monks. Every town could feed its own poor; and if it were too small, the people in the neighbouring villages should be called upon to contribute. As it is, they have to support many knaves and vagabonds under the name of beggars. If they did what I propose, they would at least know who were really poor or not. [. . .]

22. It is also to be feared that the many masses that have been founded in convents and foundations, instead of doing any good, arouse God's anger; wherefore it would be well to endow no more masses and to abolish many of those that have been endowed; for we see that they are only looked upon as sacrifices and good works, though in truth they are sacraments like baptism and confession, and as such profit him only that receives them. [. . .]

23. As for the fraternities, together with indulgences, letters of indulgence, dispensations for Lent, and masses, and all the rest of such things, let them all be drowned and abolished; there is no good in them at all. If the Pope has the authority to grant dispensation in the matter of eating butter and hearing masses, let him allow priests to do the same; he has no right to take the power from them. I speak also of the fraternities in which indulgences, masses, and good works are distributed. My friend, in baptism you joined a fraternity of which Christ, the angels,

and saints, and all Christians are members; be true to this, and satisfy it, and you will have fraternities enough. [. . .]

24. It is high time to take up earnestly and truthfully the cause of the Bohemians, to unite them with ourselves and ourselves with them, so that all mutual accusations, envy, and hatred may cease. I will be the first, in my folly, to give my opinion, with all due deference to those of better understanding.

First of all, we must honestly confess the truth, without attempting self-justification, and own one thing to the Bohemians, namely that John Huss and Jerome of Prague were burnt at Constance in violation of the papal, Christian, and imperial oath and safe-conduct, and that thus God's commandment was broken and the Bohemians excited to great anger. [. . .]

25. The universities also require a good, sound reformation. . . . my advice would be that the books of Aristotle, the Physics, the Metaphysics, Of the Soul, Ethics, which have hitherto been considered the best, be altogether abolished, with all others that profess to treat of nature, though nothing can be learned from them, either of natural or of spiritual things. [. . .]

I would, however, gladly consent that Aristotle's books of Logic, Rhetoric, and Poetry, should be retained, or they might be usefully studied in a condensed form, to practise young people in speaking and preaching; but the notes and comments should be abolished, and, just as Cicero's Rhetoric is read without note or comment, Aristotle's Logic should be read without such long commentaries. . . . Besides this, there are languages-Latin, Greek, and Hebrew-the mathematics, history; which I recommend to men of higher understanding . . .

26. let the Pope give up [the Holy Roman Empire], all he has of the empire, and free our country from his unbearable taxes and robberies, and give back to us our liberty, authority, wealth, honour, body, and soul, rendering to the empire those things that are the empire's, so as to act in accordance with his words and pretences. [. . .]

27. [. . .] In the first place, we require a general law and consent of the German nation against **profusion and extravagance in dress**, which is the cause of so much poverty among the nobles and the people. [. . .]

It is similarly necessary to diminish **the use of spices**, which is one of the ships in which our gold is sent away from Germany. [. . .]

But without doubt the greatest misfortune of the Germans is **buying on usury**. But for this, many a man would have to leave unbought his silk, velvet, cloth of gold, spices, and all other luxuries. The system has not been in force for more than one hundred years, and has already brought poverty, misery, and destruction on almost all princes, foundations, cities, nobles, and heirs. If it continues for another hundred years Germany will be left without a farthing, and we shall be reduced to eating one another. The devil invented this system, and the Pope has done an injury to the whole world by sanctioning it. [. . .]

Then there is the **excess in eating and drinking**, for which we Germans have an ill reputation in foreign countries, as our special vice, and which has become so common, and gained so much the upper hand, that sermons avail nothing. The loss of money caused by it is not the worst; but in its train come murder, adultery, theft, blasphemy, and all vices. The temporal power should do something to prevent it; otherwise it will come to pass, as Christ foretold, that the last day shall come as a thief in the night, and shall find them eating and drinking, marrying and giving in marriage, planting and building, buying and selling (Matt. xxiv. 38; Luke xvii. 26), just as things go on now, and that so strongly that I apprehend lest the day of judgment be at hand, even now when we least expect it.

Lastly, is it not a terrible thing that we Christians should maintain **public brothels**, though we all vow chastity in our baptism? I well know all that can be said on this matter: that it is not peculiar to one nation, that it would be difficult to demolish it, and that it is better thus than that virgins, or married women, or honourable women should be dishonoured. But should not the spiritual and temporal powers combine to find some means of meeting these difficulties without any such heathen practice? If the people of Israel existed without this scandal, why should not a Christian nation be able to do so? How do so many towns and villages manage to exist without these houses? Why should not great cities be able to do so? [. . .]

But this may suffice for the present. For of what concerns the temporal authority and the nobles I have, I think, said enough in my tract on Good Works. For their lives and governments leave room enough for improvement; but there is no comparison between spiritual and temporal abuses, as I have there shown. I daresay I have sung a lofty strain, that I have proposed many things that will be thought impossible, and attacked many points too sharply. But what was I to do? I was bound to say this: if I had the power, this is what I would do. I had rather incur the world's anger than God's; they cannot take from me more than my life. I have hitherto made many offers of peace to my adversaries; but, as I see, God has forced me through them to open my mouth wider and wider, and, because they do not keep quiet, to give them enough cause for speaking, barking, shouting, and writing. Well, then, I have another song still to sing concerning them and Rome; if they wish to hear it, I will sing it to them, and sing with all my might. Do you understand, my friend Rome, what I mean?

I have frequently offered to submit my writings for inquiry and examination, but in vain, though I know, if I am in the right, I must be condemned upon earth and justified by Christ alone in heaven. For all the Scriptures teach us that the affairs of Christians and Christendom must be judged by God alone; they have never yet been justified by men in this world, but the opposition has always been too strong. My greatest care and fear is lest my cause be not condemned by men, by which I should know for certain that it does not please God. Therefore let them go freely to work, pope, bishop, priest, monk, or doctor; they are the true people to persecute the truth, as they have always done. May God grant us all a Christian understanding, and especially to the Christian nobility of the German nation true spiritual courage, to do what is best for our unhappy Church. Amen!

At Wittenberg, in the year 1520.

Source:

Martin Luther: *Address to the Christian nobility of the German nation respecting the reformation of the Christian estate*, tr. by C. A. Buchheim.

from *The prince / by Niccolo Machiavelli. Utopia / by Sir Thomas More. Ninety-five theses; Address to the German nobility ; Concerning Christian liberty / by Martin Luther ; with introductions and notes*. (New York : P.F. Collier, c1910) Harvard classics 36, ed. by C.W.Eliot

Title page from ***The Babylonian Captivity of the Church***

Martin Luther

The Babylonian Captivity of the Church (Oct 1520)

Source: *Works of Martin Luther with Introductions and Notes* (Philadelphia: A. J. Holman Company, 1915), pp. 167-293, Translated by Albert T. W. Steinhaeuser,

Martin Luther, Augustinian, to his friend, Herman Tulich,

Greeting

1.1 Like it or not, I am compelled to learn more every day, with so many and such able masters vying with one another to improve my mind. Some two years ago I wrote a little book on indulgences, which I now deeply regret having published. For at the time I still clung to the Roman tyranny with great superstition and held that indulgences should not be altogether rejected, seeing they were approved by the common consent of men. Nor was this to be wondered at, for I was then engaged single-handed in my Sisyphean task. Since then, however, through the kindness of Sylvester and the friars, who so strenuously defended indulgences, I have come to see that they are nothing but an fraud of the Roman flatterers by which they rob people of their faith and fortunes. I wish I could convince the booksellers and all my readers to burn up the whole of my writings on indulgences and to substitute for them this proposition:

INDULGENCES are a Swindler's Trick of the Roman flatterers.

1.3 Next, Eck and Emser, with their fellows, undertook to instruct me concerning the **PRIMACY OF THE POPE**. Here too, not to be ungrateful to such learned folk, I acknowledge how greatly I have profited by their labors. For, while denying the divine authority of the papacy, I still admitted its human authority. But after hearing and reading the subtle subtleties of these pretentious and conceited men, with which they skilfully prop their idol – for in these matters my mind is not altogether unreachable – I now know of a certainty that:

THE PAPACY is the kingdom of Babylon and the power of Nimrod the mighty hunter.

Once more, therefore, that all may fall out to my friends' advantage, I beg both booksellers and readers to burn what I have published on that subject and to hold to this proposition:

1.4 THE PAPACY IS THE MIGHTY prey of the Roman Bishop.

This follows from the arguments of Eck, Emser and the Leipzig lecturer on the Holy Scriptures.

[. . .]

1.18 AT THE OUTSET I must deny that there are seven sacraments, and hold for the present to but three – baptism, penance and the bread. These three have been subjected to a miserable captivity by the Roman curia, and the Church has been deprived of all her liberty. To be sure, if I desired to use the term in its scriptural sense, I should allow but a single sacrament, with three sacramental signs. But of this I shall treat more fully at the proper time.

The Sacrament of the Altar

2.1 Now, about the Sacrament of the Bread, the most important of all sacraments:

2.2 Let me tell you what progress I have made in my studies on the administration of this sacrament. For when I published my treatise on the Eucharist, I clung to the common usage, being in no way concerned with the question whether the papacy was right or wrong. But now, challenged and attacked, no, forcibly thrust into the arena, I shall freely speak my mind, let all the papists laugh or weep together. [. . .]

2.5 Now there are two passages that do clearly bear upon this matter – the Gospel narratives of the institution of the Lord's Supper, and Paul in 1 Corinthians 11. Let us examine these. Matthew, Mark and Luke agree that Christ gave the whole sacrament to all the disciples, and it is certain that Paul delivered both kinds. No one has ever had the temerity to assert the contrary. Further, Matthew reports that Christ did not say of the bread, "All of you, eat of it," but of the cup, " Drink of it all of you." Mark likewise does not say, "They all ate from it," but, " They all drank from it."

Both Matthew and Mark attach the note of universality to the cup, not to the bread, as though the Spirit saw this schism coming, by which some would be forbidden to partake of the cup, which Christ desired should be common to all. How furiously, do you think, would they rave against us, if they had found the word "all" attached to the bread instead of the cup! They would not leave us a loophole to escape, they would cry out against us and set us down as heretics, they would damn us for schismatics. But now, since it stands on our side and against them, they will not be bound by any force of logic – these men of the most free will, who change and change again even the things that are God's, and throw everything into confusion. [. . .]

2.20 I conclude, then, that it is wicked and despotic to deny both kinds to the laity, and that this is not in the power of any angel, much less of any pope or council. Nor does the Council of Constance give me pause, for if its authority carries weight, why does not that of the Council of Basel also carry weight? For the latter council decided, on the contrary, after much disputing, that the Bohemians might use both kinds, as the extant records and documents of the council prove. And to that council this ignorant flatterer refers in support of his dream. In such wisdom does his whole treatise abound.

2.21 The first captivity of this sacrament, therefore, concerns its substance or completeness, of which we have been deprived by the despotism of Rome. Not that they sin against Christ, who use the one kind, for Christ did not command the use of either kind, but left it to every one's free will, when He said: "As often as you do this, do it in remembrance of me." But they sin who forbid the giving of both kinds to such as desire to exercise this free will. The fault lies not with the laity, but with the priests. The sacrament does not belong to the priests, but to all, and the priests are not lords but ministers, in duty bound to administer both kinds to those who desire them, and as often as they desire them. If they wrest this right from the laity and forcibly withhold it, they are tyrants. But the laity are without fault, whether they lack one kind or both kinds. They must meanwhile be sustained by their faith and by their desire for the complete sacrament. The priests, being ministers, are bound to administer baptism and absolution to whoever seeks them, because he has a right to them. But if they do not administer them, he that seeks them has at least the full merit of his faith, while they will be accused before Christ as wicked servants. In like manner the holy Fathers of old who dwelt in the desert did not receive the sacrament in any form for many years together.

2.22 Therefore I do not urge that both kinds be seized by force, as though we were bound to this form by a rigorous command. But I instruct men's consciences that they may endure the Roman tyranny, knowing well they have been deprived of their rightful share in the sacrament because of their own sin. This only do I desire – that no one justify the tyranny of Rome, as though it did well to forbid one of the two kinds to the laity. We ought rather to abhor it, withhold our consent, and endure it just as we should do if we were held captive by the Turk and not permitted to use either kind. That is what I meant by saying it seemed well to me that this captivity should be ended by the decree of a general council, our Christian liberty restored to us out of the hands of the Roman tyrant, and every one left free to seek and receive this sacrament, just as he is free to receive baptism and penance. But now they compel us, by the same tyranny, to receive the one kind year after year. So utterly lost is the liberty which Christ has given us. This is but the due reward of our godless ingratitude.

2.23 The second captivity of this sacrament is less grievous so far as the conscience is concerned, yet the very gravest danger threatens the man who would attack it, to say nothing of condemning it. Here I shall be called a Wycliffite and a heretic a thousand times over. But what of that? Since the Roman bishop has ceased to be a bishop and become a tyrant, I fear none of his decrees, for I know that it is not in his power, nor even in that of a general council, to make new articles of faith. Years ago, when I was delving into scholastic theology, the Cardinal of

Cambrai gave me food for thought, in his comments on the fourth Book of the Sentences, where he argues with great acumen that to hold that real bread and real wine, and not their accidents only, are present on the altar, is much more probable and requires fewer unnecessary miracles – if only the Church had not decreed otherwise. When I learned later what church it was that had decreed this – namely, the Church of Thomas, i.e., of Aristotle – I waxed bolder, and after floating in a sea of doubt, at last found rest for my conscience in the above view – namely, that it is real bread and real wine, in which Christ's real flesh and blood are present, not otherwise and not less really than they assume to be the case under their accidents. I reached this conclusion because I saw that the opinions of the Thomists, though approved by pope and council, remain but opinions and do not become articles of faith, even though an angel from heaven were to decree otherwise. For what is asserted without Scripture or an approved revelation, may be held as an opinion, but need not be believed. But this opinion of Thomas hangs so completely in the air, devoid of Scripture and reason, that he seems here to have forgotten both his philosophy and his logic. For Aristotle writes about subject and accidents so very differently from St. Thomas, that I think this great man is to be pitied, not only for drawing his opinions in matters of faith from Aristotle, but for attempting to base them on him without understanding his meaning – an unfortunate superstructure upon an unfortunate foundation.

2.24 I therefore permit every man to hold either of these views, as he chooses. My one concern at present is to remove all scruples of conscience, so that no one may fear to become guilty of heresy if he should believe in the presence of real bread and real wine on the altar, and that every one may feel at liberty to ponder, hold and believe either one view or the other, without endangering his salvation. However, I shall now more fully set forth my own view. In the first place, I do not intend to listen or attach the least importance to those who will cry out that this teaching of mine is Wycliffite, Hussite, heretical, and contrary to the decision of the Church, for they are the very persons whom I have convicted of manifold heresies in the matter of indulgences, the freedom of the will and the grace of God, good works and sin, etc. If Wycliffe was once a heretic, they are heretics ten times over, and it is a pleasure to be suspected and accused by such heretics and perverse sophists, whom to please is the height of godlessness. Besides, the only way in which they can prove their opinions and disprove those of others, is by saying, "That is Wycliffite, Hussite, heretical!" They have this feeble retort always on their tongue, and they have nothing else. If you demand a Scripture passage, they say, "This is our opinion, and the decision of the Church – that is, of ourselves!" Thus these men, " reprobate concerning the faith" and untrustworthy, have the audacity to set their own fancies before us in the name of the Church as articles of faith.

2.25 But there are good grounds for my view, and this above all – no violence is to be done to the words of God, whether by man or angel. But they are to be retained in their simplest meaning wherever possible, and to be understood in their grammatical and literal sense unless the context plainly forbids, lest we give our adversaries occasion to make a mockery of all the Scriptures. Thus Origen was repudiated, in ancient times, because he despised the grammatical sense and turned the trees, and all things else written concerning Paradise, into allegories. For it might be concluded from this that God did not create trees. Even so here, when the Evangelists plainly write that Christ took bread and broke it, and the book of Acts and Paul, in their turn, call it bread, we have to think of real bread and real wine, just as we do of a real cup. For even they do not maintain that the cup is transubstantiated. But since it is not necessary to assume a transubstantiation wrought by Divine power, it is to be regarded as a figment of the human mind, for it rests neither on Scripture nor on reason, as we shall see.

2.26 Therefore it is an absurd and unheard-of juggling with words, to understand "bread" to mean "the form, or accidents of bread," and "wine" to mean "the form, or accidents of wine." Why do they not also understand all other things to mean their forms, or accidents? Even if this might be done with all other things, it would yet not be right thus to emasculate the words of God and arbitrarily to empty them of their meaning.

2.27 Moreover, the Church had the true faith for more than twelve hundred years, during which time the holy Fathers never once mentioned this transubstantiation – certainly, a monstrous word for a monstrous idea – until the pseudo-philosophy of Aristotle became rampant in the Church these last three hundred years. During these centuries many other things have been wrongly defined, for example, that the Divine essence neither is begotten nor begets, that the soul is the substantial form of the human body, and the like assertions, which are made without reason or sense, as the Cardinal of Cambray himself admits.

2.28 Perhaps they will say that the danger of idolatry demands that bread and wine be not really present. How ridiculous! The laymen have never become familiar with their subtle philosophy of substance and accidents, and could not grasp it if it were taught them. Besides, there is the same danger in the case of the accidents which remain and which they see, as in the case of the substance which they do not see. For if they do not adore the accidents, but Christ hidden under them, why should they adore the bread, which they do not see?

2.29 But why could not Christ include His body in the substance of the bread just as well as in the accidents? The two substances of fire and iron are so mingled in the heated iron that every part is both iron and fire. Why could not much rather Christ's body be thus contained in every part of the substance of the bread? [. . .]

2.37 The third captivity of this sacrament is that most wicked abuse of all, in consequence of which there is today no more generally accepted and firmly believed opinion in the Church than this – that the mass is a good work and a sacrifice. This abuse has brought an endless host of others in its wake, so that the faith of this sacrament has become utterly extinct and the holy sacrament has truly been turned into a fair, tavern, and place of merchandise. Hence participations, brotherhoods, intercessions, merits, anniversaries, memorial days, and the like wares are bought and sold, traded and bartered in the Church, and from this priests and monks derive their whole living. [. . .]

2.60 Now there are two roadblocks that commonly prevent us from gathering the fruits of the mass. First, the fact that we are sinners and unworthy of such great things because of our exceeding vileness. Secondly, the fact that, even if we were worthy, these things are so high that our faint-hearted nature dare not aspire to them or ever hope to attain to them. For to have God for our Father, to be His sons and heirs of all His goods – these are the great blessings that come to us through the forgiveness of sins and life everlasting. If you see these things clearly, aren't you more likely to stand in awe before them than to desire to possess them? Against this twofold faintness of ours we must lay hold on the word of Christ and fix our gaze on it much more firmly than on those thoughts of our weakness. For "great are the works of the Lord; all who enjoy them study them," " who is able to do exceeding abundantly above all that we ask or think." If they did not surpass our worthiness, our grasp and all our thoughts, they would not be divine. Thus Christ also encourages us when He says: "Fear not, little flock, for your Father is pleased to give you a kingdom." For it is just this overflowing goodness of the incomprehensible God, lavished upon us through Christ, that moves us to love Him again with our whole heart above all things, to be drawn to Him with all confidence, to despise all things else, and be ready to suffer all things for Him. For this reason, this sacrament is correctly called "a fount of love."

2.61 Let us take an illustration of this from human experience. If a thousand gold coins were bequeathed by a rich lord to a beggar or an unworthy and wicked servant, it is certain that he would boldly claim and take them regardless of his unworthiness and the greatness of the bequest. And if any one should seek to oppose him by pointing out his unworthiness and the large amount of the legacy, what do you suppose he would say? Certainly, he would say: "What is that to you? What I accept, I accept not on my merits or by any right that I may personally have to it. I know that I am unworthy and receive more than I have deserved, no, I have deserved the very opposite. But I claim it because it is so written in the will, and on the account of another's goodness. If it was not an unworthy thing for him to bequeath so great a sum to an unworthy person, why should I refuse to accept this other man's gracious gift?" With such thoughts we need to fortify the consciences of men against all qualms and scruples, that they may lay hold of the promise of Christ with unwavering faith, and take the greatest care to approach the sacrament, not trusting in their confession, prayer and preparation, but rather despairing of these and with a proud confidence in Christ Who gives the promise. For, as we have said again and again, the word of promise must here reign supreme in a pure and unalloyed faith, and such faith is the one and all-sufficient preparation. [. . .]

THE SACRAMENT OF BAPTISM

3.1 Blessed be the God and Father of our Lord Jesus Christ, Who according to the riches of His mercy has preserved in His Church this sacrament at least, untouched and untainted by the ordinances of men, and has made it free to all nations and every estate of mankind, nor suffered it to be oppressed by the filthy and godless monsters of greed and superstition. For He desired that by it little children, incapable of greed and superstition, might be initiated and sanctified in the simple faith of His Word. Even today baptism's chief blessing is for them. But if this sacrament were to be given to adults and older people, I think it could not possibly have retained its power and its glory against the tyranny of greed and superstition which has everywhere laid waste to divine things. Doubtless the wisdom of the flesh would here too have devised its preparations and worthinesses, its reservations, restrictions, and I know not what other snares for taking money, until water fetched as high a price as parchment does now. [. . .]

3.6 Therefore a penitent will gain much by laying hold of the memory of his baptism above all else, confidently calling to mind the promise of God, which he has forsaken. He should plead it with His Lord, rejoicing that he is baptised and therefore is yet within the fortress of salvation. He should detest his wicked ingratitude in falling away from its faith and truth. His soul will find wondrous comfort, and will be encouraged to hope for mercy, when he considers that the divine promise which God made to him and which cannot possibly lie, still stands unbroken and unchanged, yes, unchangeable by any sins, as Paul says in 2 Timothy 2. "If we do not believe, He continues to be faithful, He cannot deny Himself." Yes, this truth of God will sustain him, so that if all else should sink in ruins, this truth, if he believes it, will not fail him. For in it he has a shield against all assaults of the enemy, an answer to the sins that disturb his conscience, an antidote for the dread of death and judgment, and a comfort in every temptation – namely, this one truth – he can say, " God is faithful that promised, Whose sign I have received in my baptism. If God be for me, who is against me?" [. . .]

3.15 The second part of baptism is the sign, or sacrament, which is that immersion into water from this also it derives its name. For the Greek baptize means "I immerse," and baptisma means "immersion." For, as has been said, signs are added to the divine promises to represent that which the words signify, or, as they now say, that which the sacrament "effectively signifies." We shall see how much of truth there is in this. [. . .]

3.22 Baptism, then, signifies two things –death and resurrection – that is, full and complete justification. When the minister immerses the child in the water, baptism signifies death. When he draws the child forth again, baptism signifies life. Thus Paul expounds on this in Romans 6, "We are buried together with Christ by baptism into death. As Christ is risen from the dead by the glory of the Father, so we also may walk in newness of life." This death and resurrection we call the new creation, regeneration, and the spiritual birth. And this must not be understood only in a figurative sense, of the death of sin and the life of grace, as many understand it, but of actual death and resurrection. The significance of baptism is not an imaginary significance, and sin does not completely die, nor does grace completely rise, until the body of sin that we carry about in this life is destroyed. This the Apostle teaches in the same chapter. For as long as we are in the flesh, the desires of the flesh stir and are stirred. When we begin to believe, we also begin to die to this world and to live to God in the life to come. Faith is truly a death and a resurrection, that is, it is that spiritual baptism in which we are submerged and from which we rise.

3.23 Hence it is indeed correct to say that baptism washes sins away, but that expression is too weak and mild to bring out the full significance of baptism, which is rather a symbol of death and resurrection. For this reason I would have the candidates for baptism completely immersed in the water, as the word says and as the sacrament signifies. Not that I deem this necessary, but it would be well to give to so perfect and complete a thing a perfect and complete sign. Thus it was also doubtless instituted by Christ. The sinner does not so much need to be washed as he needs to die, in order to be wholly renewed and made another creature, and to be conformed to the death and resurrection of Christ, with Whom, through baptism, he dies and rises again. Although you may properly say that Christ was washed clean of mortality when He died and rose again, yet that is a weaker way of putting it than if you said He was completely changed and renewed. In the same way it is far more forceful to say that baptism signifies that we die completely and rising to eternal life, than to say that it signifies merely our being washed clean from sins.

3.24 Here, again, you see that the sacrament of baptism, even in respect to its sign, does not last only for a moment, but continues on forever. Although its administration is soon over, yet the thing it signifies continues until we die, no, until we rise at the last day. For as long as we live we are continually doing that which our baptism signifies, that is, we die and rise again. We die, that is, not only spiritually and in our affections, by renouncing the sins and vanities of this world, but in reality we die. We begin to leave this bodily life and to lay hold on the life to come. So there is, as they say, a real and even a bodily leaving of this world to go to the Father.

3.25 We must, therefore, beware of those who have reduced the power of baptism, making it something thin and small. While they do say that baptism indeed pours the grace of God into us, but afterwards sin pours it out again. So, they say, one must reach heaven by another way. As if baptism had then become entirely useless! Do not hold such a viewpoint, but know that baptism signifies that you die and live again. Therefore, whether it is by penance or by any other way, you can only return to the power of your baptism, and once again do what you were baptised to do and what your baptism signified. Never does baptism lose its power, unless you despair and refuse to return to its salvation. You may, indeed, for a time wander away from the sign, but that does not mean that the sign is powerless. You have, thus, been baptised once in the sacrament, but you must be constantly baptised again through faith, you must constantly die, you must constantly live again. Baptisms absorbs your whole body, and gives it back again. Even so that which baptism signifies should absorb your whole life in body and soul, and give it back again at the last day, clothed in robes of glory and immortality. We are, therefore, never without the sign of baptism nor yet without the thing it signifies. No, we must be baptised ever more and more completely, until we perfectly fulfill the sign, at the last day. [. . .]

THE SACRAMENT OF PENANCE

4.1 We come in the third place to the sacrament of penance. On this subject I have already given no little offense by my published treatise and disputations, in which I have amply set forth my views. These I must now briefly rehearse, in order to unmask the tyranny that is rampant here no less than in the sacrament of the bread. For because these two sacraments furnish opportunity for gain and profit, the greed of the shepherds rages in them with incredible zeal against the flock of Christ; although baptism, too, has sadly declined among adults and become the servant of avarice, as we have just seen in our discussion of vows. [. . .]

4.13 Of private confession, which is now observed, I am hearty in favor, even though, it cannot be proved from the Scriptures; it is useful and necessary, nor would I have it abolished – no, I rejoice that it exists in the Church of Christ, for it is a cure without an equal for distressed consciences. For when we have laid bare our conscience to our brother and privately made known to him the evil that lurked within, we receive from our brother's lips the word of comfort spoken by God Himself; and, if we accept it in faith, we find peace in the mercy of God speaking to us through our brother. This alone do I abominate – that this confession has been subjected to the despotism and extortion of the pontiffs. They reserve to themselves, even hidden sins, and command that they be made known to confessors named by them, only to trouble the consciences of men. They merely play the pontiff, while they utterly despise the true duties of pontiffs, which are to preach the Gospel and to care for the poor. Yes, the godless despots leave the great sins to the plain priests, and reserve to themselves those sins only which are of less consequence, such as those ridiculous and fictitious things in the bull Coenadoinini. No, to make the wickedness of their error the more apparent, they not only do not reserve, but actually teach and approve, the sins, against the service of God, against faith and the chief commandments; such as their running on pilgrimages, the perverse worship of the saints, the lying saints'? Legends, the various forms of trust in works and ceremonies, and the practicing of them, by all of which faith in God is extinguished and idolatry encouraged, as we see in our day. We have the same kind of priests today as Jereboam ordained of old in Dan and Beersheba,(1 Kings 12:26 ff.) ministers of the golden calves, men who are ignorant of the law of God, of faith and of whatever pertains to the feeding of Christ's sheep, and who inculcate in the people nothing but their own inventions with terror and violence. [. . .]

4.20 But this must suffice in repetition of what I have more fully said on indulgences, and in general this must suffice for the present concerning the three sacraments, which have been treated, and yet not treated, in so many harmful books, theological as well as juristic. It remains to attempt some discussion of the other sacraments also, lest I seem to have rejected them without cause.

CONFIRMATION

5.1 I wonder what could have possessed them to make a sacrament of confirmation out of the laying on of hands, (Mark 16:18; Acts 6:6, Acts 8:17, Acts 19:6) which Christ employed when He blessed young children, (Mark 10:16) and the apostles when they imparted the Holy Spirit, ordained elders and cured the sick, as the Apostle writes to Timothy, "Lay hands suddenly on no man." (1 Timothy 5:22) Why have they not also turned the sacrament of the bread into confirmation? For it is written in Acts 9:19, "And when he had taken meat he was strengthened," and in Psalm 104:15, "And that bread may cheer man's heart." Confirmation would thus include three sacraments – the bread, ordination, and confirmation itself. But if everything the apostles did is a sacrament, why have they not rather made preaching a sacrament?

5.2 I do not say this because I condemn the seven sacraments, but because I deny that they can be proved from the Scriptures. Would to God we had in the Church such a laying on of hands as there was in apostolic times, whether we called it confirmation or healing! But there is nothing left of it now but what we ourselves have invented to adorn the office of the bishops, that they may have at least something to do in the Church. For after they relinquished to their inferiors those arduous sacraments together with the Word, as being too common for themselves – since, forsooth, whatever the divine Majesty has instituted has to be despised of men – it was no more than right that we should discover something easy and not too burdensome for such delicate and great heroes to do, and should by no means entrust it to the lower clergy as something common – for whatever human wisdom has decreed has to be held in honor among men! Therefore, as are the priests, so let their ministry and duty be. For a bishop who does not preach the Gospel or care for souls, what is he but an idol in the world, having but the name and appearance of a bishop? (1 Corinthians 8:4) But we seek, instead of this, sacraments that have been divinely instituted, among which we see no reason for numbering confirmation. For, in order that there be a sacrament, there is required above all things a word of divine promise, whereby faith, may be trained. But we read nowhere that Christ ever gave a promise concerning confirmation, although He laid hands on many and included the laying on of hands among the signs in Mark 16:18 "They shall lay their hands on the sick, and they shall recover." Yet no one referred this to a sacrament, nor can this be done.

5.3 Hence it is sufficient to regard confirmation as a certain churchly rite or sacramental ceremony, similar to other ceremonies, such as the blessing of holy water and the like. For if every other creature is sanctified by the word and by prayer, (1 Timothy 4:4 f.) why should not much rather man be sanctified by the same means? Still, these things cannot be called sacraments of faith, because there is no divine promise connected with them, neither do they save; but sacraments do save those who believe the divine promise.

MARRIAGE

6.1 Not only is marriage regarded as a sacrament without the least warrant of Scripture, but the very traditions which extol it as a sacrament have turned it into a farce. Let me explain.

6.2 We said that there is in every sacrament a word of divine promise, to be believed by whoever receives the sign, and that the sign alone cannot be a sacrament. Now we read nowhere that the man who marries a wife receives any grace of God. No, there is not even a divinely instituted sign in marriage, or nowhere do we read that marriage was instituted by God to be a sign of anything. To be sure, whatever takes place in a visible manner may be regarded as a type or figure of something invisible; but types and figures are not sacraments in the sense in which we use this term.

6.3 Furthermore, since marriage existed from the beginning of the world and is still found among unbelievers, it cannot possibly be called a sacrament of the New Law and the exclusive possession of the Church. The marriages of the ancients were no less sacred than are ours, nor are those of unbelievers less true marriages than those of believers, and yet they are not regarded, as sacraments. Besides, there are even among believers married folk who are wicked and worse than any heathen; why should marriage be called a sacrament in their case and not among the heathen? Or are we going to rant so foolishly of baptism and the Church as to hold that marriage is a sacrament only in the Church, just as some make the mad claim that temporal power exists only in the Church? That is childish and foolish talk, by which we expose our ignorance and our arrogance to the ridicule of unbelievers.

6.4 But they will say: The Apostle writes in Ephesians 5:31, "They shall be two in one flesh. This is a great sacrament." Surely you are not going to contradict so plain a statement of the Apostle!

I reply: This argument, like the others, betrays great shallowness and a negligent and thoughtless reading of Scripture. Nowhere in Holy Scripture is this word sacrament employed in the meaning to which we are accustomed; it has an entirely different meaning. For wherever it occurs it signifies not the sign of a sacred thing, but a sacred, secret, hidden thing. Thus Paul writes in 1 Corinthians 4:1, "Let a man so account of us as the ministers of Christ, and dispensers of the mysteries – i.e., sacraments – of God." Where we have the word sacrament the Greek text reads mystery, which word our version sometimes translates and sometimes retains in its Greek form. Thus our verse reads in the Greek: "They Shall be two in one flesh; this is a great mystery." (Ephesians 5:31 f.) This explains how they came to find a sacrament of the New Law here – a thing they would never have done if they had read the word "mystery", as it is in the Greek.

6.5 Thus Christ Himself is called a sacrament in 1 Timothy 3:16, "And evidently great is the sacrament – i.e., mystery – of godliness, which was manifested in the flesh, was justified in the spirit, appeared to angels, has been preached to the Gentiles, is believed, by the world, is taken up in glory." Why have they not drawn out of this passage an eighth sacrament of the New Law, since they have the clear authority of Paul? But if they restrained themselves here, where they had a most excellent opportunity to unearth a new sacrament, why are they so wanton in the former passage? It was their ignorance, forsooth, of both words and things; they clung to the mere sound of the words, no, to their own fancies. For, having once arbitrarily taken the word sacrament to mean a sign, they immediately, without thought or scruple, made a sign of it every time they came upon it in the Sacred Scriptures. Such new meanings of words and such human customs they have also elsewhere dragged into Holy Writ, and conformed it to their dreams, making anything out of any passage whatsoever. Thus they continually chatter nonsense about the terms: good and evil works, sin, grace, righteousness, virtue, and well-nigh every one of the fundamental words and things. For they employ them all after their own arbitrary judgment, learned from the writings of men, to the detriment both of the truth of God and of our salvation.

6.6 Therefore, sacrament, or mystery, in Paul's writings, is that wisdom of the Spirit, hidden in a mystery, as he says in 1 Corinthians 2, which is Christ, Who is for this very reason not known to the princes of this world, wherefore they also crucified Him, and Who still is to them foolishness, an offense, a stone of stumbling, and a sign which is spoken against. (1 Corinthians 1:23; Romans 9:33; Luke 2:34; 1 Corinthians 1:23 f., 1 Corinthians 4:1) The preachers he calls dispensers of these mysteries because they preach Christ, the power and the wisdom of God, yet so that one cannot receive this unless one believe. Therefore, a sacrament is a mystery, or secret thing, which is set forth in words and is received by the faith of the heart. Such a sacrament is spoken of in the verse before us – "They shall be two in one flesh. This is a great sacrament" (Ephesians 5:31 f.) – which they understand as spoken of marriage, while Paul wrote these words of Christ and the Church, and clearly explained his meaning by adding, "But I speak in Christ and in the Church." Yes, how well they agree with Paul! He declares he is setting forth a great sacrament in Christ and the Church, but they set it forth in a man and a woman! If such wantonness be permitted in the Sacred Scriptures, it is small wonder if one find there anything one please, even a hundred sacraments.

6.7 Christ and the Church are, therefore, a mystery, that is, a great and secret thing, which it was possible and proper to represent by marriage as by a certain outward allegory, but that was no reason for their calling marriage a sacrament. The heavens are a type of the apostles, as Psalm 19:1 declares; the sun is a type of Christ; the waters, of the peoples; but that does not make those things sacraments, for in every case there are lacking both the divine institution and the divine promise, which constitute a sacrament.6.8 Hence Paul, in Ephesians 5, following his own mind, applies to Christ these words in Genesis 2 about marriage, or else, following the general view, he teaches that the spiritual marriage of Christ is also contained therein, saying: "As Christ cherisheth the Church: because we are members, of his body, of his flesh and of his bones. For this cause shall a man leave his father and mother, and shall cleave to his wife, and they shall be two in one flesh. This is a great sacrament; I speak in Christ and in the Church." You see, he would have the whole passage apply to Christ, and is at pains to admonish the reader to find the sacrament in Christ and the Church, and not in marriage.

6.9 Therefore we grant that marriage is a type of Christ and the Church, and a sacrament, yet not divinely instituted but invented by men in the Church, carried away by their ignorance both of the word and of the thing. Which ignorance, since it does not conflict with the faith, is to be charitably borne with, just as many other practices of human weakness and ignorance are borne within the Church, so long as they do not conflict with the faith and with the Word of God. But we are now dealing with the certainty and purity of the faith and the Scriptures; so that our faith be not exposed to ridicule, when after affirming that a certain thing is contained in the Sacred Scriptures and in the articles of our faith, we are refuted and shown that it is not contained therein, and, being found ignorant of our own affairs, become a stumbling block to our opponents and to the weak; no, that we destroy not the authority of the Holy Scriptures. For those things which have been delivered to us by God in the Sacred Scriptures must be sharply distinguished from those that have been invented by men in the Church, it matters not how eminent they be for saintliness and scholarship. [. . .]

6.26 As to divorce, it is still a moot question whether it be allowable. For my part I so greatly detest divorce that I should prefer bigamy to it, but whether it be allowable, I do not venture to decide. Christ Himself, the Chief Pastor, says in Matthew 5:32, "Whosoever shall put away his wife, Matthew excepting for the cause of fornication, maketh her commit adultery; and he that shall marry her that is put away, committeth adultery." Christ, then, permits divorce, but for the cause of fornication only. The pope must, therefore, be in error whenever he grants a divorce for any other cause, and no one should feel safe who has obtained a dispensation by this temerity (not authority) of the pope. Yet it is a still greater wonder to me, why they compel a man to remain, unmarried after bring separated from his wife, and why they will not permit him to remarry. For if Christ pennies divorce for the cause, of fornication and compels no one to remain unmarried, and if Paul would rather have one marry than burn, (1 Corinthians 7:9) then He certainly seems to permit a man to marry another woman in the stead of the one who has been put away. Would to God this matter were thoroughly threshed out and derided, so that counsel might be given in the infinite perils of those who, without any fault of their own, are nowadays compelled to remain unmarried, that is, of those whose wives or husbands have run away and deserted them, to come back perhaps after ten years, perhaps never. This matter troubles and distresses me; I meet cases of it every day, whether it happen by the special malice of Satan or because of our neglect of the word of God.

6.27 I, indeed, who, alone against all, can decide nothing in this matter, would yet greatly desire at least the passage in 1 Corinthians 7 to be applied here – "But if the unbeliever depart, let him depart. For a brother or sister is not under servitude in such cases." Here the Apostle gives permission to put away the unbeliever who departs and to set the believing spouse free to marry again. Why should not the same hold true when a believer – that is, a believer in name, but in truth as much an unbeliever as the one Paul speaks of – deserts his wife, especially if he never intends to return? I certainly can see no difference between the two. But I believe that if in the Apostle's day an unbelieving deserter had returned and had become a believer or had promised to live again with his believing wife, he would not have been taken back, but he too would have been given the right to marry again. Nevertheless, in these matters I decide nothing, as I have said, although there is nothing I would rather see decided, since nothing at present more grievously perplexes me and many more with me. I would have nothing decided here on the mere authority of the pope or the bishops; but if two learned and pious men agreed in the name of Christ (Matthew 18:19 f.) and published their opinion in the spirit of Christ, I should prefer their judgment even to such councils as are nowadays assembled, famous only for numbers and authority, not for scholarship and saintliness. Herewith I hang up my harp, until another and a better man shall take up this matter with me. (Psalm 137:2).

ORDINATION

7.1 Of this sacrament the Church of Christ knows nothing; it is an invention of the pope's church. Not only is there nowhere any promise of grace attached to it, but there is not the least mention of it in the whole New Testament. Now it is ridiculous to put forth as a sacrament of God that which cannot be proved to have been instituted by God. I do not hold that this rite, which has been observed for so many centuries, should be condemned; but in sacred things I am opposed to the invention of human fictions, nor is it right to give out as divinely instituted what was not divinely instituted, lest we become a laughing-stock to our opponents. We ought to see to it that every article of faith of which we boast be certain, pure, and based on clear passages of Scripture. But that we are utterly unable to do in the case of the sacrament under consideration. [. . .]

THE SACRAMENT OF EXTREME UNCTION

8.1 To the rite of anointing the sick our theologians have made two additions which are worthy of them; first, they call it a sacrament, and secondly, they make it the last sacrament. So that it is now the sacrament of extreme unction, which may be administered only to such as are at the point of death. Being such subtle dialecticians, perchance they have done this in order to relate it to the first unction of baptism and the two succeeding unctions of confirmation and ordination. But here they are able to cast in my teeth, that in the case of this sacrament there are, on the authority of James the Apostle, both promise and sign, which, as I have all along maintained, constitute a sacrament. For does not James say: (James 5:14 f.) "Is any man sick among you? Let him bring in the priests of the church, and let them pray over him, anointing him with oil in the name of the Lord. And the prayer of faith shall raise him up: and if he be in sins, they shall be forgiven him." There, say they, you have the promise of the forgiveness of sins, and the sign of the oil.

8.2 But I reply: If ever there was a mad conceit, here is one indeed. I will say nothing of the fact that many assert with much probability that this Epistle is not by James the Apostle, nor worthy of an apostolic spirit, although, whoever be its author, it has come to be esteemed as authoritative. But even if the Apostle James did write it, I yet should say, no Apostle has the right on his own authority to institute a sacrament, that is, to give a divine promise with a sign attached; for this belongs to Christ alone. Thus Paul says that he received from the Lord the sacrament of the Eucharist, (1 Corinthians 11:23) and that he was not sent to baptise but to preach the Gospel. (1 Corinthians 1:17) And we read nowhere in the Gospel of this sacrament of extreme unction. But let us also waive that point. Let us examine the words of the Apostle, or whoever was the author of the Epistle, and we shall at once see how little heed these multipliers of sacraments have given to them.

8.3 In the first place, then, if they believe the Apostle's words to be true and binding, by what right do they change and contradict them? Why do they make an extreme and a particular kind of unction of that which the Apostle wished to be general? For he did not desire it to be an extreme unction or administered only to the dying; but he says quite generally: "If any man be sick" – not, "If any man be dying." I care not what learned discussions Dionysius has on this point in his Ecclesiastical Hierarchy; the Apostle's words are clear enough, on which words he as well as they rely, without, however, following them. It is evident, therefore, that they have arbitrarily and without any authority made a sacrament and an extreme unction out of the misunderstood words of the Apostle, to the detriment of all other sick persons, whom they have deprived of the benefit of the unction which the Apostle enjoined.

8.4 But what follows is still better. The Apostle's promise expressly declares that the prayer of faith shall save the sick man, and the Lord shall raise him up. The Apostle commands us to anoint the sick man and to pray, in order that he may be healed and raised up; that is, that he may not die, and that it may not be an extreme unction. This is proved also by the prayers which are said, during the anointing, for the recovery of the one who is sick. But they say, on the contrary, that the unction must be administered to none but the dying; that is, that they may not be healed and raised up. If it were not so serious a matter, who could help laughing at this beautiful, apt and sound exposition of the Apostle's words? Is not the folly of the sophists, here shown in its true colors? As here, so in many other places, they affirm what the Scriptures deny, and deny what they affirm. Why should we not give thanks to these excellent magisters of ours? I therefore spoke truth when I said they never conceived a crazier notion than this?

8.5 Furthermore, if this unction is a sacrament it must necessarily be, as they say, an effective sign of that which it signifies and promises. Now it promises health and recovery to the sick, as the words plainly say: "The prayer of faith shall save the sick man, and the Lord shall raise him up." But who does not see that this promise is seldom if ever fulfilled? Scarce one in a thousand is restored to health, and when one is restored nobody believes that it came about through the sacrament, but through the working of nature or the medicine; for to the sacrament they ascribe the opposite power. What shall we say then? Either the Apostle lies in making this promise or else this unction is no sacrament. For the sacramental promise is certain; but this promise deceives in the majority of cases. Indeed – and here again we recognize the shrewdness and foresight of these theologians – for this very reason they would have it to be extreme unction, that the promise should not stand; in other words, that the sacrament should be no sacrament. For if it is extreme unction, it does not heal, but gives way to the disease; but if it heals, it cannot be extreme unction. Thus, by the interpretation of these magisters, James is shown to have contradicted himself, and to have instituted a sacrament in order not to institute one; for they must have an extreme unction just to make untrue what the Apostle intends, namely, the healing of the sick. If that is not madness, pray what is?

8.6 These people exemplify the word of the Apostle in 1 Timothy 1:7, "Desiring to be teachers of the law, understanding neither the things they say, nor whereof they affirm." Thus they read and follow all things without judgment. With the same thoughtlessness they have also found auricular confession in our Apostle's words – "Confess your sins one to another." (James 5:16) But they do not observe the command of the Apostle, that the priests of the church be called, and prayer be made for the sick. Scarce a single priestling is sent nowadays, although the Apostle would have many present, not because of the unction but of the prayer. Wherefore he says: "The prayer of faith shall save the sick man," etc. I have my doubts, however, whether he would have us understand priests when he says presbyters, that is, elders. For one who is an elder is not therefore a priest or minister; so that the suspicion is justified that the Apostle desired the older and graver men in the Church to visit the sick; these should perform a work of mercy and pray in faith and thus heal him. Still it cannot be denied that the ancient churches were ruled by elders, chosen for this purpose, without these ordinations and consecrations, solely on account of their age and their long experience.

8.7 Therefore, I take it, this unction is the same as that which the Apostles practiced, in Mark 6:13, "They anointed with oil many that were sick, and healed them." It was a ceremony of the early Church, by which they wrought miracles on the sick, and which has long since ceased; even as Christ, in the last chapter of Mark, gave them that believe the power to take up serpents, to lay hands on the sick, etc. (Mark 16:17) It is a wonder that they have not made sacraments also of these things; for they have the same power and promise as the words of James. Therefore, this extreme – that is, this fictitious – unction is not a sacrament, but a counsel of James, which whoever will may use, and it is derived from Mark 6, as I have shown. I do not believe it was a counsel given to all sick persons, (Romans 5:3) for the Church's infirmity is her glory and death is gain; (Philippians 1:21) but it was given only to such as might bear their sickness impatiently and with little faith. These the Lord allowed to remain in the Church, in order that miracles and the power of faith might be manifest in them. [. . .]

9.2 There are yet a few other things it might seem possible to regard as sacraments; namely, all those to which a divine promise has been given, such as prayer, the Word, and the cross. Christ promised, in many places, that those who pray should be heard; especially in Luke 11, where He invites us in many parables to pray. Of the Word He says: "Blessed are they that hear the word of God, and keep it." (Luke 11.28) And who will tell how often He promises aid and glory to such as are afflicted, suffer, and are cast down? no, who will recount all the promises of God? The whole Scripture is concerned with provoking us to faith; now driving us with precepts and threats, now drawing us with promises and consolations. Indeed, whatever things are written are either precepts or promises; the precepts humble the proud with their demands, the promises exalt the humble with. their forgiveness.

9.3 Nevertheless, it has seemed best to restrict the name of sacrament to such promises as have signs attached to them. The remainder, not being bound to signs, are bare promises. Hence there are, strictly speaking, but two sacraments in the Church of God – baptism and bread; for only in these two do we find both the divinely instituted sign and the promise of forgiveness of sins. The sacrament of penance, which I added to these two, lacks the divinely instituted visible sign, and is, as I have said, nothing but a return to baptism. Nor can the scholastics say that their definition fits penance, for they too ascribe to the sacrament a visible sign, which is to impress upon the senses the form of that which it effects invisibly. But penance, or absolution, has no such sign; wherefore they are constrained by their own definition, either to admit that penance is not a sacrament, and thus to reduce the number of sacraments, or else to bring forward another definition.

9.4 Baptism, however, which we have applied to the whole of life, will truly be a sufficient substitute for all the sacraments we might need as long as we live. And the bread is truly the sacrament of the dying; for in it we commemorate the passing of Christ out of this world, that we may imitate Him. Thus we may apportion these two sacraments as follows: baptism belongs to the beginning and the entire course of life, the bread belongs to the end and to death. And the Christian should use them both as long as he is in this poor body, until, fully baptised and strengthened, he passes out of this world and is born to the new life of eternity, to eat with Christ in the Kingdom of His Father, as He promised at the Last Supper – "Amen I say to you, I will not drink from henceforth of this fruit of the vine, until it is fulfilled in the kingdom of God." (Matthew 26:29) Thus He seems clearly to have instituted the sacrament of the bread with a view to our entrance into the life to come. Then, when the meaning of both sacraments is fulfilled, baptism and bread will cease.

9.5 Herewith I conclude this prelude, and freely and gladly offer it to all pious souls who desire to know the genuine sense of the Scriptures and the proper use of the sacraments. For it is a gift of no mean importance, to know the things that are given us, as it is said in 1 Corinthians 2, and what use we ought to make of them. Endowed with this spiritual judgment, we shall not mistakenly rely on that which does not belong here. These two things our theologians never taught us, no, I think they took particular pains to conceal them from us. If I have not taught them, I certainly did not conceal them, and have given occasion to others to think out something better. It has at least been my endeavor to set forth these two things. Nevertheless, not all can do all things. To the godless, on the other hand, and those who in obstinate tyranny force on us their own teachings inas God's representative's, I confidently and freely oppose these pages, utterly indifferent to their senseless fury. Yet I wish even them a sound mind, and do not despise their efforts, but only distinguish them from such as are sound and truly Christian.

9.6 I hear a rumour of new bulls and papal curses sent out against me, in which I am urged to recant or be declared a heretic. If that is true, I desire this book to be a portion of the recantation I shall make; so that these tyrants may not complain of having had their pains for nothing. The remainder I will publish ere long, and it will, please Christ, be such as the Roman See has hitherto neither seen nor heard. I shall give ample proof of my obedience. In the name of our Lord Jesus Christ. Amen.

9.7 Why doth that impious Herod fear

When told that Christ the King is near?

He takes not earthly realms away,

Who gives the realms that ne'er decay.

Title page **Von der Freiheit eines Christen menschen.**
Martinus Luther. Wittembergae. 1520.

Martin Luther
On the Freedom of a Christian (November, 1520)

DEDICATION TO POPE LEO X (excerpts)

Among those monstrous evils of this age, with which I have now for three years been waging war, I am sometimes compelled to look to you and to call you to mind, most blessed father **Leo**. In truth, since you alone are everywhere considered as being the cause of my engaging in war, I cannot at any time fail to remember you; and although I have been compelled by the causeless raging of your impious flatterers against me to appeal from your seat to a future council -- fearless of the futile decrees of your predecessors **Pius** and **Julius**, who in their foolish tyranny prohibited such an action--yet I have never been so alienated in feeling from your Blessedness as not to have sought with all my might, in diligent prayer and crying to God, every best gift for you and for your See. But those who have hitherto endeavored to terrify me with the majesty of your name and authority, I have begun quite to despise and triumph over. One thing I see remaining, which I cannot despise, and this has been the reason of my writing anew to your Blessedness; namely, that I find that blame is cast on me, and that that rashness, in which I am judged to have spared not even your person, is imputed to me as a great offence.[. . .]

I have indeed inveighed sharply against impious doctrines, and I have not been slack to censure my adversaries on account, not of their bad morals, but of their impiety. And for this I am so far from being sorry, that I have brought my mind to despise the judgments of men, and to persevere in this vehement zeal, according to the example of Christ, who, in his zeal, calls his adversaries a generation of vipers, blind, hypocrites, and children of the devil. . . .

Your See, however, which is called the Court of Rome, and which neither you nor any man can deny to be more corrupt than any Babylon or Sodom, and quite, as I believe, of a lost, desperate, and hopeless impiety, this I have verily abominated, and have felt indignant that the people of Christ should be cheated under your name and the pretext of the Church of Rome and so I have resisted, and will resist, as long as the spirit of faith shall live in me. Not that I am striving after impossibilities, or hoping that by my labors alone, against the furious opposition of so many flatterers, any good can be done in that most disordered Babylon, but that I feel myself a debtor to my brethren, and am bound to take thought for them, that fewer of them may be ruined, or that their ruin may be less complete, by the plagues of Rome. For many years now, nothing else has overflowed from Rome into the world--as you are not ignorant--than the laying waste of goods, of bodies, and of souls, and the worst examples of all the worst things. These things are clearer than the light to all men; and the Church of Rome, formerly the most holy of all churches, has become the most lawless den of thieves, the most shameless of all brothels, the very kingdom of sin, death, and hell; so that not even Antichrist, if he were to come, could devise any addition to its wickedness. Meanwhile you, Leo, are sitting like a lamb in the midst of wolves, like Daniel in the midst of lions, and, with Ezekiel, you dwell among scorpions. What opposition can you alone make to these monstrous evils? Take to yourself three or four of the most learned and best of the Cardinals. What are these among so many? You would all perish by poison, before you could undertake to decide on a remedy. It is all over with the Court of Rome; the wrath of God has come upon her to the uttermost. She hates councils, she dreads to be reformed, she cannot restrain the madness of her impiety, she fills up the sentence passed on her mother, of whom it is said, "We would have healed Babylon, but she is not healed; let us forsake her." It had been your duty and that of your Cardinals, to apply a remedy to these evils, but this gout laughs at the physician's hand, and the chariot does not obey the reins. Under the influence of these feelings I have always grieved that you, most excellent Leo, who were worthy of a better age, have been made Pontiff in this. For the Roman Court is not worthy of you and those like you, but of Satan himself, who in truth is more the ruler in that Babylon than you are. [. . .]

Therefore, **Leo** my Father, beware of listening to those Sirens, who make you out to be not simply a man, but partly a God, so that you can command and require whatever you will. It will not happen so, nor will you prevail. You are the servant of servants, and, more than any other man, in a most pitiable and perilous position. Let not those men deceive you, who pretend that you are Lord of the world; who will not allow anyone to be a Christian without your authority; who babble of your having power over heaven, hell, and purgatory. These men are your enemies and are seeking your soul to destroy it, as Isaiah says: "My people, they that call thee blessed are themselves deceiving thee." They are in error, who raise you above councils and the universal Church. They are in error, who attribute to you alone the right of interpreting Scripture. All these men are seeking to set up their own impieties in the Church under your name, and alas! Satan has gained much through them in the time of your predecessors. [. . .]

That I may not approach you empty handed, Blessed Father, I bring with me this little treatise, published under your name, as a good omen of the establishment of peace, and of good hope. By this you may perceive in what pursuits I should prefer and be able to occupy myself to more profit, if I were allowed, or had been hitherto allowed, by your impious flatterers. It is a small matter, if you look to its exterior, but, unless I mistake, it is a summary of the Christian life put together in small compass, if you apprehend its meaning. I, in my poverty, have no other present to make you; nor do you need anything else than to be enriched by a spiritual gift. I commend myself to your Paternity and Blessedness, whom may the Lord Jesus preserve forever. Amen. Wittenberg; 6th September, 1520.

CONCERNING CHRISTIAN LIBERTY (excerpted)

CHRISTIAN faith has appeared to many an easy thing; nay, not a few even reckon it among the social virtues, as it were; and this they do, because they have not made proof of it experimentally, and have never tasted of what efficacy it is. For it is not possible for any man to write well about it, or to understand well what is rightly written, who has not at some time tasted of its spirit, under the pressure of tribulation. While he who has tasted of it, even to a very small extent, can never write, speak, think, or hear about it sufficiently. For it is a living fountain, springing up unto eternal life, as Christ calls it in the 4th chapter of St. John.

Now, though I cannot boast of my abundance, and though I know how poorly I am furnished, yet I hope that, after having been vexed by various temptations, I have attained some little drop of faith, and that I can speak of this matter, if not with more elegance, certainly with more solidity than those literal and too subtle disputants who have hitherto discoursed upon it, without understanding their own words. That I may open, then, an easier way for the ignorant-- for these alone I am trying to serve--I first lay down these two propositions, concerning spiritual liberty and servitude.

A Christian man is the most free lord of all, and subject to none; a Christian man is the most dutiful servant of all, and subject to everyone.

Although these statements appear contradictory, yet, when they are found to agree together, they will be highly serviceable to my purpose. They are both the statements of Paul himself, who says: "Though I be free from all men, yet have I made myself servant unto all" (1 Cor. ix. 19), and: "Owe no man anything, but to love one another." (Rom. xiii. 8.) Now love is by its own nature dutiful and obedient to the beloved object. Thus even Christ, though Lord of all things, was yet made of a woman; made under the law; at once free and a servant; at once in the form of God and in the form of a servant.[. . .]

Let us therefore hold it for certain and firmly established, that the soul can do without everything, except the word of God, without which none at all of its wants are provided for. But, having the word, it is rich and want for nothing; since that is the word of life, of truth, of light, of peace, of justification, of salvation, of joy, of liberty, of wisdom, of virtue, of grace, of glory, and of every good thing. It is on this account that the prophet in a whole psalm (Ps. cxix.), and in many other places, sighs for and calls upon the word of God with so many groanings and words.

Again, there is no more cruel stroke of the wrath of God than when He sends a famine of hearing His words (Amos viii. 11); just as there is no greater favor from Him than the sending forth of His word, as it is said: "He sent his word and healed them, and delivered them from their destructions." (Ps. cvii. 20.) Christ was sent for no other office than that of the word, and the order of apostles, that of bishops, and that of the whole body of the clergy, have been called and instituted for no object but the ministry of the word.

But you will ask:--"What is this word, and by what means is it to be used, since there are so many words of God?" I answer, the Apostle Paul (Rom. i.) explains what it is, namely, the Gospel of God, concerning His Son, incarnate, suffering, risen, and glorified through the Spirit, the sanctifier. To preach Christ is to feed the soul, to justify it, to set it free, and to save it, if it believes the preaching. For faith alone, and the efficacious use of the word of God, bring salvation. "If thou shalt confess with thy mouth the Lord Jesus, and shalt believe in thine heart that God hath raised him from the dead, thou shalt be saved." (Rom. x. 9.) And again: "Christ is the end of the law for righteousness to everyone that believeth" (Rom. x. 4); and "The just shall live by faith." (Rom. i. 17.) For the word of God cannot be received and honored by any works, but by faith alone. Hence it is clear that, as the soul needs the word alone for life and justification, so it is justified by faith alone and not by any works. For if it could be justified by any other means, it would have no need of the word, nor consequently of faith.

But this faith cannot consist at all with works; that is, if you imagine that you can be justified by those works, whatever they are, along with it. For this would be to halt between two opinions, to worship Baal, and to kiss the hand to him, which is a very great iniquity, as Job says. Therefore, when you begin to believe, you learn at the same time that all that is in you is utterly guilty, sinful, and damnable; according to that saying: "All have sinned, and come short of the glory of God." (Rom. iii. 23.) And also: "There is none righteous, no, not one; they are all gone out of the way; they are together become unprofitable; there is none that doeth good, no, not one." (Rom. iii. 10-12.) When you have learnt this, you will know that Christ is necessary for you, since He has suffered and risen again for you, that, believing on Him, you might by this faith become another man, all your sins being remitted, and you being justified by the merits of another, namely, of Christ alone.

Since then this faith can reign only in the inward man, as it is said: "With the heart man believeth unto righteousness" (Rom. x. 10); and since it alone justifies, it is evident that by no outward work or labor can the inward man be at all justified, made free, and saved; and that no works whatever have any relation to him. And so, on the other hand, it is solely by impiety and incredulity of heart that he becomes guilty, and a slave of sin, deserving condemnation; not by any outward sin or work. Therefore the first care of every Christian ought to be, to lay aside all reliance on works, and strengthen his faith alone more and more, and by it grow in the knowledge, not of works, but of Christ Jesus, who has suffered and risen again for him; as Peter teaches, when he makes no other work to be a Christian one. Thus Christ, when the Jews asked Him what they should do that they might work the works of God, rejected the multitude of works, with which He saw that they were puffed up, and commanded them one thing only, saying: "This is the work of God, that ye believe on him whom He hath sent, for him hath God the Father sealed." (John vi. 27, 29.)Hence a right faith in Christ is an incomparable treasure, carrying with it universal salvation, and preserving from all evil, as it is said: "He that believeth and is baptized shall be saved; but he that believeth not shall be damned." (Mark xvi. 16.) Isaiah, looking to this treasure, predicted: "The consumption decreed shall overflow with righteousness. For the Lord God of hosts shall make a consumption, even determined, in the midst of the land." (Is. x. 22, 23.) As if he said:--"Faith, which is the brief and complete fulfill ling of the law, will fill those who believe with such righteousness, that they will need nothing else for justification." Thus too Paul says: "For with the heart man believeth unto righteousness." (Rom. x. 10.)But you ask how it can be the fact that faith alone justifies, and affords without works so great a treasure of good things, when so many works, ceremonies, and laws are prescribed to us in the Scriptures? I answer: before all things bear in mind what I have said, that faith alone without works justifies, sets free, and saves, as I shall show more clearly below.

Meanwhile it is to be noted, that the whole Scripture of God is divided into two parts, precepts and promises. The precepts certainly teach us what is good, but what they teach is not forthwith done. For they show us what we ought to do, but do not give us the power to do it. They were ordained, however, for the purpose of showing man to himself; that through them he may learn his own impotence for good, and may despair of his own strength. For this reason they are called the Old Testament, and are so.

For example: "thou shalt not covet," is a precept by which we are all convicted of sin; since no man can help coveting, whatever efforts to the contrary he may make. In order therefore that he may fulfill l the precept, and not covet, he is constrained to despair of himself and to seek elsewhere and through another the help which he cannot find in himself; as it is said: "O Israel, thou hast destroyed thyself; but in me is thine help." (Hosea xiii. 9.) Now what is done by this one precept, is done by all; for all are equally impossible of fulfillment by us.

Now when a man has through the precepts been taught his own impotence, and become anxious by what means he may satisfy the law--for the law must be satisfied, so that no jot or tittle of it may pass away; otherwise he must be hopelessly condemned--then, being truly humbled and brought to nothing in his own eyes, he finds in himself no resource for justification and salvation.

Then comes in that other part of Scripture, the promises of God, which declare the glory of God, and say: "If you wish to fulfill the law, and, as the law requires, not to covet, lo! believe in Christ, in whom are promised to you grace, justification, peace, and liberty." All these things you shall have, if you believe, and shall be without them, if you do not believe. For what is impossible for you by all the works of the law, which are many and yet useless, you shall fulfill in an easy and summary way through faith; because God the Father has made everything to depend on faith, so that whosoever has it, has all things, and he who has it not, has nothing.

"For God hath concluded them all in unbelief, that He might have mercy upon all." (Rom. xi. 32.) Thus the promises of God give that which the precepts exact, and, fulfill what the law commands; so that all is of God alone, both the precepts and their fulfillment. He alone commands. He alone also fulfills. Hence the promises of God belong to the New Testament; nay, are the New Testament.

Now since these promises of God are words of holiness, truth, righteousness, liberty, and peace, and are full of universal goodness; the soul, which cleaves to them with a firm faith, is so united to them, nay, thoroughly absorbed by them, that it not only partakes in, but is penetrated and saturated by, all their virtue. For if the touch of Christ was healing, how much more does that most tender spiritual touch, nay, absorption of the word, communicate to the soul all that belongs to the word. In this way, therefore, the soul, through faith alone, without works, is from the word of God justified, sanctified, endued with truth, peace, and liberty, and filled full with every good thing, and is truly made the child of God; as it is said: "To them gave he power to become the sons of God, even to them that believe on his name." (John i. 12.)From all this it is easy to understand why faith has such great power, and why no good works, nor even all good works put together, can compare with it; since no work can cleave to the word of God, or be in the soul. Faith alone and the word reign in it; and such as is the word, such is the soul made by it; just as iron exposed to fire glows like fire, on account of its union with the fire. It is clear then that to a Christian man his faith suffices for everything, and that he has no need of works for justification. But if he has no need of works, neither has he need of the law; and, if he has no need of the law, he is certainly free from the law, and the saying is true: "The law is not made for a righteous man." (1 Tim. i. 9.) This is that Christian liberty, our faith, the effect of which is, not that we should be careless or lead a bad life, but that no one should need the law or works for justification and salvation.[. . .]

The third incomparable grace of faith is this, that it unites the soul to Christ, as the wife to the husband; by which mystery, as the Apostle teaches, Christ and the soul are made one flesh. Now if they are one flesh, and if a true marriage -- nay, by far the most perfect of all marriages--is accomplished between them (for human marriages are but feeble types of this one great marriage), then it follows that all they have becomes theirs in common, as well good things as evil things; so that whatsoever Christ possesses, that the believing soul may take to itself and boast of as its own, and whatever belongs to the soul, that Christ claims as his.

If we compare these possessions, we shall see how inestimable is the gain. Christ is full of grace, life, and salvation; the soul is full of sin, death, and condemnation. Let faith step in, and then sin, death, and hell will belong to Christ, and grace, life, and salvation to the soul. For, if he is a husband, he must needs take to himself that which is his wife's, and, at the same time, impart to his wife that which is his. For, in giving her his own body and himself, how can he but give her all that is his? And, in taking to himself the body of his wife, how can he but take to himself all that is hers?

In this is displayed the delightful sight, not only of communion, but of a prosperous warfare, of victory, salvation, and redemption. For since Christ is God and man, and is such a person as neither has sinned, nor dies, nor is condemned,--nay, cannot sin, die, or be condemned; and since his righteousness, life, and salvation are invincible, eternal, and almighty; when, I say, such a person, by the wedding-ring of faith, takes a share in the sins, death, and hell of his wife, nay, makes them his own, and deals with them no otherwise than as if they were his, and as if he himself had sinned; and when he suffers, dies, and descends to hell, that he may overcome all things, since sin, death, and hell cannot swallow him up, they must needs be swallowed up by him in stupendous conflict. For his righteousness rises above the sins of all men; his life is more powerful than all death; his salvation is more unconquerable than all hell.

Thus the believing soul, by the pledge of its faith in Christ, becomes free from all sin, fearless of death, safe from hell, and endowed with the eternal righteousness, life, and salvation of its husband Christ. Thus he presents to himself a glorious bride, without spot or wrinkle, cleansing her with the washing of water by the word; that is, by faith in the word of life, righteousness, and salvation. Thus he betrothes her unto himself "in faithfulness, in righteousness, and in judgment, and in lovingkindness, and in mercies." (Hosea ii. 19, 20.) Who then can value highly enough these royal nuptials? Who can comprehend the riches of the glory of this grace?

Christ, that rich and pious husband, takes as a wife a needy and impious harlot, redeeming her from all her evils, and supplying her with all his good things. It is impossible now that her sins should destroy her, since they have been laid upon Christ and swallowed up in Him, and since she has in her husband Christ a righteousness which she may claim as her own, and which she can set up with confidence against all her sins, against death and hell, saying: "If I have sinned, my Christ, in whom I believe, has not sinned; all mine is His, and all His is mine;" as it is written, "My beloved is mine, and I am his. (Cant. ii. 16.) This is what Paul says: "Thanks be to God, which giveth us the victory through our Lord Jesus Christ;" victory over sin and death, as he says: "The sting of death is sin, and the strength of sin is the law." (I Cor. xv. 56, 57.) From all this you will again understand, why so much importance is attributed to faith, so that it alone can fulfill the law, and justify without any works. For you see that the first commandment, which says, "Thou shalt worship one God only," is fulfill led by faith alone. If you were nothing but good works from the soles of your feet to the crown of your head, you would not be worshipping God, nor fulfill ling the first commandment, since it is impossible to worship God, without ascribing to Him the glory of truth and of universal goodness, as it ought in truth to be ascribed. Now this is not done by works, but only by faith of heart. It is not by working, but by believing, that we glorify God, and confess Him to be true. On this ground faith is the sole righteousness of a Christian man, and the fulfill ling of all the commandments. For to him who fulfill s the first, the task of fulfill ling all the rest is easy.

Works, since they are irrational things, cannot glorify God; although they may be done to the glory of God, if faith be present. But at present we are enquiring, not into the quality of the works done, but into him who does them, who glorifies God, and brings forth good works. This is faith of heart, the head and the substance of all our righteousness. Hence that is a blind and perilous doctrine which teaches that the commandments are fulfill led by works. The commandments must have been fulfilled, previous to any good works, and good works follow their fulfillment, as we shall see. [. . .]

From these considerations any one may clearly see how a Christian man is free from all things; so that he needs no works in order to be justified and saved, but receives these gifts in abundance from faith alone. Nay, were he so foolish as to pretend to be justified, set free, saved, and made a Christian, by means of any good work, he would immediately lose faith with all its benefits. Such folly is prettily represented in the fable, where a dog, running along in the water, and carrying in his mouth a real piece of meat, is deceived by the reflection of the meat in the water, and, in trying with open mouth to seize it, loses the meat and its image at the same time. [. . .]

And now let us turn to the other part, to the outward man. Here we shall give an answer to all those who, taking offence at the word of faith and at what I have asserted, say: "If faith does everything, and by itself suffices for justification, why then are good works commanded? Are we then to take our ease and do no works, content with faith?" Not so, impious man, I reply; not so. That would indeed really be the case, if we were thoroughly and completely inner and spiritual persons; but that will not happen until the last day, when the dead shall be raised. As long as we live in the flesh, we are but beginning and making advances in that which shall be completed in a future life. On this account the Apostle calls that which we have in this life, the first-fruits of the Spirit. (Rom. viii. 23.) In future we shall have the tenths, and the fullness of the Spirit. To this part belongs the fact I have stated before, that the Christian is the servant of all and subject to all. For in that part in which he is free, he does no works, but in that in which he is a servant, he does all works. Let us see on what principle this is so.

Although, as I have said, inwardly, and according to the spirit, a man is amply enough justified by faith, having all that lie requires to have, except that this very faith and abundance ought to increase from day to day, even till the future life; still he remains in this mortal life upon earth, in which it is necessary that he should rule his own body, and have intercourse with men. Here then works begin; here he must not take his ease; here he must give heed to exercise his body by fastings, watchings, labour, and other moderate discipline, so that it may be subdued to the spirit, and obey and conform itself to the inner man and faith, and not rebel against them nor hinder them, as is its nature to do if it is not kept under. For the inner man, being conformed to God, and created after the image of God through faith, rejoices and delights itself in Christ, in whom such blessings have been conferred on it; and hence has only this task before it, to serve God with joy and for naught in free love.

In doing this he offends that contrary will in his own flesh, which is striving to serve the world, and to seek its own gratification. This the spirit of faith cannot and will not bear; but applies itself with cheerfulness and zeal to keep it down and restrain it; as Paul says: "I delight in the law of God after the inward man; but I see another law in my members, warring against the law of my mind, and bringing me into captivity to the law of sin." (Rom. vii. 22, 23.) And again: "I keep under my body, and bring it into subjection, lost that by any means, when I have preached to others, I myself should be a castaway." (1 Cor. ix. 27.) And: "They that are Christ's have crucified the flesh with the affections and lusts." (Gal. v. 24.) These works, however, must not be done with any notion that by them a man can be justified before God--for faith, which alone is righteousness before God, will not bear with this false notion--but solely with this purpose, that the body may be brought into subjection, and be purified from its evil lusts, so that our eyes may be turned only to purging away those lusts. For when the soul has been cleansed by faith and made to love God, it would have all things to be cleansed in like manner; and especially in its own body, so that all things might unite with it in the love and praise of God. Thus it comes that from the requirements of his own body a man cannot take his ease, but is compelled on its account to do many good works, that he may bring it into subjection. Yet these works are not the means of his justification before God, he does them out of disinterested love to the service of God; looking to no other end than to do what is well-pleasing to Him whom he desires to obey dutifully in all things.[. . .]

A bishop, when he consecrates a church, confirms children, or performs any other duty of his office, is not consecrated as bishop by these works; nay, unless he had been previously consecrated as bishop, not one of those works would have any validity; they would be foolish, childish, and ridiculous. Thus a Christian, being consecrated by his faith, does good works; but he is not by these works made a more sacred person, or more a Christian. That is the effect of faith alone; nay, unless he were previously a believer and a Christian, none of his works would have any value at all; they would really be impious and damnable sins.

True then are these two sayings: Good works do not make a good man, but a good man does good works. Bad works do not make a bad man, but a bad man does bad works. Thus it is always necessary that the substance or person should be good before any good works can be done, and that good works should follow and proceed from a good person. As Christ says: "A good tree cannot bring forth evil fruit, neither can a corrupt tree bring forth good fruit." (Matt. vii. 18) Now it is clear that the fruit does not bear the tree, nor does the tree grow on the fruit; but, on the contrary, the trees bear the fruit and the fruit grows on the trees.

As then trees must exist before their fruit, and as the fruit does not make the tree either good or bad, but, on the contrary, a tree of either kind produces fruit of the same kind; so must first the person of the man be good or bad, before he can do either a good or a bad work; and his works do not make him tad or good, but he himself makes his works either bad or good.

We may see the same thing in all handicrafts. A bad or good house does not make a bad or good builder, but a good or bad builder makes a good or bad house. And in general, no work makes the workman such as it is itself; but the workman makes the work such as he is himself. Such is the case too with the works of men. Such as the man himself is, whether in faith or in unbelief, such is his work; good if it be done in faith, bad if in unbelief. But the converse is not true--that, such as the work is, such the man becomes in faith or in unbelief. For as works do not make a believing man, so neither do they make a justified man; but faith, as it makes a man a believer and justified, so also it makes his works good.

Since, then, works justify no man, but a man must be justified before he can do any good work, it is most evident that it is faith alone which, by the mere mercy of God through Christ, and by means of His word, can worthily and sufficiently justify and save the person; and that a Christian man needs no work, no law, for his salvation; for by faith be is free from all law, and in perfect freedom does gratuitously all that he does, seeking nothing either of profit or of salvation--since by the grace of God he is already saved and rich in all things through his faith--but solely that which is well-pleasing to God.[. . .]

We do not then reject good works; nay, we embrace them and teach them in the highest degree. It is not on their own account that we condemn them, but on account of this impious addition to them, and the perverse notion of seeking justification by them. These things cause them to be only good in outward show, but in reality not good; since by them men are deceived and deceive others, like ravening wolves in sheep's clothing.[. . .]

Here is the truly Christian life; here is faith really working by love; when a man applies himself with joy and love to the works of that freest servitude, in which he serves others voluntarily and for naught; himself abundantly satisfied in the fullness and riches of his own faith.

Thus, when Paul had taught the Philippians how they had been made rich by that faith in Christ, in which they had obtained all things, he teaches them further in these words--"If there be therefore any consolation in Christ, if any comfort of love, if any fellowship of the Spirit, if any bowels and mercies, fulfill ye my joy, that ye be like-minded, having the same love, being of one accord, of one mind. Let nothing be done through strife or vainglory; but in lowliness of mind let each esteem other better than themselves. Look not every man on his own things, but every man also on the things of others." (Phil. ii. 1-4.)In this we see clearly that the Apostle lays down this rule for a Christian life, that all our works should be directed to the advantage of others; since every Christian has such abundance through his faith, that all his other works and his whole life remain over and above, wherewith to serve and benefit his neighbor of spontaneous good will.

To this end he brings forward Christ as an example, saying: "Let this mind be in you, which was also in Christ Jesus: who, being in the form of God, thought it not robbery to be equal with God: but made himself of no reputation, and took upon him the form of a servant, and was made in the likeness of men; and being found in fashion as a man, he humbled himself, and became obedient unto death." (Phil. ii. 5-8.) This most wholesome saying of the Apostle has been darkened to us by men who, totally misunderstanding the expressions: "form of God," "form of a servant," " fashion," "likeness of men," have transferred them to the natures of Godhead and manhood. Paul's meaning is this: Christ, when He was full of the form of God, and abounded in all good things, so that He had no need of works or sufferings to be justified and saved--for all those things He had from the very beginning--yet was not puffed up with these things, and did not raise Himself above us, and arrogate to Himself power over us, though He might lawfully have done so, but on the contrary so acted in laboring, working, suffering, and dying, as to be like the rest of men, and no otherwise than a man in fashion and in conduct, as if he were in want of all things, and had nothing of the form of God; and yet all this He did for our sakes, that He might serve us, and that all the works He should do under that form of a servant, might become ours. [. . .]

Who then can comprehend the riches and glory of the Christian life? It can do all things, has all things, and is in want of nothing; is lord over sin, death, and hell, and at tile same time is the obedient and useful servant of all. But alas! It is at this day unknown throughout the world; it is neither preached nor sought after, so that we are quite ignorant about our own name, why we are and are called Christians. We are certainly called so from Christ, who is not absent, but dwells among us, provided, that is, that we believe in Him, and are reciprocally and mutually one the Christ of the other, doing to our neighbor as Christ does to us. But now, in the doctrine of men, we are taught only to seek after merits, rewards, and things which are already ours, and we have made of Christ a taskmaster far more severe than Moses. [. . .]

We give this rule: the good things which we have from God ought to flow from one to another, and become common to all, so that every one of us may, as it were, put on his neighbor, and so behave towards him its if he were himself in his place. They flowed and do flow from Christ to us; he put us on, and acted for us as if he himself were what we are. From us they flow to those who have need of them; so that my faith and righteousness ought to be laid down before God as a covering and intercession for the sins of my neighbor, which I am to take on myself, and so labor and endure servitude in them, as if they were my own; for thus has Christ done for us. This is true love and the genuine truth of Christian life. But only there is it true and genuine, where there is true and genuine faith. Hence the Apostle attributes to Charity this quality, that she seeketh not her own.

We conclude therefore that a Christian man does not live in himself, but in Christ, and in his neighbor, or else is no Christian; in Christ by faith, in his neighbor by love. By faith he is carried upwards above himself to God, and by love he sinks back below himself to his neighbor, still always abiding in God and His love, as Christ says: "verily I say unto you, hereafter ye shall see heaven open, and the angels of God ascending and descending upon the Son of man." (John i. 51.) [. . .]

Thus too we do not scorn works and ceremonies; nay, we set the highest value on them; but we scorn the belief in works, which no one should consider to constitute true righteousness; as do those hypocrites who employ and throw away their whole life in the pursuit of works, and yet never attain to that for the sake of which the works are done. As the Apostle says, they are "ever learning, and never able to come to the knowledge of the truth." (2 Tim. iii. 7). They appear to wish to build, they make preparations, and yet they never do build; and thus they continue in a show of godliness, but never attain to its power.

Meanwhile they please themselves with this zealous pursuit, and even dare to judge all others, whom they do not see adorned with such a glittering display of works; while, if they had been imbued with faith, they might have done great things for their own and others' salvation, at the same cost which they now waste in abuse of the gifts of God. But since human nature and natural reason, as they call it, are naturally superstitious, and quick to believe that justification can be attained by any laws or works proposed to them; and since nature is also exercised and confirmed in the same view by the practice of all earthly lawgivers, she can never, of her own power, free herself from this bondage to works, and come to a recognition of the liberty of faith.

We have therefore need to pray that God will lead us, and make us taught of God, that is, ready to learn from God; and will Himself, as He has promised, write His law in our hearts; otherwise there is no hope for us. For unless He himself teach us inwardly this wisdom hidden in a mystery, nature cannot but condemn it and judge it to be heretical. She takes offence at it and it seems folly to her; just as we see that it happened of old in the case of the prophets and apostles; and just as blind and impious pontiffs, with their flatterers, do now in my case and that of those who are like me; upon whom, together with ourselves, may God at length have mercy, and lift up the light of His countenance upon them, that we may know His way upon earth and His saving health among all nations, Who is blessed for evermore. Amen. In the year of the Lord MDXX.

Source: Text from Henry Wace and C. A. Buchheim, *First Principles of the Reformation*, London: John Murray, 1883.

Martin Luther
Preface to the Letter of St. Paul to the Romans
in Luther's German translation of the New Testament

Source: "Vorrede auff die Epistel S. Paul: an die Romer" in *D. Martin Luther: Die gantze Heilige Schrifft Deudsch 1545 aufs new zurericht*, ed. Hans Volz and Heinz Blanke. Munich: Roger & Bernhard. 1972, vol. 2, pp. 2254-2268. Translated by Bro. Andrew Thornton, OSB

Translator's Note: The material between square brackets is explanatory in nature and is not part of Luther's preface. The terms "just, justice, justify" in this piece are synonymous with the terms "righteous, righteousness, make righteous." Both sets of English words are common translations of German "gerecht" and related words. A similar situation exists with the word "faith"; it is synonymous with "belief." Both words can be used to translate German "Glaube." Thus, "We are justified by faith" translates the same original German sentence as does "We are made righteous by belief."

This letter is truly the most important piece in the New Testament. It is purest Gospel. It is well worth a Christian's while not only to memorize it word for word but also to occupy himself with it daily, as though it were the daily bread of the soul. It is impossible to read or to meditate on this letter too much or too well. The more one deals with it, the more precious it becomes and the better it tastes. Therefore I want to carry out my service and, with this preface, provide an introduction to the letter, insofar as God gives me the ability, so that everyone can gain the fullest possible understanding of it. Up to now it has been darkened by glosses [explanatory notes and comments which accompany a text] and by many a useless comment, but it is in itself a bright light, almost bright enough to illumine the entire Scripture.

To begin with, we have to become familiar with the vocabulary of the letter and know what St. Paul means by the words law, sin, grace, faith, justice, flesh, spirit, etc. Otherwise there is no use in reading it.

You must not understand the word law here in human fashion, i.e., a regulation about what sort of works must be done or must not be done. That's the way it is with human laws: you satisfy the demands of the law with works, whether your heart is in it or not. God judges what is in the depths of the heart. Therefore his law also makes demands on the depths of the heart and doesn't let the heart rest content in works; rather it punishes as hypocrisy and lies all works done apart from the depths of the heart. All human beings are called liars (Psalm 116), since none of them keeps or can keep God's law from the depths of the heart. Everyone finds inside himself an aversion to good and a craving for evil. Where there is no free desire for good, there the heart has not set itself on God's law. There also sin is surely to be found and the deserved wrath of God, whether a lot of good works and an honorable life appear outwardly or not.

Therefore in chapter 2, St. Paul adds that the Jews are all sinners and says that only the doers of the law are justified in the sight of God. What he is saying is that no one is a doer of the law by works. On the contrary, he says to them, "You teach that one should not commit adultery, and you commit adultery. You judge another in a certain matter and condemn yourselves in that same matter, because you do the very same thing that you judged in another." It is as if he were saying, "Outwardly you live quite properly in the works of the law and judge those who do not live the same way; you know how to teach everybody. You see the speck in another's eye but do not notice the beam in your own."

Outwardly you keep the law with works out of fear of punishment or love of gain. Likewise you do everything without free desire and love of the law; you act out of aversion and force. You'd rather act otherwise if the law didn't exist. It follows, then, that you, in the depths of your heart, are an enemy of the law. What do you mean, therefore, by teaching another not to steal, when you, in the depths of your heart, are a thief and would be one outwardly too, if you dared. (Of course, outward work doesn't last long with such hypocrites.) So then, you teach others but not yourself; you don't even know what you are teaching. You've never understood the law rightly. Furthermore, the law increases sin, as St. Paul says in chapter 5. That is because a person becomes more and more an enemy of the law the more it demands of him what he can't possibly do.

In chapter 7, St. Paul says, "The law is spiritual." What does that mean? If the law were physical, then it could be satisfied by works, but since it is spiritual, no one can satisfy it unless everything he does springs from the depths of the heart. But no one can give such a heart except the Spirit of God, who makes the person be like the law, so that he actually conceives a heartfelt longing for the law and henceforward does everything, not through fear or coercion, but from a free heart. Such a law is spiritual since it can only be loved and fulfilled by such a heart and such a spirit. If the Spirit is not in the heart, then there remain sin, aversion and enmity against the law, which in itself is good, just and holy.

You must get used to the idea that it is one thing to do the works of the law and quite another to fulfill it. The works of the law are everything that a person does or can do of his own free will and by his own powers to obey the law. But because in doing such works the heart abhors the law and yet is forced to obey it, the works are a total loss and are completely useless. That is what St. Paul means in chapter 3 when he says, "No human being is justified before God through the works of the law." From this you can see that the schoolmasters [i.e., the scholastic theologians] and sophists are seducers when they teach that you can prepare yourself for grace by means of works. How can anybody prepare himself for good by means of works if he does no good work except with aversion and constraint in his heart? How can such a work please God, if it proceeds from an averse and unwilling heart?

But to fulfill the law means to do its work eagerly, lovingly and freely, without the constraint of the law; it means to live well and in a manner pleasing to God, as though there were no law or punishment. It is the Holy Spirit, however, who puts such eagerness of unconstrained love into the heart, as Paul says in chapter 5. But the Spirit is given only in, with, and through faith in Jesus Christ, as Paul says in his introduction. So, too, faith comes only through the word of God, the Gospel, that preaches Christ: how he is both Son of God and man, how he died and rose for our sake. Paul says all this in chapters 3, 4 and 10.

That is why faith alone makes someone just and fulfills the law; faith it is that brings the Holy Spirit through the merits of Christ. The Spirit, in turn, renders the heart glad and free, as the law demands. Then good works proceed from faith itself. That is what Paul means in chapter 3 when, after he has thrown out the works of the law, he sounds as though the wants to abolish the law by faith. No, he says, we uphold the law through faith, i.e. we fulfill it through faith.

Sin in the Scriptures means not only external works of the body but also all those movements within us which bestir themselves and move us to do the external works, namely, the depth of the heart with all its powers. Therefore the word *do* should refer to a person's completely falling into sin. No external work of sin happens, after all, unless a person commit himself to it completely, body and soul. In particular, the Scriptures see into the heart, to the root and main source of all sin: unbelief in the depth of the heart. Thus, even as faith alone makes just and brings the Spirit and the desire to do good external works, so it is only unbelief which sins and exalts the flesh and brings desire to do evil external works. That's what happened to Adam and Eve in Paradise (cf. Genesis 3).

That is why only unbelief is called sin by Christ, as he says in John, chapter 16, "The Spirit will punish the world because of sin, because it does not believe in me." Furthermore, before good or bad works happen, which are the good or bad fruits of the heart, there has to be present in the heart either faith or unbelief, the root, sap and chief power of all sin. That is why, in the Scriptures, unbelief is called the head of the serpent and of the ancient dragon which the offspring of the woman, i.e. Christ, must crush, as was promised to Adam (cf. Genesis 3). *Grace* and *gift* differ in that grace actually denotes God's kindness or favor which he has toward us and by which he is disposed to pour Christ and the Spirit with his gifts into us, as becomes clear from chapter 5, where Paul says, "Grace and gift are in Christ, etc." The gifts and the Spirit increase daily in us, yet they are not complete, since evil desires and sins remain in us which war against the Spirit, as Paul says in chapter 7, and in Galatians, chapter 5. And Genesis, chapter 3, proclaims the enmity between the offspring of the woman and that of the serpent. But grace does do this much: that we are accounted completely just before God. God's grace is not divided into bits and pieces, as are the gifts, but grace takes us up completely into God's favor for the sake of Christ, our intercessor and mediator, so that the gifts may begin their work in us.

In this way, then, you should understand chapter 7, where St. Paul portrays himself as still a sinner, while in chapter 8 he says that, because of the incomplete gifts and because of the Spirit, there is nothing damnable in those who are in Christ. Because our flesh has not been killed, we are still sinners, but because we believe in Christ and have the beginnings of the Spirit, God so shows us his favor and mercy, that he neither notices nor judges such sins. Rather he deals with us according to our belief in Christ until sin is killed.

Faith is not that human illusion and dream that some people think it is. When they hear and talk a lot about faith and yet see that no moral improvement and no good works result from it, they fall into error and say, "Faith is not enough. You must do works if you want to be virtuous and get to heaven." The result is that, when they hear the Gospel, they stumble and make for themselves with their own powers a concept in their hearts which says, "I believe." This concept they hold to be true faith. But since it is a human fabrication and thought and not an experience of the heart, it accomplishes nothing, and there follows no improvement.

Faith is a work of God in us, which changes us and brings us to birth anew from God (cf. John 1). It kills the old Adam, makes us completely different people in heart, mind, senses, and all our powers, and brings the Holy Spirit with it. What a living, creative, active powerful thing is faith! It is impossible that faith ever stop doing good. Faith doesn't ask whether good works are to be done, but, before it is asked, it has done them. It is always active. Whoever doesn't do such works is without faith; he gropes and searches about him for faith and good works but doesn't know what faith or good works are. Even so, he chatters on with a great many words about faith and good works.

Faith is a living, unshakeable confidence in God's grace; it is so certain, that someone would die a thousand times for it. This kind of trust in and knowledge of God's grace makes a person joyful, confident, and happy with regard to God and all creatures. This is what the Holy Spirit does by faith. Through faith, a person will do good to everyone without coercion, willingly and happily; he will serve everyone, suffer everything for the love and praise of God, who has shown him such grace. It is as impossible to separate works from faith as burning and shining from fire. Therefore be on guard against your own false ideas and against the chatterers who think they are clever enough to make judgments about faith and good works but who are in reality the biggest fools. Ask God to work faith in you; otherwise you will remain eternally without faith, no matter what you try to do or fabricate.

Now *justice* is just such a faith. It is called God's justice or that justice which is valid in God's sight, because it is God who gives it and reckons it as justice for the sake of Christ our Mediator. It influences a person to give to everyone what he owes him. Through faith a person becomes sinless and eager for God's commands. Thus he gives God the honor due him and pays him what he owes him. He serves people willingly with the means available to him. In this way he pays everyone his due. Neither nature nor free will nor our own powers can bring about such a justice, for even as no one can give himself faith, so too he cannot remove unbelief. How can he then take away even the smallest sin? Therefore everything which takes place outside faith or in unbelief is lie, hypocrisy and sin (Romans 14), no matter how smoothly it may seem to go.

You must not understand flesh here as denoting only unchastity or spirit as denoting only the inner heart. Here St. Paul calls flesh (as does Christ in John 3) everything born of flesh, i.e. the whole human being with body and soul, reason and senses, since everything in him tends toward the flesh. That is why you should know enough to call that person "fleshly" who, without grace, fabricates, teaches and chatters about high spiritual matters. You can learn the same thing from Galatians, chapter 5, where St. Paul calls heresy and hatred works of the flesh. And in Romans, chapter 8, he says that, through the flesh, the law is weakened. He says this, not of unchastity, but of all sins, most of all of unbelief, which is the most spiritual of vices.

On the other hand, you should know enough to call that person "spiritual" who is occupied with the most outward of works as was Christ, when he washed the feet of the disciples, and Peter, when he steered his boat and fished. So then, a person is "flesh" who, inwardly and outwardly, lives only to do those things which are of use to the flesh and to temporal existence. A person is "spirit" who, inwardly and outwardly, lives only to do those things which are of use to the spirit and to the life to come.

Unless you understand these words in this way, you will never understand either this letter of St. Paul or any book of the Scriptures. Be on guard, therefore against any teacher who uses these words differently, no matter who he be, whether Jerome, Augustine, Ambrose, Origen or anyone else as great as or greater than they. Now let us turn to the letter itself.

The first duty of a preacher of the Gospel is, through his revealing of the law and of sin, to rebuke and to turn into sin everything in life that does not have the Spirit and faith in Christ as its base. [Here and elsewhere in Luther's preface, as indeed in Romans itself, it is not clear whether "spirit" has the meaning "Holy Spirit" or "spiritual person," as Luther has previously defined it.] Thereby he will lead people to a recognition of their miserable condition, and thus they will become humble and yearn for help. This is what St Paul does. He begins in chapter 1 by rebuking the gross sins and unbelief which are in plain view, as were (and still are) the sins of the pagans, who live without God's grace. He says that, through the Gospel, God is revealing his wrath from heaven upon all mankind because of the godless and unjust lives they live. For, although they know and recognize day by day that there is a God, yet human nature in itself, without grace, is so evil that it neither thanks nor honors God. This nature blinds itself and continually falls into wickedness, even going so far as to commit idolatry and other horrible sins and vices. It is unashamed of itself and leaves such things unpunished in others.

In chapter 2, St. Paul extends his rebuke to those who appear outwardly pious or who sin secretly. Such were the Jews, and such are all hypocrites still, who live virtuous lives but without eagerness and love; in their heart they are enemies of God's law and like to judge other people. That's the way with hypocrites: they think that they are pure but are actually full of greed, hate, pride and all sorts of filth (cf. Matthew 23). These are they who despise God's goodness and, by their hardness of heart, heap wrath upon themselves. Thus Paul explains the law rightly when he lets no one remain without sin but proclaims the wrath of God to all who want to live virtuously by nature or by free will. He makes them out to be no better than public sinners; he says they are hard of heart and unrepentant.

In chapter 3, Paul lumps both secret and public sinners together: the one, he says, is like the other; all are sinners in the sight of God. Besides, the Jews had God's word, even though many did not believe in it. But still God's truth and faith in him are not thereby rendered useless. St. Paul introduces, as an aside, the saying from Psalm 51, that God remains true to his words. Then he returns to his topic and proves from Scripture that they are all sinners and that no one becomes just through the works of the law but that God gave the law only so that sin might be perceived.

Next St. Paul teaches the right way to be virtuous and to be saved; he says that they are all sinners, unable to glory in God. They must, however, be justified through faith in Christ, who has merited this for us by his blood and has become for us a mercy seat [cf. Exodus 25:17, Leviticus 16:14ff, and John 2:2] in the presence of God, who forgives us all our previous sins. In so doing, God proves that it is his justice alone, which he gives through faith, that helps us, the justice which was at the appointed time revealed through the Gospel and, previous to that, was witnessed to by the Law and the Prophets. Therefore the law is set up by faith, but the works of the law, along with the glory taken in them, are knocked down by faith. [As with the term "spirit," the word "law" seems to have for Luther, and for St. Paul, two meanings. Sometimes it means "regulation about what must be done or not done," as in the third paragraph of this preface; sometimes it means "the Torah," as in the previous sentence. And sometimes it seems to have both meanings, as in what follows.]

In chapters 1 to 3, St. Paul has revealed sin for what it is and has taught the way of faith which leads to justice. Now in chapter 4 he deals with some objections and criticisms. He takes up first the one that people raise who, on hearing that faith make just without works, say, "What? Shouldn't we do any good works?" Here St. Paul holds up Abraham as an example. He says, "What did Abraham accomplish with his good works? Were they all good for nothing and useless?" He concludes that Abraham was made righteous apart from all his works by faith alone. Even before the "work" of his circumcision, Scripture praises him as being just on account of faith alone (cf. Genesis 15). Now if the work of his circumcision did nothing to make him just, a work that God had commanded him to do and hence a work of obedience, then surely no other good work can do anything to make a person just. Even as Abraham's circumcision was an outward sign with which he proved his justice based on faith, so too all good works are only outward signs which flow from faith and are the fruits of faith; they prove that the person is already inwardly just in the sight of God.

St. Paul verifies his teaching on faith in chapter 3 with a powerful example from Scripture. He calls as witness David, who says in Psalm 32 that a person becomes just without works but doesn't remain without works once he has become just. Then Paul extends this example and applies it against all other works of the law. He concludes that the Jews cannot be Abraham's heirs just because of their blood relationship to him and still less because of the works of the law. Rather, they have to inherit Abraham's faith if they want to be his real heirs, since it was prior to the Law of Moses and the law of circumcision that Abraham became just through faith and was called a father of all believers. St. Paul adds that the law brings about more wrath than grace, because no one obeys it with love and eagerness. More disgrace than grace come from the works of the law. Therefore faith alone can obtain the grace promised to Abraham. Examples like these are written for our sake, that we also should have faith.

In chapter 5, St. Paul comes to the fruits and works of faith, namely: joy, peace, love for God and for all people; in addition: assurance, steadfastness, confidence, courage, and hope in sorrow and suffering. All of these follow where faith is genuine, because of the overflowing good will that God has shown in Christ: he had him die for us before we could ask him for it, yes, even while we were still his enemies. Thus we have established that faith, without any good works, makes just. It does not follow from that, however, that we should not do good works; rather it means that morally upright works do not remain lacking. About such works the "works-holy" people know nothing; they invent for themselves their own works in which are neither peace nor joy nor assurance nor love nor hope nor steadfastness nor any kind of genuine Christian works or faith.

Next St. Paul makes a digression, a pleasant little side-trip, and relates where both sin and justice, death and life come from. He opposes these two: Adam and Christ. What he wants to say is that Christ, a second Adam, had to come in order to make us heirs of his justice through a new spiritual birth in faith, just as the old Adam made us heirs of sin through the old fleshy birth.

St. Paul proves, by this reasoning, that a person cannot help himself by his works to get from sin to justice any more than he can prevent his own physical birth. St. Paul also proves that the divine law, which should have been well-suited, if anything was, for helping people to obtain justice, not only was no help at all when it did come, but it even increased sin. Evil human nature, consequently, becomes more hostile to it; the more the law forbids it to indulge its own desires, the more it wants to. Thus the law makes Christ all the more necessary and demands more grace to help human nature.

In chapter 6, St. Paul takes up the special work of faith, the struggle which the spirit wages against the flesh to kill off those sins and desires that remain after a person has been made just. He teaches us that faith doesn't so free us from sin that we can be idle, lazy and self-assured, as though there were no more sin in us. Sin *is* there, but, because of faith that struggles against it, God does not reckon sin as deserving damnation. Therefore we have in our own selves a lifetime of work cut out for us; we have to tame our body, kill its lusts, force its members to obey the spirit and not the lusts. We must do this so that we may conform to the death and resurrection of Christ and complete our Baptism, which signifies a death to sin and a new life of grace. Our aim is to be completely clean from sin and then to rise bodily with Christ and live forever.

St. Paul says that we can accomplish all this because we are in grace and not in the law. He explains that to be "outside the law" is not the same as having no law and being able to do what you please. No, being "under the law" means living without grace, surrounded by the works of the law. Then surely sin reigns by means of the law, since no one is naturally well-disposed toward the law. That very condition, however, is the greatest sin. But grace makes the law lovable to us, so there is then no sin any more, and the law is no longer against us but one with us.

This is true freedom from sin and from the law; St. Paul writes about this for the rest of the chapter. He says it is a freedom only to do good with eagerness and to live a good life without the coercion of the law. This freedom is, therefore, a spiritual freedom which does not suspend the law but which supplies what the law demands, namely eagerness and love. These silence the law so that it has no further cause to drive people on and make demands of them. It's as though you owed something to a moneylender and couldn't pay him. You could be rid of him in one of two ways: either he would take nothing from you and would tear up his account book, or a pious man would pay for you and give you what you needed to satisfy your debt. That's exactly how Christ freed us from the law. Therefore our freedom is not a wild, fleshy freedom that has no obligation to do anything. On the contrary, it is a freedom that does a great deal, indeed everything, yet is free of the law's demands and debts.

In chapter 7, St. Paul confirms the foregoing by an analogy drawn from married life. When a man dies, the wife is free; the one is free and clear of the other. It is not the case that the woman may not or should not marry another man; rather she is now for the first time free to marry someone else. She could not do this before she was free of her first husband. In the same way, our conscience is bound to the law so long as our condition is that of the sinful old man. But when the old man is killed by the spirit, then the conscience is free, and conscience and law are quit of each other. Not that conscience should now do nothing; rather, it should now for the first time truly cling to its second husband, Christ, and bring forth the fruit of life.

Next St. Paul sketches further the nature of sin and the law. It is the law that makes sin really active and powerful, because the old man gets more and more hostile to the law since he can't pay the debt demanded by the law. Sin is his very nature; of himself he can't do otherwise. And so the law is his death and torture. Now the law is not itself evil; it is our evil nature that cannot tolerate that the good law should demand good from it. It's like the case of a sick person, who cannot tolerate that you demand that he run and jump around and do other things that a healthy person does.

St. Paul concludes here that, if we understand the law properly and comprehend it in the best possible way, then we will see that its sole function is to remind us of our sins, to kill us by our sins, and to make us deserving of eternal wrath. Conscience learns and experiences all this in detail when it comes face to face with the law. It follows, then, that we must have something else, over and above the law, which can make a person virtuous and cause him to be saved.

Those, however, who do not understand the law rightly are blind; they go their way boldly and think they are satisfying the law with works. They don't know how much the law demands, namely, a free, willing, eager heart. That is the reason that they don't see Moses rightly before their eyes. [In both Jewish and Christian teaching, Moses was commonly held to be the author of the Pentateuch, the first five books of the bible. Cf. the involved imagery of Moses' face and the veil over it in 2 Corinthians 3:7-18.] For them he is covered and concealed by the veil.

Then St. Paul shows how spirit and flesh struggle with each other in one person. He gives himself as an example, so that we may learn how to kill sin in ourselves. He gives both spirit and flesh the name "law," so that, just as it is in the nature of divine law to drive a person on and make demands of him, so too the flesh drives and demands and rages against the spirit and wants to have its own way. Likewise the spirit drives and demands against the flesh and wants to have its own way. This feud lasts in us for as long as we live, in one person more, in another less, depending on whether spirit or flesh is stronger. Yet the whole human being is both: spirit and flesh. The human being fights with himself until he becomes completely spiritual.

In chapter 8, St. Paul comforts fighters such as these and tells them that this flesh will not bring them condemnation. He goes on to show what the nature of flesh and spirit are. Spirit, he says, comes from Christ, who has given us his Holy Spirit; the Holy Spirit makes us spiritual and restrains the flesh. The Holy Spirit assures us that we are God's children no matter how furiously sin may rage within us, so long as we follow the Spirit and struggle against sin in order to kill it. Because nothing is so effective in deadening the flesh as the cross and suffering, Paul comforts us in our suffering. He says that the Spirit, [cf. previous note about the meaning of "spirit."] love and all creatures will stand by us; the Spirit in us groans and all creatures long with us that we be freed from the flesh and from sin. Thus we see that these three chapters, 6, 7 and 8, all deal with the one work of faith, which is to kill the old Adam and to constrain the flesh.

In chapters 9, 10 and 11, St. Paul teaches us about the eternal providence of God. It is the original source which determines who would believe and who wouldn't, who can be set free from sin and who cannot. Such matters have been taken out of our hands and are put into God's hands so that we might become virtuous. It is absolutely necessary that it be so, for we are so weak and unsure of ourselves that, if it depended on us, no human being would be saved. The devil would overpower all of us. But God is steadfast; his providence will not fail, and no one can prevent its realization. Therefore we have hope against sin.

But here we must shut the mouths of those sacrilegious and arrogant spirits who, mere beginners that they are, bring their reason to bear on this matter and commence, from their exalted position, to probe the abyss of divine providence and uselessly trouble themselves about whether they are predestined or not. These people must surely plunge to their ruin, since they will either despair or abandon themselves to a life of chance.

You, however, follow the reasoning of this letter in the order in which it is presented. Fix your attention first of all on Christ and the Gospel, so that you may recognize your sin and his grace. Then struggle against sin, as chapters 1-8 have taught you to. Finally, when you have come, in chapter 8, under the shadow of the cross and suffering, they will teach you, in chapters 9-11, about providence and what a comfort it is. [The context here and in St. Paul's letter makes it clear that this is the cross and passion, not only of Christ, but of each Christian.] Apart from suffering, the cross and the pangs of death, you cannot come to grips with providence without harm to yourself and secret anger against God. The old Adam must be quite dead before you can endure this matter and drink this strong wine. Therefore make sure you don't drink wine while you are still a babe at the breast. There is a proper measure, time and age for understanding every doctrine.

In chapter 12, St. Paul teaches the true liturgy and makes all Christians priests, so that they may offer, not money or cattle, as priests do in the Law, but their own bodies, by putting their desires to death. Next he describes the outward conduct of Christians whose lives are governed by the Spirit; he tells how they teach, preach, rule, serve, give, suffer, love, live and act toward friend, foe and everyone. These are the works that a Christian does, for, as I have said, faith is not idle.

In chapter 13, St. Paul teaches that one should honor and obey the secular authorities. He includes this, not because it makes people virtuous in the sight of God, but because it does insure that the virtuous have outward peace and protection and that the wicked cannot do evil without fear and in undisturbed peace. Therefore it is the duty of virtuous people to honor secular authority, even though they do not, strictly speaking, need it. Finally, St. Paul sums up everything in love and gathers it all into the example of Christ: what he has done for us, we must also do and follow after him.

In chapter 14, St. Paul teaches that one should carefully guide those with weak conscience and spare them. One shouldn't use Christian freedom to harm but rather to help the weak. Where that isn't done, there follow dissention and despising of the Gospel, on which everything else depends. It is better to give way a little to the weak in faith until they become stronger than to have the teaching of the Gospel perish completely. This work is a particularly necessary work of love especially now when people, by eating meat and by other freedoms, are brashly, boldly and unnecessarily shaking weak consciences which have not yet come to know the truth.

In chapter 15, St. Paul cites Christ as an example to show that we must also have patience with the weak, even those who fail by sinning publicly or by their disgusting morals. We must not cast them aside but must bear with them until they become better. That is the way Christ treated us and still treats us every day; he puts up with our vices, our wicked morals and all our imperfection, and he helps us ceaselessly. Finally Paul prays for the Christians at Rome; he praises them and commends them to God. He points out his own office and the message that he preaches. He makes an unobtrusive plea for a contribution for the poor in Jerusalem. Unalloyed love is the basis of all he says and does.

The last chapter consists of greetings. But Paul also includes a salutary warning against human doctrines which are preached alongside the Gospel and which do a great deal of harm. It's as though he had clearly seen that out of Rome and through the Romans would come the deceitful, harmful Canons and Decretals along with the entire brood and swarm of human laws and commands that is now drowning the whole world and has blotted out this letter and the whole of the Scriptures, along with the Spirit and faith. Nothing remains but the idol Belly, and St. Paul depicts those people here as its servants. God deliver us from them. Amen.

We find in this letter, then, the richest possible teaching about what a Christian should know: the meaning of law, Gospel, sin, punishment, grace, faith, justice, Christ, God, good works, love, hope and the cross. We learn how we are to act toward everyone, toward the virtuous and sinful, toward the strong and the weak, friend and foe, and toward ourselves. Paul bases everything firmly on Scripture and proves his points with examples from his own experience and from the Prophets, so that nothing more could be desired. Therefore it seems that St. Paul, in writing this letter, wanted to compose a summary of the whole of Christian and evangelical teaching which would also be an introduction to the whole Old Testament. Without doubt, whoever takes this letter to heart possesses the light and power of the Old Testament. Therefore each and every Christian should make this letter the habitual and constant object of his study. God grant us his grace to do so. Amen.

Ulrich Zwingli
pastor of the Grossmünster in Zürich

Ulrich Zwingli
The Sixty-Seven Articles (1523)

Source: **Selected Works of Huldreich Zwingli**, edited by Samuel Macauley Jackson. Philadelphia: University of Pennsylvania, 1901.

The articles and opinions below, I, Ulrich Zwingli confess to have preached in the worthy city of Zurich as based upon the Scriptures which are called inspired by God, and I offer to protect and conquer with the said articles, and where I have not now correctly understood said Scriptures I shall allow myself to be taught better but only from said Scriptures

I. All who say that the Gospel is invalid without the confirmation of the Church err and slander God .

II. The sum and substance of the Gospel is that our Lord Jesus Christ, the true Son of God, has made known to us the will of his heavenly Father, and has with his innocence released us from death and reconciled God .

III. Hence Christ is the only way to salvation for all who ever were, are and shall be.

IV. Who seeks or points out another door errs, yea, he is a murderer of souls and a thief.

V. Hence all who consider other teachings equal to or higher than the Gospel err, and do not know what the Gospel is.

VI. For Jesus Christ is the guide and leader, promised by God to all human beings which promise was fulfilled.

VII. That he is an eternal salvation and head of all believers, who are his body, but which is dead and can do nothing without him.

VIII. From this follows first that all who dwell in the head are members and children of God, and that is the church or communion of the saints the bride of Christ, *Ecclesia catholica*.

IX. Furthermore, that as the members of the body can do nothing without the control of the head, so no one in the body of Christ can do the least without his head Christ.

X. As that man is mad whose limbs (try to) do something without his head, tearing, wounding, injuring himself; thus when the members of Christ undertake something without their head, Christ, they are mad, and injure and burden themselves with unwise ordinances.

XI. Hence we see in the clerical (so-called) ordinances, concerning their splendor, riches, classes, titles, laws, a cause of all foolishness, for they do not also agree with the head.

XII. Thus they still rage, not on account of the head (for that one is eager to bring forth in these times from the grace of God,) but because one will not let them rage, but tries to compel them to listen to the head.

XIII. Where this (the head) is hearkened to, one learns clearly and plainly the will of God, and man is attracted by his spirit to him and changed into him.

XIV. Therefore all Christian people shall use their best diligence that the Gospel of Christ be preached alike everywhere.

XV. For in the faith rests our salvation, and in unbelief our damnation; for all truth is clear in him.

XVI. In the Gospel one learns that human doctrines and decrees do not aid in salvation.

ABOUT THE POPE

XVII. That Christ is the only eternal high priest, wherefrom it follows that those who have called themselves high priests have opposed the honor and power of Christ, yea cast it out.

ABOUT THE MASS

XVIII. That Christ, having sacrificed himself once, is to eternity a certain and valid sacrifice for the sins of all faithful, wherefrom it follows that the mass is not a sacrifice, but is a remembrance of the sacrifice and assurance of the salvation which Christ has given us.

XIX. That Christ is the only mediator between God and us.

ABOUT THE INTERCESSION OF THE SAINTS

XX. That God desires to give us all things in his name, whence it follows that outside of this life we need no mediator except himself.

XXI. That when we pray for each other on earth, we do so in such fashion that we believe that all things are given to us through Christ alone.

ABOUT GOOD WORKS

XXII. That Christ is our justice, from which follows that our works in so far as they are good, so far they are of Christ, but in so far as they are ours, they are neither right nor good.

CONCERNING CLERICAL PROPERTY

XXIII. That Christ scorns the property and pomp of this world, whence from it follows that those who attract wealth to themselves in his name slander him terribly when they make him a pretext for their avarice and willfulness.

CONCERNING THE FORBIDDING OF FOOD

XXIV. That no Christian is bound to do those things which God has not decreed, therefore one may eat at all tunes all food, wherefrom one learns that the decree about cheese and butter is s Roman swindle.

ABOUT HOLIDAY AND PILGRIMAGE

XXV. That time and place is under the jurisdiction of Christian people, and man with them, wherefrom is learnt that those who fix time and place deprive the Christians of their liberty.

ABOUT HOODS DRESS INSIGNIA

XXVI. That God is displeased with nothing so much as with hypocrisy; whence is learnt that all is gross hypocrisy and profligacy which is mere show before men. Under this condemnation fall hoods, insignia, plates, etc.

ABOUT ORDER AND SECTS

XXVII. That all Christian men are brethren of Christ and brethren of one another, and shall create no father (for themselves) on earth. Under this condemnation fall orders, sects, brotherhoods, etc.

ABOUT THE MARRIAGE OF ECCLESIASTS

XXVIII. That all which God has allowed or not forbidden is righteous, hence marriage is permitted to all human beings.

XXIX. That all who are called clericals sin when they do not protect themselves by marriage after they have become conscious that God has not enabled them to remain chaste.

ABOUT THE VOW OF CHASTITY

XXX. That those who promise chastity [outside of matrimony] take foolishly or childishly too much upon themselves, whence is learnt that those who make such vows do wrong to the pious being.

ABOUT THE BAN

XXXI. That no special person can impose the ban upon any one, but the Church, that is the congregation of those among whom the one to be banned dwells, together with their watchman, i.e. the pastor .

XXXII. That one may ban only him who gives public offence.

ABOUT ILLEGAL PROPERTY

XXXIII. That property unrighteously acquired shall not be given to temples, monasteries, cathedrals, clergy, or nuns, but to the needy, if it cannot be returned to the legal owner.

ABOUT MAGBTRY

XXXIV. The spiritual {so-called) power has no justification for its pomp in the teaching of Christ.

XXXV. But the lay has power and confirmation from the deed and doctrine of Christ.

XXXVI. All that the spiritual (so-called) state claims to have of power and protection belongs to the lay, if they wish to be Christians.

XXXVII. To them, furthermore, all Christians owe obedience without exception.

XXXVIII. In so far as they do not command that which it contrary to God.

XXXIX. Therefore all their laws shall be in harmony with the divine will, so that they protect the oppressed, even if he does not complain.

XL. They alone may put to death justly, also, only those who give public offence (if God is not offended let another thing be commanded).

XLI. If they give good advice and help to those for whom they must account to God, then these owe to them bodily assistance.

XLII. But if they are unfaithful and transgress the laws of Christ they may be deposed in the name of God.

XLIII. In short, the realm of him is best and most stable who rules in the name of God alone, and his is worst and most unstable who rules in accordance with his own will.

ABOUT PRAYER

XLIV. Real petitioners call to God in spirit and truly, without great ado before men.

XLV. Hypocrites do their work so that they may be seen by men, also receive their reward in this life.

XLVI. Hence it must always follow that church-song and outcry without devoutness, and only for reward, is seeking either fame before the men or gain.

ABOUT OFFENCE

XLVII. Bodily death a man should suffer before he offend or scandalize a Christian.

XLVIII. Who through stupidness or ignorance is offended without cause, he should not be left sick or weak, but he should be made strong, that he may not consider as a sin which is not a sin.

XLIX. Greater offence I know not than that one does not allow priests to have wives, but permits them to hire prostitutes. Out upon the shame I

ABOUT REMITTANCE OF SIN

L. God alone remits sin through Jesus Christ, his Son, and alone our Lord.

LI. Who assigns this to creatures detracts from the honor of God and gives it to him who is not God; this is real idolatry.

LII. Hence the confession which is made to the priest or neighbor shall not be declared to be a remittance of sin, but only a seeking for advice.

LIII. Works of penance coming from the counsel of human beings (except the ban) do not cancel sin; they are imposed as a menace to others.

LIV. Christ has borne all our pains and labor. Hence whoever assigns to works of penance what belongs to Christ errs and slanders God.

LV. Whoever pretends to remit to a penitent being any sin would not be a vicar of God or St Peter, but of the devil .

LVI. Whoever remits any sin only for the sake of money is the companion of Simon and Balaam, and the real messenger of the devil personified.

ABOUT PURGATORT

LVII. The true divine Scriptures know naught about purgatory after this life.

LVIII. The sentence of the dead is known to God only.

LIX. And the less God has let us know concerning, it the less we should undertake to know about it.

LX. That man earnestly calls to God to show mercy to the dead I do not condemn, but to determine a period of time therefor (seven years for a mortal sin) and to lie for the sake of gain, is not human, but devilish.

ABOUT THE PRIESTHOOD

LXI. About the consecration which the priests have received in late times the Scriptures know nothing.

LXII. Furthermore, they know no priests except those who proclaim the word of God.

LXIII. They command honor should be shown, i.e., to furnish them with food for the body.

ABOUT THE CESSATION OF MISUSAGES

LXIV. All those who recognize their errors shall not be allowed to suffer, but to die in peace, and thereafter arrange in a Christian manner their bequests to the Church.

LXV. Those who do not wish to confess, God will probably take care of. Hence no force shall be used against their body, unless it be that they behave so criminally that one cannot do without that.

LXVI. All the clerical superiors shall at once settle down, and with unanimity set up the cross of Christ, not the money chests, or they will perish, for I tell thee the ax is raised against the tree.

LXVII. If any one wishes conversation with me concerning interes,t tithes, unbaptized children or confirmation, I am willing to answer.

Let no one undertake here to argue with sophistry or human foolishness, but come to the Scriptures to accept them as the judge (*foras cares*l the Scriptures breathe the Spirit of God), so that the truth either may be found, or if found, as I hope, retained. Amen.

Thus may God rule.

The basis and commentary of these articles will soon appear in print.

Conrad Grebel

Letters to Thomas Muntzer

from *The Sources of Swiss Anabaptism: The Grebel Letters and Related Documents*. Edited by Leland Harder, Herald Press: 1985. Used by permission.

Letter 63
Grebel to Muntzer
Zurich, September 5, 1524

Letters 63 and 64 comprise what J. C. Wenger calls "the programmatic letters of Conrad Grebel" because they contain, more than any other document in this collection, the vision of a believers' church free of the state which he and his friends had developed before the autumn of 1524. These letters were first translated into English in 1905 by Walter Rauschenbusch, father of the "social gospel." This version was revised and republished by George H. Williams in 1957. Then in 1970, J. C. Wenger published his own translation. These are the first of Grebel's extant letters written in the German language. As far as is known, he had previously used German only in brief phrases and postscripts, such as in 51/195/28ff. Following the present two epistles, Letters 65, 66, and 67 were written in German.

Latin was used primarily by scholars and clergy and was not understood by the masses. Most of the day?to?day commercial and civil business was transacted in German, including all of the court records. Although Muntzer and Vadian were proficient Latinists, Grebel's resort to German reflects a new interest in using the vernacular for Reformation discourse (see 57C/245/ 8?18). His decision to write letters to Muntzer, Carlstadt, and Luther was announced to Vadian in Letter 62.

Muntzer was preacher at the Church of St. John's in Allstedt from Easter 1523 until the middle of August 1524. Grebel did not know that he had already fled to Muhlhausen. It is not known whether he received the letter; but the fact that the original is extant in the Vadian archives in St. Gallen may indicate that it was returned to Vadian undelivered, perhaps by the messenger himself since Grebel expressly states in 63/294/15?16 that he had not kept a copy.

Another obvious possibility is that having informed Vadian about his intention to write to Muntzer he decided to send Vadian a copy of his own, so that he could better know what Grebel's new approach to the Reformation was. Perhaps this is "the question which I said I would put to you" (61/281/31), namely.. What do you think of this free church vision for the Reformation of the church?

Peace, grace, and mercy from God our Father and Jesus Christ our Lord be with us all, Amen.

Dear Brother Thomas.

For the sake of God, please do not let it surprise you that we address you without title and ask you as a brother henceforth to exchange ideas with us by correspondence, and that we, unsolicited and unknown to you, have dared to initiate such future dialogue. God's Son, Jesus

Christ, who offers himself as the only Master and Head to all who are to be saved and commands us to be brethren to all brethren and believers through the one common Word, has moved and impelled us to establish friendship and brotherhood and to bring the following theses to your attention. Also the fact that you have written two booklets on phony faith has led us to write to you. Therefore, if you will accept it graciously for the sake of Christ our Savior, it may, if God wills, serve and work for the good. Amen.

Just as our forefathers had fallen away from the true God and knowledge of Jesus Christ and true faith in him, from the one true common divine Word and from the godly practices of the Christian love and way, and lived without God's law and gospel in human, useless, unchristian practices and ceremonies and supposed they would find salvation in them but fell far short of it, as the evangelical preachers have shown and are still in part showing, so even today everyone wants to be saved by hypocritical faith, without fruits of faith, without the baptism of trial and testing, without hope and love, without true Christian practices, and wants to remain in all the old ways of personal vices and common antichristian ceremonial rites of baptism and the Lord's Supper, dishonoring the divine Word, but honoring the papal word and the antipapal preachers, which is not like or in accord with the divine Word. In respect of persons and all manner of seduction they are in more serious and harmful error than has ever been the case since the foundation of the world. We were also in the same aberration because we were only hearers and readers of the evangelical preachers who are responsible for all this error as our sins deserved. But after we took the Scripture in hand and consulted it on all kinds of issues, we gained some insight and became aware of the great and harmful shortcomings of the shepherds as well as our own in that we do not daily cry earnestly to God with constant sighs to be led out of the destruction of all godly living and out of human abominations and enter into true faith and practices of God. In all this, a false forbearance is what leads to the suppression of God's Word and its mixture with the human. Indeed, we say it brings harm to all and does disservice to all the things of God ? no need for further analysis and detail.

While we were noting and lamenting these things, your writing against false faith and baptism was brought out here to us and we are even better informed and strengthened and were wonderfully happy to have found someone who is of a common Christian mind with us and ventures to show the evangelical preachers their shortcomings ? how in all the major issues they practice false forbearance and set their own opinions and even those of antichrist above God and against God, not as befits messengers of God to act and to preach. Therefore we ask and admonish you as a brother in the name, power, Word, Spirit, and salvation which comes to all Christians through Jesus Christ our Master and Savior, to seek earnestly to preach only God's Word unflinchingly, to establish and defend only divine practices, to esteem as good and right only what can be found in definite clear Scripture, and to reject, hate, and curse all the schemes, words, practices, and opinions of all men, even your own.

No. 1: We understand and have read that you have translated the mass into German and instituted new German chants. This cannot be good when we find in the New Testament no teaching on chanting, no example. Paul reproves the Corinthian learned more than he praises them for murmuring in their assemblies as if they were singing, as the Jews and Italians pronounce their rituals in the form of songs.

No. 2: Second, since chanting in Latin developed without divine teaching or apostolic example or practice and has not brought good or edified, it will much less edify in German and will create an outward appearing faith.

No. 3:Third, since Paul quite distinctly forbids chanting in Ephesians 5:24 and Colossians 3:21 where he says and teaches that they should address and instruct one another with psalms and spiritual songs, and if anyone would sing, he should sing in his heart and give thanks.

No. 4: Whatever we are not taught in definite statements and examples, we are to consider forbidden, as if it were written, "Do not do this, do not chant."

No. 5: Christ commanded his messengers to preach only the Word according to the Old as well as the New Testament. Paul also says that we should let the Word of Christ, not the chant, dwell in us. Whoever chants poorly feels chagrin; whoever can do it well feels conceit.

No. 6: We should neither add to nor take away from the Word what seems good to us.

No. 7: If you want to abolish the mass, it cannot be done with German chanting, which is perhaps your idea or derived from Luther.

No. 8: It must be rooted out with the Word and command of Christ.

No. 9: For it was not planted by God.

No. 10: Christ instituted and planted the Supper of fellowship.

No. 11: Only the words found in Matthew 26, Mark 14, Luke 22, and 1 Corinthians 11 should be used, neither more nor less.

No. 12: The minister from the congregation shall recite them from one of the Gospels or from Paul.

No. 13: They are words of institution of the Supper of unity, not of consecration.

No. 14: There shall be an ordinary [loaf of] bread, without idolatry or addition.

No. 15. For this causes a hypocritical worship and veneration of the bread and detracts from the inward. There shall also be a common cup.

No. 16. This would do away with the veneration and would bring about a proper knowledge and understanding of the Supper, because the bread is nothing but bread. By faith it is the body of Christ and an incorporation with Christ and the brethren. For one must eat and drink in spirit and in love, as John indicates in chapter 6 and elsewhere, and Paul in [1] Corinthians 10 and 11, and is clearly observed in Acts 2.

No. 17. Although it is simply bread, if faith and brotherly love are already present, it shall be eaten with joy, for when it is thus practiced in the church it ought to show us that we are and want to be truly one loaf and body and true brethren to one another, etc.

No. 18. But if there be one who does not intend to live in a brotherly way, he eats to his condemnation, for he eats like any other meal without discernment and he brings shame upon love, the inward bond, as well as the bread, the outward bond.

No. 19. For it also does not remind him of the body and blood of Christ, the covenant of the cross, so that he is willing to live and to suffer for the sake of Christ and the brethren, the Head and the members.

No. 20. Nor should it be administered by you. Thereby the mass, the individual meal, would disappear, for the Supper is a sign of fellowship, not a mass and sacrament. Therefore no one shall eat it alone, whether on a deathbed or otherwise. Nor shall the bread be locked away, etc., for any individual person, for no one shall take the bread of the fellowship for himself alone, unless he be in unity with himself, which no one is, etc.

No. 21. According to all Scripture and history, it shall also not be practiced in temples, for it leads to false devotion.

No. 22. It shall be observed often and much.

No. 23. It should not be practiced without applying the rule of Christ in Matthew 18; otherwise it is not the Lord's Supper, for without the same [rule], everyone pursues externals. The internal, love, is neglected, if brethren and false brethren go there and eat.

No. 24. If you ever intend to administer, we would wish it would be without priestly robes and the vestments of the mass, without chanting, without addition.

No. 25. Concerning the time, we know that Christ gave it to the apostles in the evening meal and that the Corinthians had also thus observed it. We do not stipulate any specific time, etc.

With this, since you are much better informed about the Lord's Supper, and we have merely indicated our understanding, if we are incorrect, teach us better, and be willing yourself to drop chanting and the mass, and act only in accord with the Word, and proclaim and establish the practices of the apostles with the Word. If that cannot be done it would be better to leave everything in Latin, unchanged and uncompromised. If that which is right cannot be established, then still do not administer after your own or the antichristian priestly rites, and at least teach how it ought to be, as Christ does in John 6, teaching how one should eat and drink his flesh and blood. Pay no attention to the apostasy or to the unchristian forbearance, which the very learned foremost evangelical preachers established as an actual idol and planted throughout the world. It is far better that a few be correctly instructed through the Word of God and believe and live right in virtues and practices than that many believe deceitfully out of adulterated false doctrine. Although we admonish and implore you, we do hope that you will do it of your own accord and are therefore admonishing you in deepest affection because you listened so kindly to our brother and have confessed to him that you have been too lax, and because you and Carlstadt are regarded among us as the purest proclaimers and preachers of the purest Word of God. And if you both properly impugn those who mix human word and practice with the divine, you should also logically break away from the priesthood, benefices, and all kinds of new and ancient practices and from your own and ancient opinions and become completely pure. If your benefices, like ours, are based on interest and tithes, both of which are actual usury, and if you are not supported by one entire congregation, we hope you will withdraw from the benefices. You know well enough how a shepherd is to be supported.

We await much good from Jacob Strauss and several others who are little regarded by the negligent theologians and doctors at Wittenberg. We are likewise rejected by our learned shepherds. All men adhere to them because they preach a sinful sweet Christ and they lack the power to discern as you show in your booklets, which have almost immeasurably instructed and strengthened us, the poor in spirit. And so we think alike in everything except that we learned with sorrow that you have set up tablets, for which we can find neither text nor example in the New Testament. In the Old, it was of course to be written outwardly, but now in the New it is to be written on the fleshly tablets of the heart, as a comparison of the two Testaments shows, as we are taught by Paul in 2 Corinthians 3, in Jeremiah 31, in Hebrews 8, and in Ezekiel 36. Unless we are in error, which we do not think and believe, we hope you will again destroy the tablets. It developed out of your own opinions; it is a useless expenditure which would continue to increase and become entirely idolatrous and implant itself throughout the world as idols did. It would also create a suspicion that some outward object from which the unlearned could learn had to stand and be erected in place of the idols, whereas the outward Word alone should be used according to all example and commands of Scripture, as shown to us especially in 1 Corinthians 14 and Colossians 3. This kind of learning from a single word might in time become somewhat obstructing, and even if it would never cause any harm I would never invent or establish any such innovation and thereby follow or imitate the negligent, misleading, falsely forbearing scholars, nor out of my own opinion invent, teach, or institute a single item.

March forward with the Word and create a Christian church with the help of Christ and his rule such as we find instituted in Matthew 18 and practiced in the epistles. Press on in earnest with common prayer and fasting, in accord with faith and love without being commanded and compelled. Then God will help you and your lambs to all purity, and the chanting and the tablets will fall away. There is more than enough wisdom and counsel in the Scripture on how to teach, govern, direct, and make devout all classes and all men. Anyone who will not reform or believe and strives against the Word and acts of God and persists therein, after Christ and his Word and rule have been preached to him, and he has been admonished with the three witnesses before the church, such a man we say on the basis of God's Word shall not be put to death but regarded as a heathen and publican and left alone.

Moreover, the gospel and its adherents are not to be protected by the sword, nor [should] they [protect] themselves, which as we have heard through our brother is what you believe and maintain. True believing Christians are sheep among wolves, sheep for the slaughter. They must be baptized in anguish and tribulation, persecution, suffering, and death, tried in fire, and must reach the fatherland of eternal rest not by slaying the physical but the spiritual. They use neither worldly sword nor war, since killing has ceased with them entirely, unless indeed we are still under the old law, and even there (as far as we can know) war was only a plague after they had once conquered the Promised Land. No more of this.

On the subject of baptism, your writing pleases us well, and we ask for further instruction from you. We are taught that without Christ's rule of binding and loosing, even an adult should not be baptized. The Scriptures describe baptism for us, that it signifies the washing away of sins by faith and the blood of Christ (that the nature of the baptized and believing one is changing before and after), that it signifies one has died and shall (die) to sin and walks in newness of life and Spirit and one will surely be saved if one through the inward baptism lives the faith according to this meaning, so that the water does not strengthen and increase faith and give a very great comfort and last resort on the deathbed, as the scholars at Wittenberg say. Also that it does not save, as Augustine, Tertullian, Theophylact, and Cyprian taught, thus dishonoring faith and the suffering of Christ for mature adults and dishonoring the suffering of Christ for unbaptized infants. On the basis of the following Scriptures ? Genesis 8, Deuteronomy 1, 30?31; 1 Corinthians 14; Wisdom 12; also 1 Peter 2; Romans 1, 2, 7, 10; Matthew 18?19; Mark 9? 10; Luke 18, etc we hold that all children who have not attained the knowledge to discern between good and evil and have not eaten of the tree of knowledge are surely saved through the suffering of Christ, the new Adam, who has restored the life that has been distorted, because they would have been subject to death and damnation only if Christ had not suffered, not afterward risen to the infirmity of our broken nature, unless it can be proved to us that Christ did not die for children. But in answer to the charge that faith is required of all who are to be saved, we exclude children and on the basis of the above texts accept that they will be saved without faith and that they do not believe; and we conclude from the description of baptism and from Acts (according to which no child was baptized) and also from the above texts, which are the only ones which deal with the subject of children, and all other Scriptures which do not concern children, that infant baptism is a senseless, blasphemous abomination contrary to all Scripture and even contrary to the papacy, for we learn through Cyprian and Augustine that for many years after the time of the apostles, for six hundred years, believers and unbelievers were baptized together, etc. Since you know this ten times better than we, and have published your protestation against infant baptism, we hope that you will not act contrary to God's eternal Word, wisdom, and command, according to which only believers should be baptized and will not baptize children. If you or Carlstadt do not adequately write against infant baptism and all that pertains to it, how and why one is to baptize, etc., I (Conrad Grebel) will try my hand at it and will finish writing out what I have begun against all (except for you) who have thus far written misleadingly and knowingly about baptism, and who have translated into German the senseless, blasphemous form of infant baptism, like Luther, Leo, Osiander, and the Strasbourgers and some who have acted even more shamefully. Unless God averts it, I together with all of us are and shall be more certain of persecution by the scholars, etc., than by other people. We beg you not to use or adopt the old rites of the antichrist, such as sacrament, mass, signs, etc. Hold to the Word alone and administer' as all emissaries should, especially you and Carlstadt and you will be doing more than all the preachers of all nations.

Consider us your brethren and read this epistle as our expression of great joy and hope toward you through God. Admonish, comfort, and strengthen us as you are well able. Pray to the Lord God for us that he will come to the aid of our faith, for we are very ready to believe. And if God grants it to us to pray, we too will intercede for you and for all that we may all walk according to our calling and commitment. May God grant us this through Jesus Christ our Savior. Amen.

Greet all the brethren for us, the shepherds and the sheep, who accept the Word of faith and salvation with deep desire and hunger, etc. One thing more. We desire a reply from you; and if you publish anything, send it to us by this messenger or another. We would also like to know whether you and Carlstadt are of one mind. We hope and believe you are. We commend to you this messenger, who has also carried letters from us to our dear brother Carlstadt. And if you should go to Carlstadt so that you would reply jointly, that would be a great joy to us. The messenger is to return to us. Whatever we have not adequately paid him will be reimbursed when he returns.

Whatever we have not correctly understood, inform and instruct us. At Zurich, on the fifth day of September in the year 1524.

Conrad Grebel, Andreas Castelberg(er), Felix Mantz, Hans Ockenfuss, Bartlime Pur, Heinrich Aberli, and your other brethren (God willing) in Christ. Until another communication, we who have written this to you wish for you and all of us and all your flock the true Word of God, true faith, love, and hope, with all peace and grace from God through Christ Jesus, Amen.

I, C. Grebel, was going to write to Luther in the name of all of us and exhort him to desist from the forbearance which he and his followers practice without scriptural authority and planted abroad in the world, but my affliction and time did not permit. You do it according to your duty, etc.

To the true and faithful proclaimer of the gospel, Thomas Muntzer of Allstedt in the Hartz, our faithful and dear brother in Christ, etc.

Original: Stadtbibliothek (Vadiana) St. Gallen, VB.XL.97

Transcriptions: M?S, No. 14, pp. 13?19; J. C. Wenger, Conrad Grebel's Programmatic Letters of 1524

Letter 64
Grebel to Miintzer
Zurich, sent with letter of September 5, 1524

Dearly beloved brother Thomas.

After I had written in haste in the name of all of us and assumed that the messenger would not wait until we also wrote to Luther, he had to delay and wait because of rain. And so I also wrote to Luther in my name and that of the other brothers, mine and yours, and admonished him to desist from his false forbearance toward the weak, which they are themselves. Andreas Castelberg(er) wrote to Carlstadt. Meanwhile, there arrived here for Hans Hujuff of Halle, our fellow citizen and brother who visited you recently, a letter and a shameful booklet by Luther, which no one who claims to be primaries [firstfruits] like the apostles ought to write. Paul teaches otherwise: Porro servum domini, etc. ["Next, the Lord's servant, etc."] I see that he wants to deliver you to the ax and hand you over to the prince, to whom he has bound his gospel, just as Aaron had to have Moses as a god. As for your booklets and protestations, 1 find you guiltless. I do not gather from them that you utterly repudiate baptism, but that you condemn infant baptism and the misunderstanding of baptism. What water means in John 3 we want to examine further in your booklet and in the Scripture.

Hujuff's brother writes that you have preached against the princes, that they should be combatted with the fist. If that is true, or if you intend to defend war, the tablets, chanting, or other things for which you do not find a clear word (as you do not find for any of these aforementioned points), I admonish you by the salvation common to all of us that if you will desist from them and all opinions of your own now and henceforth, you will become completely pure, for you satisfy us on all other points better than anyone else in this German and other lands. If you fall into the hands of Luther and the duke, drop the aforementioned articles and stand by the other like a hero and a soldier of God. Be strong. You have the Bible (which Luther rendered "bible bubel ballet") as defense against Luther's idolatrous forbearance, which he and the learned shepherds around here have spread throughout the world against the deceitful lax faith, against their preaching in which they do not teach Christ as they ought. They have just opened up the gospel to all the world so that many can read it for themselves (or ought to read it), but not many do, for everyone depends on them. Around here there are not even twenty who believe the Word of God. They only believe humans ? Zwingli, Leo, and others who are regarded elsewhere as learned. And if you should have to suffer for it, you know that it cannot be otherwise. Christ must suffer still more in his members, but he will strengthen them and keep them steadfast to the end. God grant you and us grace, for our shepherds are also fierce and enraged against us, reviling us from the public pulpit as rascals and Satanas in angelos lucis conversos [Satans turned into angels of light]. In time we too will see persecution come upon us through them. Therefore pray to God for us. Once more we admonish you, because we love and respect you so sincerely for the clarity of your words, and we confidently venture to write to you: Do not act, teach, or establish anything according to human opinion, your own or borrowed, repeal what has been established, and teach only the clear Word and rites of God, including the rule of Christ, the unadulterated baptism and unadulterated Supper, which we touched upon in our first letter and upon which you are better informed than a hundred of us. If you and Carlstadt, Jacob Strauss, and Michael Stiefel should not deliberately strive to be wholly pure (as I and my brethren hope you will do) it will be a sorry gospel indeed that has come into the world. But you are far purer than our clergy here or those at Wittenberg who daily fall from one perversion of Scripture into another and from one blindness into another that is worse. I believe and am sure that they want to become true papists and popes. No more now. God our captain with his Son Jesus Christ our Savior and his Spirit and Word be with you and us all.

Conrad Grebel, Andreas Castelberg(er), Felix Mantz, Heinrich Aberli, John Pannicellus, Hans Ockenfuss, Hans Hujuff your countryman of Halle, brethren to you, and seven new young Muntzers to Luther.

In case you are allowed to continue to preach and nothing happens to you, we will send you a copy of our letter to Luther and his answer if he replies to us. We have admonished him and our clergy here too. In this way, unless God prevents, we want to show them their shortcomings and not fear what may happen to us for it. We have kept no copy except for the letter we wrote to Martin, your adversary. Please accept favorably our unlearned, unpolished letter, and be sure that we have written out of genuine love, for we are one in Word and trial and adversaries, although you are more learned and stronger in spirit. Because of this common identity, we have spoken or rather written at length. Give our greetings to the Christians there, God willing, and write us a long letter in reply from all of you together. You will give us great joy and stir in us an even greater love for you.

This letter also is for Thomas Muntzer of Allstedt in the Hartz.

Original: Stadtbibliothek (Vadiana) St. Gallen, V13.11.204
Transcription: M-S, No. 14, pp. 19-21

Michael Sattler
The Schleitheim Confession

Source: Rod and Staff Publishers, Inc., Crockett, KY via http://www.anabaptists.org

Adopted by a Swiss Brethren Conference, February 24, 1527
Brotherly Union of a Number of Children of God concerning Seven Articles

The articles which we discussed and on which we were of one mind are these:

I.   Baptism;
II. The Ban (Excommunication);
III. Breaking of Bread;
IV. Separation from the Abomination;
V.   Pastors in the Church;
VI. The Sword;
VII. The Oath.

I. Observe concerning baptism: Baptism shall be given to all those who have learned repentance and amendment of life, and who believe truly that their sins are taken away by Christ, and to all those who walk in the resurrection of Jesus Christ, and wish to be buried with Him in death, so that they may be resurrected with Him and to all those who with this significance request it (baptism) of us and demand it for themselves. This excludes all infant baptism, the highest and chief abomination of the Pope. In this you have the foundation and testimony of the apostles. Matt. 28, Mark 16, Acts 2, 8, 16, 19. This we wish to hold simply, yet firmly and with assurance.

II. We are agreed as follows on the ban: The ban shall be employed with all those who have given themselves to the Lord, to walk in His commandments, and with all those who are baptized into the one body of Christ and who are called brethren or sisters, and yet who slip sometimes and fall into error and sin, being inadvertently overtaken. The same shall be admonished twice in secret and the third time openly disciplined or banned according to the command of Christ. Matt. 18. But this shall be done according to the regulation of the Spirit (Matt. 5) before the breaking of bread, so that we may break and eat one bread, with one mind and in one love, and may drink of one cup.

III. In the breaking of bread we are of one mind and are agreed (as follows): All those who wish to break one bread in remembrance of the broken body of Christ, and all who wish to drink of one drink as a remembrance of the shed blood of Christ, shall be united beforehand by baptism in one body of Christ which is the church of God and whose Head is Christ. For as Paul points out, we cannot at the same time drink the cup of the Lord and the cup of the devil. That is, all those who have fellowship with the dead works of darkness have no part in the light. Therefore all who follow the devil and the world have no part with those who are called unto God out of the world. All who lie in evil have no part in the good.

Therefore it is and must be (thus): Whoever has not been called by one God to one faith, to one baptism, to one Spirit, to one body, with all the children of God's church, cannot be made (into) one bread with them, as indeed must be done if one is truly to break bread according to the command of Christ.

IV. We are agreed (as follows) on separation: A separation shall be made from the evil and from the wickedness which the devil planted in the world; in this manner, simply that we shall not have fellowship with them (the wicked) and not run with them in the multitude of their abominations. This is the way it is: Since all who do not walk in the obedience of faith, and have not united themselves with God so that they wish to do His will, are a great abomination before God, it is not possible for anything to grow or issue from them except abominable things. For truly all creatures are in but two classes, good and bad, believing and unbelieving, darkness and light, the world and those who (have come) out of the world, God's temple and idols, Christ and Belial; and none can have part with the other.

To us then the command of the Lord is clear when He calls upon us to be separate from the evil and thus He will be our God and we shall be His sons and daughters.

He further admonishes us to withdraw from Babylon and earthly Egypt that we may not be partakers of the pain and suffering which the Lord will bring upon them.

From this we should learn that everything which is not united with our God and Christ cannot be other than an abomination which we should shun and flee from. By this is meant all Catholic and Protestant works and church services, meetings and church attendance, drinking houses, civic affairs, the oaths sworn in unbelief and other things of that kind, which are highly regarded by the world and yet are carried on in flat contradiction to the command of God, in accordance with all the unrighteousness which is in the world. From all these things we shall be separated and have no part with them for they are nothing but an abomination, and they are the cause of our being hated before our Christ Jesus, Who has set us free from the slavery of the flesh and fitted us for the service of God through the Spirit Whom He has given us.

Therefore there will also unquestionably fall from us the unchristian, devilish weapons of force - such as sword, armor and the like, and all their use (either) for friends or against one's enemies - by virtue of the Word of Christ. Resist not (him that is) evil.

V. We are agreed as follows on pastors in the church of God: The pastor in the church of God shall, as Paul has prescribed, be one who out-and-out has a good report of those who are outside the faith. This office shall be to read, to admonish and teach, to warn, to discipline, to ban in the church, to lead out in prayer for the advancement of all the brethren and sisters, to lift up the bread when it is to be broken, and in all things to see to the care of the body of Christ, in order that it may be built up and developed, and the mouth of the slanderer be stopped.

This one moreover shall be supported of the church which has chosen him, wherein he may be in need, so that he who serves the Gospel may live of the Gospel as the Lord has ordained. But if a pastor should do something requiring discipline, he shall not be dealt with except (on the testimony of) two or three witnesses. And when they sin they shall be disciplined before all in order that the others may fear.

But should it happen that through the cross this pastor should be banished or led to the Lord (through martyrdom) another shall be ordained in his place in the same hour so that God's little flock and people may not be destroyed.

VI. We are agreed as follows concerning the sword: The sword is ordained of God outside the perfection of Christ. It punishes and puts to death the wicked, and guards and protects the good. In the Law the sword was ordained for the punishment of the wicked and for their death, and the same (sword) is (now) ordained to be used by the worldly magistrates.

In the perfection of Christ, however, only the ban is used for a warning and for the excommunication of the one who has sinned, without putting the flesh to death - simply the warning and the command to sin no more.

Now it will be asked by many who do not recognize (this as) the will of Christ for us, whether a Christian may or should employ the sword against the wicked for the defense and protection of the good, or for the sake of love.

Our reply is unanimously as follows: Christ teaches and commands us to learn of Him, for He is meek and lowly in heart and so shall we find rest to our souls. Also Christ says to the heathenish woman who was taken in adultery, not that one should stone her according to the Law of His Father (and yet He says, As the Father has commanded me, thus I do), but in mercy and forgiveness and warning, to sin no more. Such (an attitude) we also ought to take completely according to the rule of the ban.

Secondly, it will be asked concerning the sword, whether a Christian shall pass sentence in worldly disputes and strife such as unbelievers have with one another. This is our united answer. Christ did not wish to decide or pass judgment between brother and brother in the case of the inheritance, but refused to do so. Therefore we should do likewise.

Thirdly, it will be asked concerning the sword, Shall one be a magistrate if one should be chosen as such? The answer is as follows: They wished to make Christ king, but He fled and did not view it as the arrangement of His Father. Thus shall we do as He did, and follow Him, and so shall we not walk in darkness. For He Himself says, He who wishes to come after Me, let him deny himself and take up his cross and follow Me. Also, He Himself forbids the (employment of) the force of the sword saying, The worldly princes lord it over them, etc., but not so shall it be with you. Further, Paul says, Whom God did foreknow He also did predestinate to be conformed to the image of His Son, etc. Also Peter says, Christ has suffered (not ruled) and left us an example, that ye should follow His steps.

Finally it will be observed that it is not appropriate for a Christian to serve as a magistrate because of these points: The government magistracy is according to the flesh, but the Christian's is according to the Spirit; their houses and dwelling remain in this world, but the Christian's are in heaven; their citizenship is in this world, but the Christian's citizenship is in heaven; the weapons of their conflict and war are carnal and against the flesh only, but the Christian's weapons are spiritual, against the fortification of the devil. The worldlings are armed with steel and iron, but the Christians are armed with the armor of God, with truth, righteousness, peace, faith, salvation and the Word of God. In brief, as in the mind of God toward us, so shall the mind of the members of the body of Christ be through Him in all things, that there may be no schism in the body through which it would be destroyed. For every kingdom divided against itself will be destroyed. Now since Christ is as it is written of Him, His members must also be the same, that His body may remain complete and united to its own advancement and upbuilding.

VII. We are agreed as follows concerning the oath: The oath is a confirmation among those who are quarreling or making promises. In the Law it is commanded to be performed in God's Name, but only in truth, not falsely. Christ, who teaches the perfection of the Law, prohibits all swearing to His (followers), whether true or false - neither by heaven, nor by the earth, nor by Jerusalem, nor by our head - and that for the reason He shortly thereafter gives, For you are not able to make one hair white or black. So you see it is for this reason that all swearing is forbidden: we cannot fulfill that which we promise when we swear, for we cannot change (even) the very least thing on us.

Now there are some who do not give credence to the simple command of God, but object with this question: Well now, did not God swear to Abraham by Himself (since He was God) when He promised him that He would be with him and that He would be his God if he would keep His commandments, - why then should I not also swear when I promise to someone? Answer: Hear what the Scripture says: God, since He wished more abundantly to show unto the heirs the immutability of His counsel, inserted an oath, that by two immutable things (in which it is impossible for God to lie) we might have a strong consolation. Observe the meaning of this Scripture: What God forbids you to do, He has power to do, for everything is possible for Him. God swore an oath to Abraham, says the Scripture, so that He might show that His counsel is immutable. That is, no one can withstand nor thwart His will; therefore He can keep His oath. But we can do nothing, as is said above by Christ, to keep or perform (our oaths): therefore we shall not swear at all (nichts schweren).

Then others further say as follows: It is not forbidden of God to swear in the New Testament, when it is actually commanded in the Old, but it is forbidden only to swear by heaven, earth, Jerusalem and our head. Answer: Hear the Scripture, He who swears by heaven swears by God's throne and by Him who sitteth thereon. Observe: it is forbidden to swear by heaven, which is only the throne of God: how much more is it forbidden (to swear) by God Himself! Ye fools and blind, which is greater, the throne or Him that sitteth thereon?

Further some say, Because evil is now (in the world, and) because man needs God for (the establishment of) the truth, so did the apostles Peter and Paul also swear. Answer: Peter and Paul only testify of that which God promised to Abraham with the oath. They themselves promise nothing, as the example indicates clearly. Testifying and swearing are two different things. For when a person swears he is in the first place promising future things, as Christ was promised to Abraham. Whom we a long time afterwards received. But when a person bears testimony he is testifying about the present, whether it is good or evil, as Simeon spoke to Mary about Christ and testified, Behold this (child) is set for the fall and rising of many in Israel, and for a sign which shall be spoken against.

Christ also taught us along the same line when He said, Let your communication be Yea, yea; Nay, nay; for whatsoever is more than these cometh of evil. He says, Your speech or word shall be yea and nay. (However) when one does not wish to understand, he remains closed to the meaning. Christ is simply Yea and Nay, and all those who seek Him simply will understand His Word. Amen.

The Seven Articles of Schleitheim
Canton Schaffhausen, Switzerland,
February 24, 1527

Michael Sattler
The Trial of Michael Sattler from The Martyr's Mirror

After a long trial on the day of his departure from this world, the articles being many, Michael Sattler requested that they should be read to him again and that he should have another hearing. This the bailiff, as the governor of his lord, opposed and would not consent to it. Michael Sattler then requested permission to speak. After a consultation, the judges returned as their answer, that if his opponents would allow it, they (the judges) would consent. Thereupon the town clerk of Ensisheim, as the attorney of said Governor spoke thus: "Prudent, honorable and wise Sirs, He has boasted of the Holy Ghost. Now, if his boast is true, it seems to me, it is unnecessary to grant him this; for if he has the Holy Ghost, as he boasts, the same will tell him what has been done here." To this Michael Sattler replied: "Ye servants of God, I hope my request will not be denied; for said articles are as yet unknown to me." The town clerk responded: "Prudent, honorable and wise Sirs, Though we are not bound to do this, yet in order to give satisfaction, we will grant him his request that it may not be thought that injustice is done him in his heresy, or that we desire to wrong him; hence let the articles be read to him."

ARTICLES OR CHARGES AGAINST MICHAEL SATTLER

First, that he and his adherents have acted contrary to the mandate of the Emperor.

Secondly, he has taught, held and believed that the body and blood of Christ are not present in the sacrament.

Thirdly, he has taught and believed that infant baptism does not conduce to salvation.

Fourthly, they have rejected the sacrament of extreme unction.

Fifthly, they have despised and condemned the mother of God and the saints.

Sixthly, he has declared that men are not to swear before the authorities.

Seventhly, he has commenced a new and unheard of custom in regard to the Lord's Supper, placing the bread and wine on a plate, and eating and drinking the same.

Eighthly, he has left the order, and married a wife.

Ninthly, he has said that if the Turks should invade the country, no resistance ought to be offered them; and if it were right to wage war, he would rather take the field against the Christians than against the Turks; and it is certainly a great matter, to set the greatest enemies of our holy faith against us.

Thereupon Michael Sattler requested permission to confer with his brethren and sisters, which was granted him. Having conferred with them for a little while, he began and undauntingly answered thus: "In regard to the articles relating to me and my brethren and sisters, hear this brief answer:

"First, That we have acted contrary to the imperial mandate, we do not admit; for the same says that the Lutheran doctrine and delusion is not to be adhered to, but only the Gospel and Word of God. This we have kept; for I am not aware that we have acted contrary to the Gospel and the Word of God; I appeal to the words of Christ.

"Secondly, That the real body of Christ the Lord is not present in the sacrament, we admit; for the Scripture says: Christ ascended into heaven and, sitteth on the right hand of His heavenly Father whence He shall come to judge the quick and the dead; from which it follows, that if He is in heaven, and not in the breads He may not be eaten bodily. Mark 16:19; Acts 1:9; Col. 3:1; Acts 10:42; 11 Tim. 4:1.

"Thirdly, As to baptism we say: Infant baptism is of no avail to salvation; for it is written, that we live by faith alone. Again: He that believeth and is baptized shall be saved. Peter likewise says

> The like figure whereunto even baptism doth also now save us (not the putting away of the filth of the flesh, but the answer of a good conscience toward God), by the resurrection of Jesus Christ. Romans 1:1 7; Mark 16:16; 1 Pet. 3:21.

"Fourthly, We have not rejected the oil; for it is a creature of God, and what God has made is good and not to be refused; but that the pope, the bishops, monks and priests can make it better, we do not believe; for the pope never made anything good. That of which the epistle of James speaks is not the pope's oil. Gen. 1:11; 1 Tim. 4:4; James 5:14.

"Fifthly, We have not condemned the mother of God and the saints; for the mother of Christ is to be blessed among all women; for to her was accorded the favor of giving birth to the Saviour of the whole world. But that she is a mediatress and advocatess, of this the Scriptures know nothing; for she must with us await the judgment. Paul said to Timothy: Christ is our Mediator and Advocate with God. As regards the saints; we say that we who live and believe are the saints; which I prove by the epistles of Paul to the Romans, Corinthians, Ephesians; and in other places where he always writes: To the beloved saints. Hence we that believe are the saints; but those who have died in faith we regard as the blessed. Luke 1:28; Matthew ' 1:21; I Tim. 2:5; I Cor. 1:2; Eph. 1:1; Rev. 14:13.

"Sixthly, We hold, that we are not to swear before the authorities: For the Lord says: Swear not; but let your communication be, Yea, yea; Nay, nay. Matt. 5:34; James 5:12.

"Seventhly, When God called me to testify of His Word, and I had read Paul, and also considered the unchristian and perilous state in which I was; beholding the pomp, pride, usury, and great whoredom of the monks and priests, I went and took unto me a wife, according to the command of God; for Paul well prophesies concerning this to Timothy: In the latter time it shall come to pass that men shall forbid to marry, and command to abstain from meats which God hath created to be received with thanksgiving. I Cor. 7:2; 1 Tim. 4:3.

"Eighthly, If the Turks should come, we ought not to resist them; for it is written: Thou shalt not kill. We must not defend ourselves against the Turks and others of our persecutors, but are to beseech God with earnest prayer to repel and resist them. But that I said, that if warring were right, I would rather take the field against the so-called Christians, who persecute, apprehend and kill pious Christians, than against the Turks,was for this reason: The Turk is a true Turk, knows nothing of the Christian faith; and is a Turk after the flesh; but you, who would be Christians, and who make your boast of Christ, persecute the pious witnesses of Christ, and are Turks after the spirit. Ex. 20:13; Matt. 7:7; Tit. 1:16.

"In conclusion: Ye ministers of God, I admonish you to consider the end for which God has appointed you, to punish the evil, and to defend and protect the pious. Whereas, then, we have not acted contrary to God and the Gospel, you will find that neither I nor my brethren and sisters have offended in word or deed against any authority. Therefore, ye ministers of God, if ye have not heard or read the Word of God, send for the most learned, and for the sacred books of the Bible, of whatsoever language they may be, and let them confer with us in the Word of God; and if they prove to us with the Holy Scriptures, that we err and are in the wrong, we will gladly desist and recant and also willingly suffer the sentence and punishment for that of which we have been accused, but if no error is proven to us, I hope to God, that you will be converted, and receive instruction." Wisd. 6:4; Acts 25:8; Rom. 13:4; Acts 25:11.

Upon this speech the judges laughed and put their heads together, and the town clerk of Ensisheim said

"O you infamous, desperate villain and monk, shall we dispute with you? The hangman shall dispute with you, I assure you."

Michael said: "God's will be done."

The town clerk said: "It were well if you had never been born."

Michael replied: "God knows what is good."

Town Clerk: "You arch-heretic, you have seduced the pious; if they would only now forsake their error, and accept grace."

Michael: "Grace is with God alone."

One of the prisoners also said: "We must not depart from the truth."

Town Clerk: "You desperate villain and archheretic, I tell you if there were no hangman here, I would hang you myself, and think that I had done God service."

Michael:. "God will judge aright."

Thereupon the town clerk said a few words to him in Latin, what we do not know.

Michael Sattler answered him "Judica."

The town clerk then admonished the judges and said: -"He will not cease from this talk today; therefore my Lord judge, proceed with the sentence; I will commit -it to the law."

The judge asked Michael Sattler whether he also committed it to the law.

He replied: "Ye ministers of God, I am not sent to judge the Word of God; we are sent to bear witness of it, and, hence, cannot. consent to any law, since we. have no command from God concerning it; but if we cannot be. discharged from the law, we are ready to suffer for the Word of God whatever sufferings are, or may be imposed upon us all for the sake of the faith in Christ Jesus our Saviour, as long as we have breath within us; unless we be dissuaded from it by the Scriptures."

The town clerk .said: "The hangman shall convince you; he shall dispute with you, arch-heretic."

Michael: . "I appeal to the Scriptures."

Then the judges arose, and went into another room, where they remained for an hour and a.half, and determined on the sentence. Matt. 6:10; John 16:2; I Cor. 4:5; John 1:8; Job 27:3.; Acts 25:11.

In the meantime, some in the room treated Michael Sattler most unmercifully, heaping reproach upon him. One of them said: "What have you in expectation -for yourself and the others, that you have so seduced them?" With this, he also drew forth a sword which lay upon the table, saying: "See, with this shall they dispute with thee." But Michael did not answer. upon a single word concerning his person, but willingly endured it all. One of the prisoners said: "We must not cast pearls before swine." Matt. 27:14; 7:6.

Being-also asked, why he had not remained a lord in the convent, Michael answered: "According to the flesh I was a lord; but it is better so." He did not say more than what is recorded here, and this he spoke fearlessly.

The judges having returned to the room, the sentence'was read. It was as follows: "In the case of the Governor of his Imperial Majesty versus Michael Sattler, judgment is passed, that Michael Sattler shall be delivered to 'the executioner, who shall lead him to the place of execution, and cut out his tongue; then throw him upon a wagon, and there tear his body twice with red hot tongs; and after he has been brought without the gate, he shall be pinched five times in the same manner."

After this had been done in the manner prescribed, he was burned to ashes as a heretic. His fellow brethren were executed with the sword, and the sisters drowned. His wife, also; after being subjected to many entreaties, admonitions and threats, under which she remained very steadfast, was drowned a few days afterwards. Done the 21st day of May, A. D. 1527:

A Letter Written by Michael Sattler, in Prison, to the Church of God at Horb

My beloved companions in the Lord! grace and mercy from God our heavenly Father, through Jesus Christ our Lord, and the power of ,their Spirit, be with you beloved of God, brethren and sisters.

I cannot forget you; though I am not present with the body (Col. 2:5), yet I continually care for and watch over you, as my fellow members, lest the body be taken away, and the whole body the church, with all its members be overwhelmed with sorrow, especially at this time, when the ferocity of the ravening wolf has risen to such a pitch; and increases in power; so that he has aroused also me to fight against him; - but eternal praise be to God, its head is completely broken, and I hope that his whole body shall soon be no more, as is written.

Dear brethren and sisters, you well know with what ardent love I admonished you the last time I was with you, that you should be upright and godly in all patience and in the love of God, by which you may be known among this adulterous and ungodly generation, as shining lights (Matthew 5:14) whom God the heavenly Father has illuminated with His knowledge and the light of the Spirit. With like fervency I now beseech and admonish you; that you walk surely and prudently towards those that are without as unbelievers, that our office, which God has imposed upon us, may in no wise be profaned and justly reproached.

Remember the Lord, who has given you the talent, for He shall require it again with usury: That the one talent may not be taken from you, put it to usury, according to the command of the Lord, who has given you the talent. Matt., 15:19.

I say to you through the grace of God, that ye be valiant, and walk as become the saints of God. Consider what the Lord metes out to idle servants; namely, to utterly lukewarm and slothful hearts; unfit and cold for all love to God and the brethren. You have experienced what I now write.

Be admonished by this, lest God let a like punishment come upon you. Beware, beware of such as act contrary to the command of God lest ye learn their abominations; but reprove it with strict attention, and excommunication, according to the command of Christ, yet with all love and compassion for their cold hearts. Matt. 18:17. If you do this, you shall readily see how the flock of God dwells among the wolves (Acts 20:29), and shall witness a brief and speedy separation of those who will not walk in the right paths and living, ways of Christ, namely, through crosses, misery, imprisonment, self-denial, and ultimately through death. Then you can present yourselves to God' your heavenly Father, a pure, godly, true church of Christ, which is cleansed through His blood (Eph. 5:26), that it may be holy and unblamable in the sight of God and men, separated from all idolatry and abomination, and redeemed, that the Lord of all dominion may dwell in it, and that it may be a tabernacle unto Him. Beloved brethren, understand whether what I write unto you be truth, and use diligence to walk according to it. Let no one divert you from your aim, as has been the case with some even until now; but go straight on in all patience, without deviating, that you do not take up the cross which God has laid upon you, only to lay it down contrary to the honor and praise of God, and to the transgression and violation of His eternal, true, just, and life-giving commandments.

Do not become weary, if you are chastened of the Lord (Heb. 12:5); for whom God loves He chastens, even as a father that is well pleased with his son. To what will you have recourse, if you would flee from God? What can help you if you forsake God? Is it not God who fills heaven and earth? Does He not know all the secrets of thy vain heart, and the lasciviousness of thy reins? All things are manifest to Him, and there is nothing concealed from Him. Vain man, whither will you go, that God shall not see you? Why do you flee the rod of your Father? (Heb. 12:8). If you will not be chastened according to the will of the Father, you cannot inherit His riches. Why do you love a short and transient rest more than the godly and moderate correction and chastisement of the Lord to your salvation? How long will you eat flesh of the fat of Egypt? How long will you be carnally-minded? (Rom. 8:8). The flesh perishes, and all its glory; the word of the Lord alone abides forever.

Beloved brethren, mark what I write to you; for it is necessary, since you see that there are but few who will endure the chastening of the Lord; for by far the greater number when they suffer a little in the flesh, become faint and weary, and do no longer look unto Jesus, the Captain and Finisher of our faith. They also forget all His commandments, and esteem the jewel which the calling of God everywhere presents and points out to those that overcome of small value; but they regard this temporal rest, which is before their eyes as far better and more profitable, than the eternal for which we must hope. Moreover, there are some who, when this is presented to them, accuse God, though very unjustly, of not being willing to keep them under His protection. You know whom I mean, take heed that you have no fellowship with them.

Furthermore, dear fellow members in Christ, be admonished that you forget not charity, without which it is not possible for you to be a Christian flock. You know what charity is, from the testimony of Paul our fellow brother, who says:

> "Charity suffereth long, and is kind; charity envieth not; charity vaunteth not itself, is not puffed up, doth not behave itself unseemly, seeketh not her own, is not easily provoked, thinketh no evil; rejoiceth not in iniquity, but rejoiceth in the truth; beareth all things, believeth all things, hopeth all things, endureth all things." I Cor. 13:4-7:

Understand this passage, and you will find the love of God and the love of your neighbor; and if you love God, you will rejoice in the truth, and believe, hope and endure all that comes from God. In this way the aforesaid failing will be removed and avoided. But if you love your neighbor, you will not punish or excommunicate with fire, you will not seek your own, think no evil, not vaunt yourselves, and, finally, not be puffed up; but will be kind, just, liberal in all giving, humble and compassionate with the weak and imperfect. Rom. 13:8.

This love has been adulterated by some brethren (I know who they are); they have not been willing to edify one another by love, but are become puffed up and unprofitable with the vain knowledge and understanding of things which God would have remain hidden to all but Himself alone. I Cor. 8:1. I do not censure nor reject the grace and revelation of God, but the puffed up make use of this revelation. What would it profit, says Paul, if I should speak with the tongues of men and of angels, and understand all mysteries and knowledge, and have all faith, tell me, what profit is all this, if love be not exercised? You have experienced what such presumptuous speaking and ignorance has produced; you still daily see their false fruits, though they have given themselves to God.

And let no man remove you from the foundation which is laid through the letter of the holy Scriptures, and is sealed with the blood of Christ and of many witnesses of Jesus. Hear not what they say of their father, for he is a liar; and do not believe their spirit, for he is entirely swallowed up in the flesh. Judge what I write to you; take these matters to heart, that this abomination may be separated far from you, and that you be found humble, fruitful and obedient children of God. Beloved brethren, marvel not that I treat this matter with such earnestness; for I do so not without reason. The brethren have doubtless informed you that some of us are in prison; and afterwards when the brethren at Horb had also been apprehended, they brought us to Binzdorf. At this time we met with various designs of our adversaries. Once they threatened us with bonds; then with fire, and afterwards with the sword. In this peril I completely surrendered myself into the will of the Lord, and together with all my fellow brethren and my wife, prepared myself even for death for His testimony and then I thought of the great number of false brethren, and of you, who are but few, namely, a little flock; and also, that there are but few faithful laborers in the Lord's vineyard (Matt. 9:37); hence I deemed it necessary to stir you up by this admonition, to follow after us in the divine warfare, in order that you may comfort yourselves with it, that you may not become weary of the chastening of the Lord.

In short, beloved brethren and sisters this letter shall be a farewell to all of you who truly love and follow God (others I do not know); and also a testimony of my love which God has given into my heart towards you, for the sake of your salvation. I did indeed desire, and it would have been profitable, I trust, if I had labored a little while longer in the work of the Lord; but it is better for me, to be released, and to await with Christ the hope of the blessed. The Lord is able to raise up another laborer to finish this work.

Pray that reapers may be constrained into the harvest; for the time of threshing is nigh at hand. Luke 10:2. The abomination of desolation is manifest among you; the chosen servants and handmaidens of God are marked with the name of their Father on their foreheads (Rev. 13:16); the world rises up against those who are delivered from its error; the Gospel is proclaimed before all the world, as a testimony against it; therefore it will be necessary that the day of the Lord do not tarry.

You know, my most beloved fellow members, that it becomes us to conduct ourselves in a godly and Christian manner. II Tim. 3:12. Take heed, watch and pray, lest your wisdom bring judgment upon you. Pray without ceasing (I Thess. 5:17) that you may stand worthy before the Son of man. Remember your forerunner Jesus Christ, and follow Him through faith and obedience, with love and patience. I Peter 2:20. Forget that which is carnal, that you may in truth be called Christians, and children of the Most High God. Endure the chastening of your father in heaven, and turn neither to the right nor to the left, that you may enter by the door (John 10:1), and will not have to walk in a strange path, in which sinners, sorcerers, idolaters, and whosoever loves and makes a lie, must go. Rev. 22:15. Remember our assembly, and strictly follow that which was resolved on therein; and if anything has been forgotten, pray the Lord for understanding. Be liberal towards all that are in want among you (Heb. 13:3), but especially towards those who labor among you in the Word, and are driven about, and cannot eat their bread in peace and quietness. Forget not to assemble yourselves together, but give diligence that you constantly meet together, and be united in prayer for all men, and in breaking of bread; and this with the more diligence, because the day of the Lord is approaching. Heb. 10:25. In this assembling you will make manifest the hearts of the false brethren, and will speedily rid yourselves of them.

Finally, beloved brethren and sisters, sanctify yourselves for Him that has made you holy, and hear what Esdras says: "Look for your Shepherd; he shall give you everlasting rest; for he is nigh at hand, that shall come in the end of the world. Be ready to the reward of the kingdom, ... Flee the shadow of this world, ... Arise up and stand, behold the number of those that be sealed in the feast of the Lord; which are departed from the shadow of the world, and have received glorious garments of the Lord. Make my number, fulfilled, and shut up those of thine that are clothed in white, which have fulfilled the law of the Lord. The number of thy children whom thou longedst for, is fulfilled . . . . I Esdras saw upon the mount Sion a great people; whom I could not number, and they all praised the Lord with songs. And in the midst of them there was a young man of a high stature, taller than all the rest, and upon everyone of their heads he set crowns, and was more exalted; which I marveled at greatly. So I asked the angel, and said, Sir, what are these? He answered and said unto me, These be they that have put off the mortal clothing, and put on the immortal, and have confessed the name of God: now are they crowned, and receive palms. Then said I unto the angel, What young person is it that crowneth them, and giveth them palms in their hands? So he answered and said unto me, It is the Son of God, whom they have confessed in the world. Then began I greatly to commend them that stood so stiffly for the name of the Lord." II Esdras 2:34-36, 38-47; Rev. 19:12; Matt. 13:43.

Bear in mind most beloved members of the body of Christ, what I indicate by this scripture, and live according to it, and if I be offered up to the Lord, do for my wife what you would for me. The peace of Jesus Christ, and the love of the heavenly Father, and the grace of their Spirit, preserve you unspotted from sin, and present you glad and pure for the beholding of their glory, at the coming of our Lord Jesus Christ, that you may be found in the number of those called to the feast (Luke 14:15) of the one essential, true God and Saviour Jesus Christ, to whom be eternal praise and glory, Amen.

Beware of false brethren (Acts 20:39); for the Lord will perhaps call me to Him; so take warning, I wait for my God. Pray without ceasing for all that are in bonds. God be with you all. Amen.

Written in the tower at Binzdorf. Brother Michael Sattler of Staufen, together with my fellow prisoners in the Lord.

William Tyndale
Excerpts from *An Answer Unto Sir Thomas More's Dialogue* (1531)

Edited for The Parker Society by the Rev. Henry Walter, B.D. F.R.S, Cambridge: The University Press, 1850

. . . What the *church* is

THIS word *church* hath divers significations. First it a place or house; whither christian people were wont in the old time to resort at times convenient, for to hear the word of doctrine, the law of God, and the faith of our Saviour Jesus Christ, and how and what to pray, and whence to ask power and strength to live godly. For the officer, thereto appointed, preached the pure word of God only, and prayed in a tongue that all men understood: and the people hearkened unto his prayers, and said thereto Amen; and prayed with him in their hearts, and of him learned to pray at home and everywhere, and to instruct every man his household.

Where now we hear but voices without significations, and buzzing, bowlings, and cryings, as it were the hallooing of foxes ,or baitings of bears; and wonder at disguisings and toys, whereof we know no meaning. By reason whereof we be fallen into such ignorance, that we know of the mercy and promises, which are in Christ ,nothing at all. And of the law of God we think as do the Turks, and as did the old heathen people; how that it is a thing which every man may do of his own power, and in doing thereof becometh good, and waxeth righteous, and deserveth heaven; yea, and are yet more mad than that: for we imagine the same of fantasies, and vain ceremonies of our own making; neither needful unto the taming of our own flesh, neither profitable unto our neighbor, neither honour unto God. And of prayer we think that no man can pray but at church; and that it is nothing else but to say Pater noster unto a post: where with yet, and with other observances of our own imagining, we believe we deserve to be sped of all that our blind hearts desire.

In another signification, it is abused and mistaken for a multitude of shaven, shorn, and oiled; which we now call the spiritualty and clergy. As when we read in the chronicles, 'King William was a great tyrant, and a wicked man unto holy church, and took much lands from them.' 'King John was also a perilous man and a wicked unto holy church; and would have had them punished for theft, murder, and whatsoever mischief they did as though they had not been people anointed, but even of the vile rascal and common lay people.' And 'Thomas Becket was a blessed and an holy man; for he died for the liberties (to do all mischief unpunished) and privileges of the church.' 'Is he a layman or a man of the church?' 'Such is the living of holy church.' 'So men say of holy church.' 'Ye must believe in holy church, and do as they teach you.' 'Will ye not obey holy church?' 'Will ye not do the penance enjoined you by holy church?' 'Will ye not forswear obedience unto holy church?' 'Beware lest ye fall into the indignation of holy church, lest they curse you,' and so forth. In which all we understand but the pope, cardinals, legates, patriarchs, archbishops, bishops, abbots, priors, chancellors, archdeacons, commissaries, officials, priests, monks, friars, black, white, pied, grey, and so forth, by (I trow) a thousand names of blasphemy and of hypocrisies, and as many sundry fashions of disguising.

It hath yet, or should have, another signification little known among the common people now-a-days. That is to wit, it signifieth a congregation; a multitude or a company gathered together in one, of all degrees of people. As a man would say, 'the church of London,' meaning not the spiritualty only (as they will be called for their diligent serving of God in the spirit, and so sore eschewing to meddle with temporal matters), but the whole body of the city, of all kinds, conditions, and degrees: and 'the church of Bristow,' all that pertain unto that town generally. And what congregation is meant thou shalt alway understand by the matter that is entreated of, and by the circumstances thereof. And in this third signification is the church of God, or Christ, taken in the scripture; even for the whole multitude of all faom that receive the name of Christ to believe in him, and not for the clergy only. For Paul saith (Galatians i), "I persecuted the church of God above measure," which was not the preachers only, but all that believed generally: as it is to see Acts xxii, where he saith: "I persecuted this way even unto the death, binding and putting in prison both men and women." And (Galatians i), "I was unknown concerning my person unto the congregations of the Jews which were in Christ." And (Rom xvi.) "I commend unto you Phoebe, the deaconess of the church of Cenchris." And, "The churches of Asia salute you." (1 Cor. the last) And, "If a man cannot rule his own house how shall he take the care of the church of God?" "If any faithful man or woman have widows, let them find them, that the church be not charged." And, "If thy brother hear thee not, tell the church or congregation," and so forth. In which places and throughout all the scripture, the church is taken for the whole multitude of them that believe in Christ in that place, in that parish, town, city, province, land, or throughout all the world, and not for the spiritualty only.

Notwithstanding yet it is sometimes taken generally for all them that embrace the name of Christ, though their faiths be naught, or though they have no faith at all. And sometimes it is taken specially for the elect; only in whose hearts God hath written his law with his holy Spirit, and given them a feeling faith of the mercy that is in Christ Jesu our Lord.

Why Tyndale used this word *congregation* rather than *church*
in the translation of the new Testament

Wherefore, inasmuch as the clergy (as the nature of those hard and indurate adamant stones is, to draw all to them) had appropriate unto themselves the term that of right is common unto all the whole congregation of them that believe in Christ; and with their false and subtle wiles had beguiled and mocked the people, and brought them into the ignorance of the word; making them understand by this word *church* nothing but the shaven flock of them that shore the whole world; therefore in the translation of the new Testament, where I found this word *ecclesia,* I interpreted it by this word *congregation*. Even therefore did I it, and not of any mischievous mind or purpose to stablish heresy, as Master More untruly reporteth of me in his dialogue, where he raileth on the translation of the new Testament.[25]

And when M More saith that this word *church* is known well enough, I report me unto the consciences of all the land, whether he say truth or otherwise; or whether the lay people understand by *church* the whole multitude of all that profess Christ, or the juggling spirits only. And when he saith that *congregation* is a more general term; if it were, it hurteth not: for the circumstance doth ever tell what congregation is meant. Nevertheless yet saith he not the truth. For wheresoever I may say a *congregation,* there may I say a *church* also; as the church of the devil, the church of Satan, the church of wretches, the church of wicked men, the church of liars, and a church of Turks thereto. For M. More must grant (if he will have *ecclesia* translated throughout all the new Testament by this word *church)* that *church* is as common as *ecclesia.* Now is *ecclesia* a Greek word, and was in use before the time of the apostles, and taken for a congregation among the heathen, where was no congregation of God or of Christ. And also Lucas himself useth *ecclesia* for a church, or congregation, of heathen people thrice in one chapter, even in the nineteenth chapter of the Acts, where Demetrius the goldsmith, or silversmith, had gathered a company against Paul for preaching against images.

Howbeit, M. More hath so long used his figures of poetry, that (I suppose) when he erreth most, he now, by the reason of a long custom, believeth himself that he saith most true. Or else, as the wise people, which when they dance naked in nets, believe that no man seeth them; even so M. More thinketh that his errors be so subtilly couched that no man can espy them. So blind he counteth all other men, in comparison of his great understanding. But charitably I exhort him in Christ to take heed; for though Judas were wilier than his fellows to get lucre, yet he proved not most wise at the last end. Neither though Baalam, the false prophet, had a clear sight to bring the curse of God upon the children of Israel for honour's sake; yet his covetousness did so blind his prophecy, that he could not see his own end. Let, therefore, M. More and his company awake by times, ere M. More, ever their sin be ripe; lest the voice of their wickedness ascend up, and awake God out of his sleep, to look upon them, and to bow his

---

[25] More had written: ". . .Why, quoth your friend, what faults were there in it ? To tell you all that, quoth I, were in a manner to rehearse you all the whole book, wherein there were found and noted, wrong and falsely translated, above a thousand texts by tale. . . .. For he hath mistranslated three words of great weight, and every one of them is, as I suppose, more than thrice three times repeated and rehearsed in the books. Ah, that may well be, quoth he; but that was not well done. But, I pray you, what words be these? The one is, quoth I, this word *Priests;* the other, *the Church;* the third, *Charity."}*

ears unto their cursed blasphemies against the open truth, and to send his harvestmen and mowers of vengeance to reap it.

But how happeth it that M. More hath not contended in like wise against his darling Erasmus all this long while? Doth he not change this word *ecclesia* into *congregation,* and that not seldom in the new Testamenti? Peradventure he oweth him favour, because he made *Moria*[26] in his house: which book, if it were in English, then should every man see how that he then was far otherwise minded than he now writeth. But, verily, I think that as Judas betrayed not Christ for any love that he had unto the high priests, scribes and Pharisees, but only to come by that wherefore he thirsted; even so M. More (as there are tokens evident) wrote not these books for any affection that he bare unto the spiritualty, or unto the opinions which he so barely defendeth, but to obtain only that which he was an hungred for. I pray God that he eat not too hastily, lest he be choked at the latter end; but that he repent, and resist not the Spirit of God, which openeth light unto the world.

Why he useth this word *elder,* and not *priest*

Another thing which he rebuketh is, that I interpret this Greek word *presbyteros* by this word *senior*. Of a truth *senior* is no very good English, though senior and junior be used in the universities; but there came no better in my mind at that time. Howbeit, I spied my fault since, long ere M. More told it me, and have mended it in all the works which I since made, and call it *an elder*. And in that he maketh heresy of it, to call *presbyteros* an *elder,* he ' condemneth their own old Latin text of heresy, which only they use yet daily in the church, and have used, I suppose, this fourteen hundred years: for that text doth call it *an elder* likewise. In the 1 Pet. v. thus standeth it in the Latin text: *Seniores ergo qui in vobis sunt obsecro consenior, pascite qui in vobis est gregem Christi:* " The elders that are among you, I beseech, which am an elder also, that ye feed the flock of Christ, which is among you." There is *presbyteros* called an *elder*. And in that he saith, "Feed Christ's flock," he meaneth even the ministers that were chosen to teach the people, and to inform them in God's word, and no lay persons. And in the second epistle of John saith the text, *Senior electee dominœ et filiis ejus:* " The elder unto the elect lady and to her children." And in the third epistle of John, *Senior Gaio dilecto*: "The elder unto the beloved Gaius." In these two epistles *presbyteros* is called an *elder*. And in Acts, chap, xx., the text saith: " Paul sent for *majores natu ecclesice,* the elders in birth of the congregation or church, and said unto them, "Take heed unto yourselves, and unto the whole flock, over which the Holy Ghost hath made you *episcopos ad regendum ecclesiam Dei,*" bishops, or overseers, to govern the church of God. There is *presbyteros* called an *elder in birth;* which same immediately is called a

---

[26] Erasmus' celebrated sarcastic production, the *Encomium Moriae* [In Praise of Folly]; in which he held up to ridicule the ignorance frequent among the popish clergy and the friars.

bishop or overseer, to declare what persons are meant. Hereof ye see that I have no more erred than their own text, which they have used since the scripture was first in the Latin tongue, and that their own text understandeth by *presbyteros* nothing save an *elder.* And they were called elders, because of their age, gravity and sadness, as thou mayest see by the text; and bishops, or overseers, by the reason of their offices. And all that were called elders (or priests, if they so will) were called bishops also, though they have divided the names now : which thing thou mayest evidently see by the first chapter of Titus, and Acts xx., and other places more.

And when he layeth Timothy unto my charge, how he was young, then he weeneth that he hath won his gilden spurs. But I would pray him to shew me where he readeth that Paul calleth him *presbyteros,* priest or elder. I durst not then call him *episcopus* properly: for those overseers, which we now call bishops after the Greek word, were in one always biding in one place, to govern the congregation there. Now was Timothy an apostle. And Paul also writeth that he came shortly again. Well, will he say, it cometh yet all to one; for if it becometh the lower minister to be of a sad and discreet age, much more it becometh the higher. It is truth. But two things are without law, God and necessity. If God, to shew his power, shall shed out his grace more upon youth than upon age at a time, who shall let him? Women be no meet vessels to rule or to preach, for both are forbidden them; yet hath God endowed them with his Spirit at sundry times, and shewed his power and goodness upon them, and wrought wonderful things by them, because he would not have them despised. We read that women have judged all Israel, and have been great prophetesses, and have clone mighty deeds. Yea, and if stories be true, women have preached since the opening of the new testament. Do not our women now christen and minister the sacrament of baptism in time of need? Might they not, by as good reason, preach also, if necessity required? If a woman were driven into some island, where Christ was never preached, might she there not preach him, if she had the gift thereto? Might she not also baptize? And why might she not, by the same reason, minister the sacrament of the body and blood of Christ, and teach them how to choose officers and ministers? O poor women, how despise ye them! The viler the better welcome unto you. An whore had ye lever than an honest wife. If only shaven and anointed may do these things, then Christ did them not, nor any of his apostles, nor any man in long time after: for they used no such ceremonies.

Notwithstanding, though God be under no law, and necessity lawless; yet be we under a law, and ought to prefer the men before the women, and age before youth, as nigh as we can. For it is against the law of nature that young men should rule the elder, and as uncomely as that women should rule the men, but when need requireth. And therefore, if Paul had had other shift, and a man of age as meet for the room, he would not have put Timothy in the office; he should no doubt have been kept back until a fuller age, and have learned in the meantime in silence. And whatsoever thou be that readest this, I exhort thee in our Lord, that thou read both the epistles of Paul to Timothy; that thou mayest see how diligently (as a mother careth for her child, if it be in peril) Paul writeth unto Timothy, to instruct him, to teach him, to exhort, to courage him, to stir him up to be wise, sober, diligent, circumspect, sad, humble and meek, saying: "These I write that thou mayest know how to behave thyself in the house of God, which is the church" (or congregation). "Avoid lusts of youth, beware of ungodly fables and old wives' tales; and avoid the company of men of corrupt minds, which waste their brains about wrangling questions. "Let no man despise thine youth." As who shall say, 'Youth is a despised thing of itself; whereunto men give none obedience naturally or reverence. See, therefore, that thy virtue exceed, to recompense thy lack of age; and that thou so behave thyself that no fault be found with thee.' And again, "Rebuke not an elder sharply, but exhort him as thy father, and young men as thy brethren, and the elder women as thy mothers, and the young women as thy sisters;" and such like in every chapter. "Admit none accusation against an elder, under less than two witnesses." And Paul chargeth him "in the sight of God and of the Lord Jesus Christ, and of his elect angels, to do nothing rashly," or of affection. And shortly, whereunto youth is most prone and ready to fall, thereof warneth he him with all diligence, even almost or altogether half a dozen times of some one thing. And finally, as a man would teach a child that had never before gone to school, so tenderly and so carefully doth Paul teach him. It is another thing to teach the people, and to teach the preacher. Here Paul teacheth the preacher, young Timothy.

And when he affirmeth that I say, how that the oiling and shaving is no part of the priesthood, that improveth he not, nor can do. And therefore I say it yet. And when he hath insearched the uttermost that he can, this is all that he can against me, that of an hundred there be not ten that have the properties which Paul requireth to be in them. Wherefore, if oiling and shaving be no part of their priesthood, then evermore of a thousand nine hundred at the least should be no priests at all. And "Quoth your friend" would confirm it with an oath, and swear deeply, that it would follow, and that it must needs so be: which argument yet, if there were no other shift, I would solve after an Oxford fashion, with *Concede consequentiam et consequens.* And I say moreover, that their anointing is but a ceremony borrowed of the Jews, though they have somewhat altered the manner; and their shaving borrowed of the heathen priests; and that they be no more of their priesthood, than the oil, salt, spittle, taper and chrisom-cloth, of the substance of baptism. Which things, no doubt, because they be of their conjuring, they would have preached of necessity unto the salvation of the child, except necessity had driven them unto the contrary. And seeing that the oil is not of necessity, let M. More tell me what more virtue is in the oil of confirmation, inasmuch as the bishop sacreth the one as well as the other; yea, and let him tell the reason why there should be more virtue in the oil wherewith the bishop anointeth his priests. Let him tell you from whence the oil cometh, how it is made, and why he selleth it to the curates wherewith they anoint the sick, or whether this be of less virtue than the other.

And finally, why used not the apostles this Greek word *hiereus,* or the interpreter this Latin word *sacerdos,* but alway this word *presbyteros* and *senior,* by which was at that time nothing signified but an elder? And it was no doubt taken of the custom of the Hebrews, where the officers were ever elderly men, as nature requireth: as it appeareth in the old Testament, and also in the new. "The scribes, Pharisees, and the elders of the people," saith the text; which were the officers and rulers, so called by the reason of their age.

Why he useth *love,* rather than *charity.*

He rebuketh me also that I translate this Greek word *agape* into *love,* and not rather into *charity,* so holy and so known a term. Verily, *charity* is not known English, in that sense which *agape* requireth. For when we say, 'Give your alms in the worship of God, and sweet St Charity;' and when the father teacheth his son to say, 'Blessing, father, for St Charity;' what mean they? In good faith they wot not. Moreover, when we say, 'God help you, I have done my charity for this day,' do we not take it for alms? and, ' The man is ever chiding and out of charity;' and, ' I beshrew him, saving my charity;' there we take it for patience. And when I say, 'A charitable man,' it is taken for merciful. And though mercifulness be a good love, or rather spring of a good love, yet is not every good love mercifulness. As when a woman loveth her husband godly, or a man his wife or his friend that is in none adversity, it is not always mercifulness. Also we say not, 'This man hath a great charity to God;' but 'a great love.' Wherefore I must have used this general term *love* in spite of mine heart oftentimes. And *agape* and *caritas* were words used among the heathen, ere Christ came; and signified therefore more than a *godly love.* And we may say well enough, and have heard it spoken, that the Turks be charitable one to another among themselves, and some of them unto the Christians too. Besides all this, *agape* is common unto all loves.

And when M. More saith, "Every love is not charity;" no more is every apostle Christ's apostle; nor every angel God's angel; nor every hope Christian hope; nor every faith, or belief, Christ's belief; and so by an hundred thousand words: so that if I should always use but a word that were no more general than the word I interpret, I should interpret nothing at all. But the matter itself and the circumstances do declare what love, what hope, and what faith is spoken of. And, finally, I say not, charity God, or charity your neighbour; but, love God, and love your neighbour; yea, and though we say a man ought to love his neighbour's wife and his daughter, a christian man doth not understand that he is commanded to defile his neighbour's wife or his neighbour's daughter.

[. . .]

Thomas Cromwell
Secretary to King Henry VIII

Henry VIII (and Thomas Cromwell)
An Act in Restraint of Appeals (February, 1533)

Where by divers sundry old authentic histories and chronicles, it is manifestly declared and expressed, that this realm of England is an empire, and so hath been accepted in the world, governed by one supreme head and king, having the dignity and royal estate of the imperial crown of the same, unto whom a body politic, compact of all sorts and degrees of people, divided in terms, and by names of spiritualty and temporalty, be bounden and ought to bear, next to God, a natural and humble obedience: he being also institute and furnished, by the goodness and sufferance of Almighty God, with plenary, whole, and entire power, preeminence, authority, prerogative and jurisdiction, to render and yield justice, and final determination to all manner of folk, residents, or subjects within this his realm, in all causes, matters, debates, and contentions, happening to occur, in- surge, or begin within the limits thereof, without restraint, or provocation to any foreign princes or potentates of the world ; the body spiritual whereof having power, when any cause of the law divine happened to come in question, or of spiritual learning, then it was declared, interpreted, and showed by that part of the said body politic, called the spiritualty, now being usually called the English Church, which always hath been reputed, and also found of that sort, that both for knowledge, integrity, and sufficiency of number, it hath been always thought, and is also at this hour, sufficient and meet of itself, without the intermeddling of any exterior person or persons, to declare and determine all such doubts, and to administer all such offices and duties, as to their rooms spiritual doth appertain; for the due administration whereof, and to keep them from corruption and sinister affection, the king's most noble progenitors, and the antecessors of the nobles of this realm, have sufficiently endowed the said Church, both with honour and possessions; and the laws temporal, for trial of property of lands and goods, and for the conservation of the people of this realm in unity and peace, without ravin or spoil, was and yet is administered, adjudged, and executed by sundry judges and ministers of the other part of the said body politic, called the temporalty; and both their authorities and jurisdictions do conjoin together in the due administration of justice, the one to help the other.

And whereas the king, his most noble progenitors, and the nobility and Commons of this said realm, at divers and sundry Parliaments, as well in the time of King Edward I, Edward III, Richard II, Henry IV, and other noble kings of this realm, made sundry ordinances, laws, statutes, and provisions for the entire and sure conservation of the prerogatives, liberties, and pre-eminences of the said imperial crown of this realm, and of the jurisdiction spiritual and temporal of the same, to keep it from the annoyance as well of the see of Rome, as from the authority of other foreign potentates, attempting the diminution or violation thereof, as often, and from time to time, as any such annoyance or attempt might be known or espied.

And notwithstanding the said good statutes and ordinances made in the time of the king's most noble progenitors, in preservation of the authority and prerogative of the 1533. said imperial crown, as is aforesaid; yet nevertheless since dangers the making of the said good statutes and ordinances, divers vided for and sundry inconveniences and dangers, not provided for therein plainly by the said former acts, statutes, and ordinances, arisen by have arisen and sprung by reason of appeals sued out of this appeals to realm to the see of Rome, in causes testamentary, causes of matrimony and divorces, right of tithes, oblations and obventions, not only to the great inquietation, vexation, trouble, cost and charges of the king's highness, and many of his subjects and residents in this his realm, but also to the great delay and let to the true and speedy determination of the said causes, for so much as the parties appealing to the said Court of Rome most commonly do the same for the delay of justice.

And forasmuch as the great distance of way is so far out of this realm, so that the necessary proofs, nor the true knowledge of the cause, can neither there be so well known, nor the witnesses there so well examined, as within this realm, so that the parties grieved by means of the said appeals be most times without remedy:

In consideration whereof the king's highness, his nobles Commons, considering the great enormities, dangers, long delays and hurts, that as well to his highness, as to his said nobles, subjects, commons, and residents of this his realm, in the said causes testamentary, causes of matrimony and divorces, tithes, oblations and obventions, do daily ensue, does therefore by his royal assent, and by the assent of the lords spiritual and temporal, and the Commons, in this present Parliament assembled, and by authority of the same, enact, establish, and ordain, that all causes testamentary, causes of matrimony and divorces, rights of tithes, oblations and obventions (the knowledge whereof by the goodness of princes of this realm, and by the laws and customs of the same, appertaineth to the spiritual jurisdiction of this realm) already commenced, moved, depending, being, happening, or hereafter coming in contention, debate, or question within this realm, or within any the king's dominions, or marches of the same, or elsewhere, whether they concern the king our sovereign lord, his heirs and successors, or any other subjects or residents within the same, of what degree soever they be, shall be from henceforth heard, examined, discussed, clearly, finally, and definitively adjudged and determined within the king's jurisdiction and authority, and not elsewhere, in such courts spiritual and temporal of the same, as the natures, conditions, and qualities of the causes and matters aforesaid in contention, or hereafter happening in contention, shall require, without having any respect to any custom, use, or sufferance, in hindrance, let, or prejudice of the same, or to any other thing used or suffered to the contrary thereof by any other manner of person or persons in any manner of wise; any foreign inhibitions, appeals, sentences, summons, citations, suspensions, interdictions, excommunications, restraints, judgments, or any other process or impediments, of what natures, names, qualities, or conditions soever they be, from the see of Rome, or any other foreign courts or potentates of the world, or from and out of this realm, or any other the king's dominions, or marches of the same, to the see of Rome, or to any other foreign courts or potentates, to the let or impediment thereof in any wise notwithstanding.

And that it shall be lawful to the king our sovereign lord, and to his heirs and successors, and to all other subjects or residents within this realm, or within any the king's dominions, or marches of the same—notwithstanding that hereafter it should happen any excommengement, excommunications, interdictions, citations, or any other censures, or foreign process out of any outward parts, to be fulminate, provulged, declared, or put in execution within this said realm, or in any other place or places, for any of the causes before rehearsed, in prejudice, derogation, or contempt of this said Act, and the very true meaning and execution thereof — may and shall nevertheless as well pursue, execute, have, and enjoy the effects, profits, benefits, and commodities of all such processes, sentences, judgments, and determinations done, or hereafter to be done, in any of the said courts spiritual or temporal, as the cases shall require, within the limits, power, and authority of this the king's said realm, and dominions and marches of the same, and those only, and none other to take place, and to be firmly observed and obeyed within the same.

As also, that all the spiritual prelates, pastors, ministers, and curates within this realm, and the dominions of the same, shall and may use, minister, execute and do, or cause to be used, ministered, executed and done, all sacraments, sacramentals, divine services, and all other things within the said realm and dominions, unto all the subjects of the same, as catholic and Christian men ought to do ; any former citations, processes, inhibitions, suspensions, interdictions, excommunications, or appeals, for or touching the causes aforesaid, from or to the see of Rome, or any other foreign prince or foreign courts, to the let or contrary thereof in any wise notwithstanding.

And if any of the said spiritual persons, by the occasion of the said fulminations of any of the same interdictions, censures, inhibitions, excommunications, appeals, suspensions, summons, or other foreign citations for the causes beforesaid, or for any of them, do at any time hereafter refuse to minister, or cause to be ministered, the said sacraments and sacramentals, and other divine services, in form as is aforesaid, shall for every such time or times that they or any of them do refuse so to do, or cause to be done, have one year's imprisonment, and to make fine and ransom at the king's pleasure.

And it is further enacted by the authority aforesaid, that if any person or persons inhabiting or resident within this realm, or within any of the king's said dominions, or marches of the same, or any other person or persons, of what estate, condition, or degree soever he or they be, at any time hereafter, for or in any the causes aforesaid, do attempt, move, purchase, or procure, from or to the see of Rome, or from or to any" other foreign court or courts out of this realm, any manner foreign process, inhibitions, appeals, sentences, summons, citations, suspensions, interdictions, excommunications, restraints, or judgments, of what nature, kind, or quality soever they be, or execute any of the same process, or do any act or acts to the let, impediment, hindrance, or derogation of any process, sentence, judgment, or determination had, made, done, or hereafter to be had, done, or made, in any courts of this realm, or the king's said dominions, or marches of the sama, for any of the causes aforesaid, contrary to the true meaning of this present Act, and the execution of the same, that then every such person or persons so doing, and their fautors, comforters, abettors, procurers, executors, and counsellors, and every of them, being convict of the same, for every such default shall incur and run in the same pains, penalties, and forfeitures, ordained and provided by the Statute of Provision and

Prasmunire, made in the sixteenth year of the reign of the right noble prince King Richard II, against such as attempt, procure, or make provision to the see of Rome, or elsewhere, for any thing or things, to the derogation, or contrary to the prerogative or jurisdiction of the crown and dignity of this realm.

And furthermore, in eschewing the said great enormities, inquietations, delays, charges, and expenses hereafter to besustained in pursuing of such appeals, and foreign process, for and concerning the causes aforesaid, or any of them, do therefore by authority aforesaid, ordain and enact, that in such cases where heretofore any of the king's subjects or residents have used to pursue, provoke, or procure any appeal to the see of Rome, and in all other cases of appeals, in or for any of the causes aforesaid, they may and shall from henceforth take, have, and use their appeals within this realm, and not elsewhere, in manner and form as hereafter ensueth, and not otherwise ; that is to say, first from the archdeacon, or his official, if the matter or cause be there begun, to the bishop diocesan of the said see, if in case any of the parties be grieved. And in like wise if it be commenced before the bishop diocesan, or his commissary, from the bishop diocesan, or his commissary, within fifteen days next ensuing the judgment or sentence thereof there given, to the Archbishop of the province of Canterbury, if it be within his province ; and if it be within the province of York, then to the Archbishop of York ; and so likewise to all other archbishops in other the king's dominions, as the case by order of justice shall require ; and there to be definitively and finally ordered, decreed, and adjudged, according to justice, without any other appellation or provocation to any other person or persons, court or courts.

And if the matter or contention for any of the causes aforesaid be or shall be commenced, by any of the king's subjects or residents, before the archdeacon of any archbishop, or his commissary, then the party grieved shall or may take his appeal within fifteen days next after judgment or sentence there given, to the Court of the Arches, or audience, of the same archbishop or archbishops ; and from the said Court of the Arches or audience, within fifteen days then next ensuing after judgment or sentence there given, to the archbishop of the same province, there to be definitively and finally determined, without any other or further process or appeal thereupon to be had or sued.

And it is further enacted by the authority aforesaid, that all and every matter, cause, and contention now depending, or that hereafter shall be commenced by any of the king's subjects or residents for any of the causes aforesaid, before anv of the said archbishops, that then the same matter or matters, contention or contentions, shall be before the same archbishop where the said matter, cause, or process shall be so commenced, definitively determined, decreed, or adjudged, without any other appeal, provocation, or any other foreign process out of this realm, to be sued to the let or derogation of the said judgment, sentence, or decree, otherwise than is by this Act limited and appointed; saving always the prerogative of the Archbishop and Church of bishop of Canterbury, in all the foresaid cases of appeals, to him and to his successors to be sued within this realm, in such and like wise as they have been accustomed and used to have heretofore.

And in case any cause, matter, or contention, now depending for the causes before rehearsed, or any of them, or that hereafter shall come in contention for any of the same causes, in any of the foresaid courts, which has, does, shall, or may touch the king, his heirs or successors, kings of this realm; that in all and every such case or cases the party grieved, as before is said, shall or may appeal from any of the said courts of this said realm, where the said matter, now being in contention, or hereafter shall come-in contention, touching the king, his heirs, or successors (as is aforesaid) shall happen to be ventilated, commenced or begun, to the spiritual prelates and other abbots and priors of the Upper House, assembled and convocate by the king's writ in the Convocation being, or next ensuing, within the province or provinces where the same matter of contention is or shall be begun; so that every such appeal be taken by the party grieved within fifteen days next after the judgment or sentence thereupon given or to be given; and that whatsoever be done, or shall be done and affirmed, determined, decreed, and adjudged by the foresaid prelates, abbots, and priors of the Upper House of the said Convocation, as is aforesaid, appertaining, concerning, or belonging to the king, his heirs, and successors, in any of these foresaid causes of appeals, shall stand and be taken for a final decree, sentence, judgment, definition, and determination, and the same matter, so determined, never after to come in question and debate, to be examined in any other court or courts.

And if it shall happen any person or persons hereafter to pursue or provoke any appeal contrary to the effect of this Act, or refuse to obey, execute, and observe all things comprised within the same, concerning the said appeals, provocations, and other foreign processes to be sued out of this realm, for any the causes aforesaid, that then every such person or persons so doing, refusing, or offending contrary to the true meaning of this Act, their procurers, fautors, advocates, counsellors, and abettors, and every of them, shall incur into the pains, forfeitures, and penalties ordained and provided in the said statute made in the said sixteenth year of King Richard II, and with like process to be made against the said offenders, as in the same statute made in the said sixteenth year more plainly appears.

Henry VIII (and Thomas Cromwell)

The Act of Supremacy (November, 1534)

Albeit the king's Majesty justly and rightfully is and ought to be the supreme head of the Church of England, and so is recognized by the clergy of this realm in their convocations,

yet nevertheless, for corroboration and confirmation thereof, and for increase of virtue in Christ's religion within this realm of England, and to repress and extirpate all errors, heresies, and other enormities and abuses heretofore used in the same,

be it enacted, by authority of this present Parliament, that the king, our sovereign lord, his heirs and successors, kings of this realm, shall be taken, accepted, and reputed the only supreme head in earth of the Church of England, called *Anglicans Ecclesia;* and shall have and enjoy, annexed and united to the imperial crown of this realm, as well the title and style thereof, as all honors, dignities, preeminences, jurisdictions, privileges, authorities, immunities, profits, and commodities to the said dignity of the supreme head of the same Church belonging and appertaining;

and that our said sovereign lord, his heirs and successors, kings of this realm, shall have full power and authority from time to time to visit, repress, redress, record, order, correct, restrain, and amend all such errors, heresies, abuses, offenses, contempts and enormities, whatsoever they be, which by any manner of spiritual authority or jurisdiction ought or may lawfully be reformed, repressed, ordered, redressed, corrected, restrained, or amended, most to the pleasure of Almighty God, the increase of virtue in Christ's religion, and for the conservation of the peace, unity, and tranquility of this realm; any usage, foreign land, foreign authority, prescription, or any other thing or things to the contrary hereof notwithstanding.

Source: **Documents Illustrative of English Church History**, by Henry Gee and William John Hardy, New York: MacMillian and Co. , 1896

Thomas More
Last Letter to his daughter Margaret

written from prison on July 5, 1535, the day before he was executed.

Our Lord bless you, good daughter, and your good husband, and your little boy, and all yours, and all my children, and all my god-children and all our friends. Recommend me when ye may to my good daughter Cecily, whom I beseech Our Lord to comfort; and I send her my blessing and to all her children, and pray her to pray for me. I send her a handkercher, and God comfort my good son, her husband. My good daughter Daunce hath the picture in parchment that you delivered me from my Lady Coniers, her name on the back. Show her that I heartily pray her that you may send it in my name to her again, for a token from me to pray for me.

I like special well Dorothy Colly. I pray you be good unto her. I would wot whether this be she that you wrote me of. If not, yet I pray you be good to the other as you may in her affliction, and to my good daughter Jane Aleyn too. Give her, I pray you, some kind answer, for she sued hitherto me this day to pray you be good to her.

I cumber you, good Margaret, much, but I would be sorry if it should be any longer than to-morrow, for it is St. Thomas's even, and the utas of St. Peter; and therefore, to-morrow long I to go to God. It were a day very meet and convenient for me.

I never liked your manner towards me better than when you kissed me last; for I love when daughterly love and dear charity hath no leisure to look to worldly courtesy. Farewell, my dear child, and pray for me, and I shall for you and all your friends, that we may merrily meet in heaven. I thank you for your great cost. I send now my good daughter Clement her algorism stone, and I send her and my godson and all hers God's blessing and mine. I pray you at time convenient recommend me to my good son John More. I liked well his natural fashion. Our Lord bless him and his good wife, my loving daughter, to whom I pray him to be good, as he hath great cause; and that, if the land of mine come to his hands, he break not my will concerning his sister Daunce. And the Lord bless Thomas and Austin, and all that they shall have.

John Calvin (Jean Cauvin)
Pastor, Geneva

John Calvin
Preface to his Commentary Upon the Psalms

English Translation by Arthur Golding, 1571

TO THE GODLY AND INGENUOUS READERS, GREETING.

IF the reading of these my Commentaries confer as much benefit on the Church of God as I myself have reaped advantage from the composition of them, I shall have no reason to regret that I have undertaken this work. Having expounded here, in our small school, the Book of Psalms, about three years ago, I thought that I had by this means sufficiently discharged my duty, and had resolved not to publish to the world what I had familiarly taught those of my own household. And, in fact, before I had undertaken to expound this book in my lectures, at the request of my brethren, I said what was true, that I had kept away from this subject, because that most faithful teacher of the Church of God, Martin Bucer, had labored in this field with such singular learning, diligence, fidelity, and success, that at least there was not so great need that I should put my hand to the work.

[. . .]

Now, if my readers derive any fruit and advantage from the labor which I have bestowed in writing these Commentaries, I would have them to understand that the small measure of experience which I have had by the conflicts with which the Lord has exercised me, has in no ordinary degree assisted me, not only in applying to present use whatever instruction could be gathered from these divine compositions, but also in more easily comprehending the design of each of the writers. And as David holds the principal place among them, it has greatly aided me in understanding more fully the complaints made by him of the internal afflictions which the Church had to sustain through those who gave themselves out to be her members, that I had suffered the same or similar things from the domestic enemies of the Church. For although I follow David at a great distance, and come far short of equaling him; or rather, although in aspiring slowly and with great difficulty to attain to the many virtues in which he excelled, I still feel myself tarnished with the contrary vices; yet if I have any things in common with him, I have no hesitation in comparing myself with him.

In reading the instances of his faith, patience, fervor, zeal, and integrity, it has, as it ought, drawn from me unnumbered groans and sighs, that I am so far from approaching them; but it has, notwithstanding, been of very great advantage to me to behold in him as in a mirror, both the commencement of my calling, and the continued course of my function; so that I know the more assuredly, that whatever that most illustrious king and prophet suffered, was exhibited to me by God as an example for imitation. My conditions no doubt, is much inferior to his, and it is unnecessary for me to stay to show this. But as he was taken from the sheepfold, and elevated to the rank of supreme authority; so God having taken me from my originally obscure and humble condition, has reckoned me worthy of being invested with the honorable office of a preacher and minister of the gospel.

When I was as yet a very little boy, my father had destined me for the study of theology. But afterwards when he considered that the legal profession commonly raised those who followed it to wealth this prospect induced him suddenly to change his purpose. Thus it came to pass, that I was withdrawn from the study of philosophy, and was put to the study of law. To this pursuit I endeavored faithfully to apply myself in obedience to the will of my father; but God, by the secret guidance of his providence, at length gave a different direction to my course.

And first, since I was too obstinately devoted to the superstitions of Popery to be easily extricated from so profound an abyss of mire, God by a sudden conversion subdued and brought my mind to a teachable frame, which was more hardened in such matters than might have been expected from one at my early period of life Having thus received some taste and knowledge of true godliness I was immediately inflamed with so intense a desire to make progress therein, that although I did not altogether leave off other studies, I yet pursued them with less ardor. I was quite surprised to find that before a year had elapsed, all who had any desire after purer doctrine were continually coming to me to learn, although I myself was as yet but a mere novice and tyro.

Being of a disposition somewhat unpolished and bashful, which led me always to love the shade and retirement, I then began to seek some secluded corner where I might be withdrawn from the public view; but so far from being able to accomplish the object of my be desire, all my retreats were like public schools. In short, whilst my one great object was to live in seclusion without being known, God so led me about through different turnings and changes, that he never permitted me to rest in any place, until, in spite of my natural disposition, he brought me forth to public notice. Leaving my native country, France, I in fact retired into Germany, expressly for the purpose of being able there to enjoy in some obscure corner the repose which I had always desired, and which had been so long denied me.

But lo! whilst I lay hidden at Basle, and known only to a few people, many faithful and holy persons were burnt alive in France; and the report of these burnings having reached foreign nations, they excited the strongest disapprobation among a great part of the Germans, whose indignation was kindled against the authors of such tyranny. In order to allay this indignation, certain wicked and lying pamphlets were circulated, stating that none were treated with such cruelty but Anabaptists and seditious persons, who by their perverse ravings and false opinions, were overthrowing not only religion but also all civil order.

Observing that the object which these instruments of the court aimed at by their disguises, was not only that the disgrace of shedding so much innocent blood might remain buried under the false charges and calumnies which they brought against the holy martyrs after their death, but also, that afterwards they might be able to proceed to the utmost extremity in murdering the poor saints without exciting compassion towards them in the breasts of any, it appeared to me, that unless I opposed them to the utmost of my ability, my silence could not be vindicated from the charge of cowardice and treachery. This was the consideration which induced me to publish my **Institute of the Christian Religion**.

My objects were, first, to prove that these reports were false and calumnious, and thus to vindicate my brethren, whose death was precious in the sight of the Lord; and next, that as the same cruelties might very soon after be exercised against many unhappy individuals, foreign nations might be touched with at least some compassion towards them and solicitude about them. When it was then published, it was not that copious and labored work which it now is, but only a small treatise containing a summary of the principal truths of the Christian religion, and it was published with no other design than that men might know what was the faith held by those whom I saw basely and wickedly defamed by those flagitious and perfidious flatterers. That my object was not to acquire fame, appeared from this, that immediately after I left Basle, and particularly from the fact that nobody there knew that I was the author.

Wherever else I have gone, I have taken care to conceal that I was the author of that performance; and I had resolved to continue in the same privacy and obscurity, until at length William Farel detained me at Geneva, not so much by counsel and exhortation, as by a dreadful imprecation, which I felt to be as if God had from heaven laid his mighty hand upon me to arrest me. As the most direct road to Strasburg, to which I then intended to retire, was as shut up by the wars, I had resolved to pass quickly by Geneva, without staying longer than a single night in that city. A little before this, Popery had been driven from it by the exertions of the excellent person whom I have named, and Peter Viret; but matters were not yet brought to a settled state, and the city was divided into unholy and dangerous factions. Then an individual who now basely apostatised and returned to the Papists, discovered me and made me known to others. Upon this, Farel, who burned with an extraordinary zeal to advance the gospel, immediately strained every nerve to detain me. And after having learned that my heart was set upon devoting myself to private studies for which I wished to keep myself free from other pursuits, and finding that he gained nothing by entreaties, he proceeded to utter an imprecation that God would curse my retirement, and the tranquility of the studies which I sought, if I should withdraw and refuse to give assistance, when the necessity seas so urgent. By this imprecation I was so stricken with terror, that I desisted from the journey which I had undertaken; but sensible of my natural bashfulness and timidity, I would not bring myself under obligation to discharge any particular office. After that, four months had scarcely elapsed, when, on the one hand, the Anabaptists began to assail us, and, on the other, a certain wicked apostate, who being secretly supported by the influence of some of the magistrates of the city, was thus enabled to give us a great deal of trouble. At the same time, a succession of dissensions fell out in the city which strangely afflicted us. Being, as I acknowledge, naturally of a timid, softer and pusillanimous disposition, I was compelled to encounter these violent tempests as part of my early training; and although I did not sink under themes yet I was not sustained by such greatness of mind, as not to rejoice more than it became me, when, in consequence of certain commotions, I was banished from Geneva.

By this means set at liberty and loosed from the tie of my vocational I resolved to live in a private station, free from the burden and cares of any public charge, when that most excellent servant of Christ, Martin Bucer, employing a similar kind of remonstrance and protestation as that to which Farel had recourse before, drew me back to a new station. Alarmed by the example of Jonas which he set before me, I still continued in the work of teaching. And although I always continued like myself, studiously avoiding celebrity; yet I was carried, I know not how, as it were by force to the Imperial assemblies, where, willing or unwilling, I was under the necessity of appearing before the eyes of many.

Afterwards, when the Lord having compassion on this city, had allayed the hurtful agitations and broils which prevailed in it, and by his wonderful power had defeated both the wicked counsels and the sanguinary attempts of the disturbers of the Republic, necessity was imposed upon me of returning to my former charge, contrary to my desire and inclination. The welfare of this church, it is true, lay so near my heart, that for its sake I would not have hesitated to lay down my life; but my timidity nevertheless suggested to me many reasons for excusing myself from again willingly taking upon my shoulders so heavy a burden. At length, however, a solemn and conscientious regard to my duty, prevailed with me to consent to return to the flock from which I had been torn; but with what grief, tears, great anxiety and distress I did this, the Lord is my best witness, and many godly persons who would have wished to see me delivered from this painful state, had it not been that that which I feared, and which made me give my consent, prevented them and shut their mouths. Were I to narrate the various conflicts by which the Lord has exercised me since that time, and by what trials he has proved me, it would make a long history.

But that I may not become tedious to my readers by a waste of words, I shall content myself with repeating briefly what I have touched upon a little before, that in considering the whole course of the life of David, it seemed to me that by his own footsteps he showed me the way, and from this I have experienced no small consolation. As that holy king was harassed by the Philistines and other foreign enemies with continual wars, while he was much more grievously afflicted by the malice and wickedness of some perfidious men amongst his own people, so I can say as to myself, that I have been assailed on all sides, and have scarcely been able to enjoy repose for a single moment, but have always had to sustain some conflict either from enemies without or within the Church. Satan has made many attempts to overthrow the fabric of this Church; and once it came to this, that I, altogether feeble and timorous as I am, was compelled to break and put a stop to his deadly assaults by putting my life in danger, and opposing my person to his blows.

Afterwards, for the space of five years, when some wicked libertines were furnished with undue influence, and also some of the common people, corrupted by the allurements and perverse discourse of such persons, desired to obtain the liberty of doing whatever they pleased, without controls I was under the necessity of fighting without ceasing to defend and maintain the discipline of the Church. To these irreligious characters. and despisers of the heavenly doctrine, it was a matter of entire indifference, although the Church should sink into ruin, provided they obtained what they sought, -- the power of acting just as they pleased. Many, too, harassed by poverty and hunger, and others impelled by insatiable ambition or avarice and a desire of dishonest gain, were become so frantic, that they chose rather, by throwing all things into confusion, to involve themselves and us in one common ruin, than to remain quiet by living peaceably and honestly.

During the whole of this lengthened period, I think that there is scarcely any of the weapons which are forged in the workshop of Satan, which has not been employed by them in order to obtain their object. And at length matters had come to such a state, that an end could be put to their machinations in no other way than cutting them off by an ignominious death; which was indeed a painful and pitiable spectacle to me. They no doubt deserved the severest punishment, but I always rather desired that they might live in prosperity, and continue safe and untouched; which would have been the case had they not been altogether incorrigible, and obstinately refused to listen to wholesome admonition. The trial of these five years was grievous and hard to bear; but I experienced not less excruciating pain from the malignity of those who ceased not to assail myself and my ministry with their envenomed calumnies. A great proportion of them, it is true, are so blinded by a passion for slander and detraction, that to their great disgracers they betray at once their impudence, while others, however crafty and cunning, cannot so cover or disguise themselves as to escape being shamefully convicted and disgraced; yet when a man has been a hundred times found innocent of a charge brought against him, and when the charge is again repeated without any cause or occasion, it is an indignity hard to bear.

Because I affirm and maintain that the world is managed and governed by the secret providence of God, a multitude of presumptuous men rise up against me, and allege that I represent God as the author of sin. This is so foolish a calumny, that it would of itself quickly come to nothing, did it not meet with persons who have tickled ears, and who take pleasure in feeding upon such discourse. But there are many whose minds are so filled with envy and spleen, or ingratitude, or malignity, that there is no falsehood, however preposterous, yea, even monstrous, which they do not receive, if it is spoken to them. Others endeavor to overthrow God's eternal purpose of predestination, by which he distinguishes between the reprobate and the elect; others take upon them to defend free will; and forthwith many throw themselves into their ranks, not so much through ignorance as by a perversity of zeal which I know not how to characterise.

If they were open and avowed enemies who brought these troubles upon me, the thing might in some way be borne. But that those who shroud themselves under the name of brethren, and not only eat Christ's sacred bread, but also administer it to others, that those, in short, who loudly boast of being preachers of the gospel, should wage such nefarious war against me, how detestable is it? In this matter I may very justly complain with David,

"Yea, mine own familiar friend, in whom I trusted, who did eat of my bread, hath lifted up his heel against me," (Psalm 41:9.)

"For it was not an enemy that reproached me; but it was thou, a man mine equal, my guide, and mine acquaintance. We took sweet counsel together, and walked unto the house of God in company," (Psalm 55:12, 13, 14.)

Others circulated ridiculous reports concerning my treasures; others, of the extravagant authority and enormous influence which they say I possess; others speak of my delicacies and magnificence. But when a man is content with scanty food and common clothing and does not require from the humblest more frugality than he shows and practices himself, shall it be said that such an one is too sumptuous, and lives in too high a style? As to the power and influence of which they envy me, I wish I could discharge this burden upon them; for they estimate my power by the multitude of affairs, and the vast weight of labors with which I am overwhelmed.

And if there are some whom I cannot persuade whilst I am alive that I am not rich, my death at length will prove it. I confess, indeed, that I am not poor; for I desire nothing more than what I have. All these are invented stories, and there is no color whatever for any one of them; but many nevertheless are very easily persuaded of their truth, and applaud them; and the reason is, because the greatest part judge that the only means of cloaking their enormities is to throw all things into disorder, and to confound black and white; and they think that the best and shortest way by which they can obtain full liberty to live with impunity just as they please, is to destroy the authority of Christ's servants. In addition to these, there are "the hypocritical mockers in feasts," of whom David complains, (Psalm 35:16;) and I mean by these not only lick-dish characters who seek a meal to fill their belly, but all those who by false reports seek to obtain the favor of the great.

Having been long accustomed to swallow such wrongs as these, I have become almost hardened; yet when the insolence of such characters increased I cannot but sometimes feel my heart wounded with bitter pangs. Nor was it enough that I should be so inhumanly treated by my neighbors. In addition to this, in a distant country towards the frozen ocean, there was raised I know not how, by the frenzy of a few, a storm which afterwards stirred up against me a vast number of persons, who are too much at leisure, and have nothing to do but by their bickering to hinder those who are laboring for the edification of the Church. [18] I am still speaking of the internal enemies of the Church--of those who, boasting mightily of the gospel of Christ, nevertheless rush against me with greater impetuosity than against the open adversaries of the Church, because I do not embrace their gross and fictitious notion concerning a carnal way of eating Christ in the sacrament; and of whom I may protest, after the example of David, "I am for peace; but when I speak, they are for war," (Psalm 120:7.)

Moreover, the cruel ingratitude of all of them is manifest in this, that they scruple not to assail both in flank and rear a man who strenuously exerts himself to maintain a cause which they have in common with him and whom therefore they ought to aid and succor. Certainly, if such persons were possessed of even a small portion of humanity, the fury of the Papists which is directed against me with such unbridled violence, would appease the most implacable animosity which they may bear towards me. But since the condition of David was such, that though he had deserved well of his own people, he was nevertheless bitterly hated by many without a cause, as he complains in Psalm 69:4, "I restored that which I took not away," it afforded me no small consolation when I was groundlessly assailed by the hatred of those who ought to have assisted and solaced me, to conform myself to the example of so great and so excellent a person.

This knowledge and experience have been of much service in enabling me to understand The Psalms, so that in my meditations upon them, I did not wander, as it were, in an unknown region. My readers, too, if I mistake not, will observe, that in unfolding the internal affections both of David and of others I discourse upon them as matters of which I have familiar experience. Moreover, since I have labored faithfully to open up this treasure for the use of all the people of God, although what I have done has not been equal to my wishes, yet the attempt which I have made deserves to be received with some measure of favor. Still I only ask that each may judge of my labors with justice and candor, according to the advantage and fruit which he shall derive from them.

Certainly, as I have said before, in reading these Commentaries, it will be clearly seen that I have not sought to please, unless in so far as I might at the same time be profitable to others. And, therefore, I have not only observed throughout a simple style of teaching, but in order to be removed the farther from all ostentation, I have also generally abstained from refuting the opinions of others, although this presented a more favorable opportunity for plausible display, and of acquiring the applause of those who shall favor my book with a perusal. I have never touched upon opposite opinions, unless where there was reason to fear, that by being silent respecting them, I might leave my readers in doubt and perplexity. At the same time, I am sensible that it would have been much more agreeable to the taste of many, had I heaped together a great mass of materials which has great show, and acquires fame for the writer; but I have felt nothing to be of more importance than to have a regard to the edification of the Church. May God, who has implanted this desire in my heart, grant by his grace that the success may correspond thereto!

Geneva, July 22, 1557.

John Calvin

The Geneva Confession (1536)

Article 1 - The Word of God

First we affirm that we desire to follow Scripture alone as rule of faith and religion, without mixing with it any other thing which might be devised by the opinion of men apart from the Word of God, and without wishing to accept for our spiritual government any other doctrine than what is conveyed to us by the same Word without addition or diminution, according to the command of our Lord.

Article 2 - One Only God

Following, then, the lines laid down in the Holy Scriptures, we acknowledge that there is one only God, whom we are both to worship and serve, and in whom we are to put all our confidence and hope: having this assurance, that in him alone is contained all wisdom, power, justice, goodness and pity. And since he is spirit, he is to be served in spirit and in truth. Therefore we think it an abomination to put our confidence or hope in any created thing, to worship anything else than him, whether angels or any other creatures, and to recognize any other Savior of our souls than him alone, whether saints or men living upon earth; and likewise to offer the service, which ought to be rendered to him, in external ceremonies or carnal observances, as if he took pleasure in such things, or to make an image to represent his divinity or any other image for adoration.

Article 3 - The Law of God Alike for All

Because there is one only Lord and Master who has dominion over our consciences, and because his will is the only principle of all justice, we confess all our life ought to be ruled in accordance with the commandments of his holy law in which is contained all perfection of justice, and that we ought to have no other rule of good and just living, nor invent other good works to supplement it than those which are there contained as follows: Exodus 20: "I am the Lord thy God, who brought thee," and so on.

Article 4 - Natural Man

We acknowledge man by nature to be blind, darkened in understanding, and full of corruption and perversity of heart, so that of himself he has no power to be able to comprehend the true knowledge of God as is proper, nor to apply himself to good works. But on the contrary, if he is left by God to what he is by nature, he is only able to live in ignorance and to be abandoned to all iniquity. Hence he has need to be illumined by God, so that he come to the right knowledge of his salvation, and thus to be redirected in his affections and reformed to the obedience of the righteousness of God.

Article 5 - Man by Himself Lost

Since man is naturally (as has been said) deprived and destitute in himself of all the light of God, and of all righteousness, we acknowledge that by himself he can only expect the wrath and malediction of God, and hence he must look outside himself for the means of his salvation.

Article 6 - Salvation in Jesus

We confess then that it is Jesus Christ who is given to us by the Father, in order that in him we should recover all of which in ourselves we are deficient. Now all that Jesus Christ has done and suffered for our redemption, we veritably hold without any doubt, as it is contained in the Creed, which is recited in the Church, that is to say: I believe in God the Father Almighty, and so on.

Article 7 - Righteousness in Jesus

Therefore we acknowledge the things which are consequently given to us by God in Jesus Christ: first, that being in our own nature enemies of God and subjects of his wrath and judgment, we are reconciled with him and received again in grace through the intercession of Jesus Christ, so that by his righteousness and guiltlessness we have remission of our sins, and by the shedding of his blood we are cleanse and purified from all our stains.

Article 8 - Regeneration in Jesus

Second, we acknowledge that by his Spirit we are regenerated into a new spiritual nature. That is to say that the evil desires of our flesh are mortified by grace, so that they rule us no longer. On the contrary, our will is rendered conformable to God's will, to follow in his way and to seek what is pleasing to him. Therefore we are by him delivered from the servitude of sin, under whose power we were of ourselves held captive, and by this deliverance we are made capable and able to do good works and not otherwise.

http://www.studylight.org/his/ad/cac/con/gen.cgi?article=8

John Calvin

Excerpts from the Reply to Cardinal Sadoleto (1539)

Translation by Henry Beveridge in John Calvin, *Tracts Relating to the Reformation*, Volume 1, pp. 25–68 (Edinburgh: Calvin Translation Society, 1844).

JOHN CALVIN TO JAMES SADOLET, CARDINAL,—HEALTH.

In the great abundance of learned men whom our age has produced, your excellent learning and distinguished eloquence having deservedly procured you a place among the few whom all, who would be thought studious of liberal arts, look up to and revere, it is with great reluctance I bring forward your name before the learned world, and address to you the following expostulation. Nor, indeed, would I have done it if I had not been dragged into this *arena* by a strong necessity. For I am not unaware how reprehensible it would be to show any eagerness in attacking a man who has deserved so well of literature, nor how odious I should become to all the learned were they to see me stimulated by passion merely, and not impelled by any just cause, turning my pen against one whom, for his admirable endowments, they, not without good reason, deem worthy of love and honor. I trust, however, that after explaining the nature of my undertaking, I shall not only be exempted from all blame, but there will not be an individual who will not admit that the cause which I have undertaken I could not on any account have abandoned without basely deserting my duty.

You lately addressed a Letter to the Senate and People of Geneva, in which you sounded their inclination as to whether, after having once shaken off the yoke of the Roman Pontiff, they would submit to have it again imposed upon them. In that letter, as it was not expedient to wound the feelings of these whose favor you required to gain your cause, you acted the part of a good pleader; for you endeavored to soothe them by abundance of flattery, in order that you might gain them over to your views. Anything of obloquy and bitterness you directed against those whose exertions had produced the revolt from that tyranny. And here (so help you) you bear down full sail upon those who, under pretence of the gospel, have by wicked arts urged on the city to what you deplore as the subversion of religion and of the Church.

I, however, Sadolet, profess to be one of those whom with so much enmity you assail and stigmatize. For though religion was already established, and the form of the Church corrected, before I was invited to Geneva, yet having not only approved by my suffrage, but studied as much as in me lay to preserve and confirm what had been done by Viret and Farel, I cannot separate my case from theirs. Still, if you had attacked me in my private character, I could easily have forgiven the attack in consideration of your learning, and in honor of letters. But when I see that my ministry, which I feel assured is supported and sanctioned by a call from God, is wounded through my side, it would be perfidy, not patience, were I here to be silent and connive.

In that Church I have held the office first of Doctor, and then of Pastor. In my own right, I maintain, that in undertaking these offices I had a legitimate vocation. How faithfully and religiously I have performed them, there is no occasion for now showing at length. Perspicuity, erudition, prudence, ability, not even industry, will I now claim for myself, but that I certainly labored with the sincerity which became me in the work of the Lord, I can in conscience appeal to Christ, my Judge, and all his angels, while all good men bear clear testimony in my favor. This ministry, therefore, when it shall appear to have been of God, (as it certainly shall appear, after the cause has been heard,) were I in silence to allow you to tear and defame, who would not condemn such silence as treachery? Every person, therefore, now sees that the strongest obligations of duty—obligations which I cannot evade—constrain me to meet your accusations, if I would not with manifest perfidy desert and betray a cause with which the Lord has entrusted me.

For though I am for the present relieved of the charge of the Church of Geneva, that circumstance ought not to prevent me from embracing it with paternal affection—God, when he gave it to me in charge, having bound me to be faithful to it forever. Now, then, when I see the worst snares laid for that Church, whose safety it has pleased the Lord to make my highest care, and grievous peril impending if not obviated, who will advise me to await the issue silent and unconcerned? How heartless, I ask, would it be to wink in idleness, and, as it were, vacillating at the destruction of one whose life you are bound vigilantly to guard and preserve? But more on this point were superfluous, since you yourself relieve me of all difficulty. For if neighborhood, and that not very near, has weighed so much with you, that while wishing to profess your love towards the Genevans, you hesitate not so bitterly to assail me and my fame, it will, undoubtedly, by the law of humanity, be conceded to me, while desiring to consult for the public good of a city entrusted to me by a far stronger obligation than that of neighborhood, to oppose your counsels and endeavors, which I cannot doubt tend to its destruction. Besides, without paying the least regard to the Genevan Church, (though assuredly I cannot cut off that charge any more than that of my own soul,) supposing I were not actuated by any zeal for it, still, when my ministry (which, knowing it to be from Christ, I am bound, if need be, to maintain with my blood) is assailed and falsely traduced, how can it he lawful for me to bear it as if I saw it not?

Wherefore, it is easy not only for impartial readers to judge, but for yourself, also, Sadolet, to consider how numerous and valid the reasons are which have compelled me to engage in this contest, if the name of contest should be given to a simple and dispassionate defense of my innocence against your calumnious accusations. I say *my* innocence, although I cannot plead for myself without, at the same time, including my colleagues, with whom all my measures in that administration were so conjoined, that whatever has been said against them I willingly take to myself. What the feelings are which I have had toward yourself in undertaking this cause, I will study to testify and prove by my mode of conducting it. For I will act so, that all may perceive that I have not only greatly the advantage of you in the goodness and justice of the cause, in conscientious rectitude, heartfelt sincerity, and candor of speech, but have also been considerably more successful in maintaining gentleness and moderation. There will doubtless be some things which will sting, or, it may be, speak daggers to your mind, but it will he my endeavor, *first*, not to allow any harsher expression to escape me than either the injustice of the accusations with which you have previously assailed me, or the necessity of the cue may extort; and, *secondly*, not to allow any degree of harshness which may amount to intemperance or passion, or which may, by its appearance of petulance, give offence to ingenuous minds.

And, first, if you had to do with any other person, he would, undoubtedly, begin with the very argument which I have determined altogether to omit. For, without much ado, he would discuss your design in writing, until he should make it plain that your object was anything but what you profess it to be. For, were it not for the great credit you formerly acquired for candor, it is somewhat suspicious that a stranger, who never before had any intercourse with the Genevans, should now suddenly profess for them so great an affection, though no previous sign of it existed, while, as one imbued, almost from a boy, with Romish arts, (such arts as am now learned in the Court of Rome, that forge of all craft and trickery,) educated, too, in the very bosom of Clement, and now, moreover, elected a cardinal, you have many things about you which, with most men, would in this matter subject you to suspicion. Then as to those insinuations by which you have supposed you might win your way into the minds of simple men, any one, not utterly stupid, might easily refute them. But things of this nature, though many will, perhaps, be disposed to believe them, I am unwilling to ascribe to you, because they seem to me unsuitable to the character of one who has been polished by all kinds of liberal learning. I will, therefore, in entering into discussion with you, give you credit for having written to the Genevans with the purest intention as becomes one of your learning, prudence, and gravity, and for having, in good faith, advised them to the course which you believed conducive to their interest and safety. But whatever may have been your intention, (I am unwilling, in this matter, to charge you with anything invidious,) when, with the bitterest and most contumelious expressions which you can employ, you distort, and endeavor utterly to destroy what the Lord delivered by our hands. I am compelled, whether I will or not, to withstand you openly. For then only do pastors edify the Church, when, besides leading docile souls to Christ, placidly, as with the hand, they are also armed to repel the machinations of those who strive to impede the work of God.

Although your Letter has many windings, its whole purport substantially is to recover the Genevans to the power of the Roman Pontiff, or to what you call the faith and obedience of the Church. But as, from the nature of the case, their feelings required to be softened, you preface with a long oration concerning the incomparable value of eternal life, You afterwards come nearer to the point, when you show that there is nothing more pestiferous to souls than a perverse worship of God; and again, that the best rule for the due worship of God is that which is prescribed by the Church, and that, therefore, there is no salvation for those who have violated the unity of the Church unless they repent. But you next contend, that separation from your fellowship is manifest revolt from the Church, and then that the gospel which the Genevans received from us is nothing but a large farrago of impious dogmas. From this you infer what kind of divine judgment awaits them if they attend not to your admonitions. But as it was of the greatest importance to your cause to throw complete discredit on our words, you labor to the utmost to fill them with sinister suspicions of the zeal which they saw us manifest for their salvation. Accordingly, you captiously allege that we had no other end in view than to gratify our avarice and ambition. Since, then, your device has been to cast some stain upon us, in order that the minds of your readers, being preoccupied with hatred, might give us no credit, I will, before proceeding to other matters, briefly reply to that objection.

Calvin responds to Sadoleto's charge that he and Farel acted from avarice and ambition

I am unwilling to speak of myself, but since you do not permit me to be altogether silent, I will say what I can consistent with modesty. Had I wished to consult my own interest, I would never have left your party. I will not, indeed, boast that there the road to preferment had been easy to me. I never desired it, and I could never bring my mind to catch at it; although I certainly know not a few of my own age who have crept up to some eminence—among them some whom I might have equaled, and others outstripped. This only I will be contented to say, it would not have been difficult for me to reach the summit of my wishes, viz., the enjoyment of literary ease with something of a free and honorable station. Therefore, I have no fear that any one not possessed of shameless effrontery will object to me, that out of the kingdom of the Pope I sought for any personal advantage which was not there ready to my hand.

And who dare make this objection to Farel? Had it been necessary for him to live by his own industry, he had already made attainments in literature, which would not have allowed him to suffer want, and he was of a more distinguished family than to require external aid. As to those of us to whom you pointed as with the finger, it seemed proper for us to reply in our own name. But since you seem to throw out indirect insinuations against all who in the present day are united with us in sustaining the same cause, I would have you understand, that not one can he mentioned for whom I cannot give you a better answer than for Farel and myself. Some of our Reformers are known to you by fame. As to them, I appeal to your own conscience. Think you it was hunger which drove them away from you, and made them in despair flee to that change as a means of bettering their fortunes? But not to go over a long catalogue, this I say, that of those who first engaged in this cause, there was none who with you might not have been in better place and fortune than require on such grounds to look out for some new plan of life.

But come and consider with me for a little what the honors and powers are which we have gained. All our bearers will bear us witness that we did not covet or aspire to any other riches or dignities than those which fell to our lot. Since in all our words and deeds they not only perceived no trace of the ambition with which you charge us; but, on the contrary, saw clear evidence of our abhorring it with our whole heart, you cannot hope that by one little word their minds are to be so fascinated as to credit a futile slander in opposition to the many certain proofs with which we furnished them. And to appeal to facts rather than words, the power of the sword, and other parts of civil jurisdiction, which bishops and priests, under the semblance of immunity, had wrested from the magistrate and claimed for themselves, have not we restored to the magistrate? All their usurped instruments of tyranny and ambition have not we detested, and struggled to abolish? If there was any hope of rising, why did we not craftily dissemble, so that those powers might have passed to us along with the office of governing the Church? And why did we make such exertion to overturn the whole of that dominion, or rather butchery, which they exercised upon souls, without any sanction from the Word of God? How did we not consider that it was just so much lost to ourselves? In regard to ecclesiastical revenues, they are still in a great measure swallowed up by these whirlpools. But if there was a hope that they will one day he deprived of them, (as at length they certainly must,) why did we not devise a way by which they might come to us? But when with clear voice we denounced as a thief any bishop who, out of ecclesiastical revenues, appropriated more to his own use than was necessary for a frugal and sober subsistence; when we protested that the Church was exposed to a deadly poison, so long as pastors were loaded with an affluence under which they themselves might ultimately sink, when we declared it inexpedient that these revenues should fall into their possession; finally, when we counseled that as much should be distributed to ministers as might suffice for a frugality befitting their order, not superabound for luxury, and that the rest should be dispensed according to the practice of the ancient Church; when we showed that men of weight ought to be elected to manage these revenues, under an obligation to account annually to the Church and the magistracy, was this to entrap any of these for ourselves, or was it not rather voluntarily to shake ourselves free of them? All these things, indeed, demonstrate not what we are, but what we wished to be. But if these things are so plainly and generally known, that not one iota can be denied, with what face can you proceed to upbraid us with aspiring to extraordinary wealth and power, and this especially in the presence of men to whom none of those things are unknown? The monstrous lies which persons of your order spread against us among their own followers we are not surprised at, (for no man is present who can either reprimand or venture to refute them,) but where men have been eye-witnesses of all the things which we have above mentioned, to try to persuade them of the contrary is the part of a man of little discretion, and strongly derogates from Sadoleto's reputation for learning, prudence, and gravity. But if you think that our intention must be judged by the result, it will be found that the only thing we aimed at was, that the kingdom of Christ might be promoted by our poverty and insignificance. So far are we from having abused His sacred name to purposes of ambition.

I pass in silence many other invectives which you thunder out against us, (open mouthed,) as it is said. You call us crafty men, enemies of Christian unity and peace, innovators on things ancient and well established, seditious, alike pestiferous to souls, and destructive both publicly and privately to society at large. Had you wished to escape rebuke, you either ought not, for the purpose of exciting prejudice, to have attributed to us a magniloquent tongue, or you ought to have kept your own magniloquence considerably more under check. I am unwilling, however, to dwell on each of these points; only I would have you to consider how unbecoming, not to say illiberal, it is, thus in many words to accuse the innocent of things, which by one word can be instantly refuted; although to inflict injury on man is a small matter, when compared with the indignity of that contumely, which, when you come to the question, you offer to Christ and his word. When the Genevans, instructed by our preaching, escaped from the gulf of error in which they were immersed, and betook themselves to a purer teaching of the gospel, you call it defection from the truth of God; when they threw off the tyranny of the Roman Pontiff, in order that they might establish among themselves a better form of Church, you call it a desertion from the Church. Come, then, and let us discuss both points in their order.

[. . .]

I have also no difficulty in conceding to you, that there is nothing more perilous to our salvation than a preposterous and perverse worship of God. The primary rudiments, by which we are wont to train to piety those whom we wish to gain as disciples to Christ, are these; viz., not to frame any new worship of God for themselves at random, and after their own pleasure, but to know that the only legitimate worship is that which he himself approved from the beginning. For we maintain, what the sacred oracle declared, that obedience is more excellent than any sacrifice (1 Sam. xv. 22.) In short, we train them, by every means, to be contented with the one rule of worship which they have received from his mouth, and bid adieu to all fictitious worship.

Which of the two parties retains true worship?

Therefore, Sadolet, when you uttered this voluntary confession, you laid the foundation of my defense. For if you admit it to be a fearful destruction to the soul, when, by false opinions, divine truth is turned into a lie, it now only remains for us to inquire which of the two parties retains that worship of God which is alone legitimate. In order that you may claim it for your party, you assume that the most certain rule of worship is that which is prescribed by the Church, although, as if we here opposed you, you bring the matter under consideration, in the manner which is usually observed in regard to doubtful questions. But, Sadolet, as I see you toiling in vain, I will relieve you from all trouble on this head. You are mistaken in supposing that we desire to head away the people from that method of worshipping God which the Catholic Church always observed. You either labor under a delusion as to the term Church, or, at least, knowingly and willingly give it a gloss. I will immediately show the latter to be the case, though it may also be that you are somewhat in error. First, in defining the term, you omit what would have helped you, in no small degree, to the right understanding of it. When you describe it as that which in all parts, as well as at the present time, in every region of the earth, being united and consenting in Christ, has been always and everywhere directed by the one Spirit of Christ, what comes of the Word of the Lord, that clearest of all marks, and which the Lord himself, in pointing out the Church, so often recommends to us? For seeing how dangerous it would be to boast of the Spirit without the Word, he declared that the Church is indeed governed by the Holy Spirit, but in order that that government might not be vague and unstable, He annexed it to the Word. For this reason Christ exclaims, that those who are of God hear the word of God— that his sheep are those which recognize his voice as that of their Shepherd, and any other voice as that of a stranger (John x. 27.) For this reason the Spirit, by the mouth of Paul, declares (Eph. ii. 20,) that the Church is built upon the foundation of the Apostles and Prophets. Also, that the Church is made holy to the Lord, by the washing of water in the word of life. The same thing is declared still more clearly by the mouth of Peter, when he teaches that people are regenerated to God by that incorruptible seed, (1 Pet. i. 23.) In short, why is the preaching of the gospel so often styled the kingdom of God, but because it is the scepter by which the heavenly King rules his people?

Nor will you find this in the Apostolic writings only, but whenever the Prophets foretell the renewal of the Church, or its extension over the whole globe, they always assign the first place to the Word. For they tell that from Jerusalem will issue forth living waters, which being divided into four rivers, will inundate the whole earth, (Zech. xiv. 8.) And what these living waters are, they themselves explain when they say, "That the law will come forth from Zion, and the word of the Lord from Jerusalem," (Is. ii. 3.) Well, then, does Chrysostom admonish us to reject all who, under the pretence of the Spirit, lead us away from the simple doctrine of the gospel—the Spirit having been promised not to reveal a new doctrine, but to impress the truth of the gospel on our minds. And we, in fact, experience in the present day how necessary the admonition was. We are assailed by two sects, which seem to differ most widely from each other. For what similitude is there in appearance between the Pope and the Anabaptists? And yet, that you may see that Satan never transforms himself so cunningly, as not in some measure to betray himself, the principal weapon with which they both assail us is the same. For when they boast extravagantly of the Spirit, the tendency certainly is to sink and bury the Word of God, that they may make room for their own falsehoods. And you, Sadolet, by stumbling on the very threshold, have paid the penalty of that affront which you offered to the Holy Spirit, when you separated him from the Word. For, as if those who seek the way of God were standing where two ways meet, and destitute of any certain sign, you are forced to introduce them as hesitating whether it be more expedient to follow the authority of the Church, or to listen to those whom you call the inventors of new dogmas. Had you known, or been unwilling to disguise the fact, that the Spirit goes before the Church, to enlighten her in understanding the Word, while the Word itself is like the Lydian Stone, by which she tests all doctrines, would you have taken refuge in that most perplexing and thorny question? Learn, then, by your own experience, that it is no less unreasonable to boast of the Spirit without the Word, than it would be absurd to bring forward the Word itself without the Spirit. Now, if you can bear to receive a truer definition of the Church than your own, say, in future, that it is the society of all the saints, a society which, spread over the whole world, and existing in all ages, yet bound together by the one doctrine, and the one Spirit of Christ, cultivates and observes unity of faith and brotherly concord. With this Church we deny that we have any disagreement. Nay, rather, as we revere her as our mother, so we desire to remain in her bosom.

[. . .]

Doctrine, Discipline, Sacraments and Ceremonies

Since there are three things on which the safety of the Church is founded, viz., doctrine, discipline, and the sacraments, and to these a fourth is added, viz., ceremonies, by which to exercise the people in offices of piety, in order that we may be most sparing of the honor of your Church, by which of these things would you have us to judge her? The truth of Prophetical and Evangelical doctrine, on which the Church ought to be founded, has not only in a great measure perished in your Church, but is violently driven away by fire and sword. Will you obtrude upon me, for the Church, a body which furiously persecutes everything sanctioned by our religion, both as delivered by the oracles of God, and embodied in the writings of holy Fathers, and approved by ancient Councils? Where, pray, exist among you any vestiges of that true and holy discipline, which the ancient bishops exercised in the Church? Have you not scorned all their institutions? Have you not trampled all the Canons under foot? Then, your nefarious profanation of the sacraments I cannot think of without the utmost horror.

Of ceremonies, indeed, you have more than enough, but, for the most part, so childish in their import, and vitiated by innumerable forms of superstition, as to be utterly unavailing for the preservation of the Church. None of these things, you must be aware, is exaggerated by me in a captious spirit. They all appear so openly, that they may be pointed out with the finger wherever there are eyes to behold them. Now, if you please, test us in the same way. You will, assuredly, fall far short of making the charges which you have brought against us.

In the Sacraments, all we have attempted is to restore the native purity from which they had degenerated, and so enable them to resume their dignity. Ceremonies we have in a great measure abolished, but we were compelled to do so, partly because by their multitude they had degenerated into a kind of Judaism, partly because they had filled the minds of the people with superstition, and could not possibly remain without doing the greatest injury to the piety which it was their office to promote. Still we have retained those which seemed sufficient for the circumstances of the times.

That our discipline is not such as the ancient Church professed we do not deny. But with what fairness is a charge of subverting discipline brought against us by those who themselves have utterly abolished it, and in our attempts to re-instate it in its rights have hitherto opposed us? As to our doctrine, we hesitate not to appeal to the ancient Church. And since, for the sake of example, you have touched on certain heads, as to which you thought you had some ground for accusing us, I will briefly show how unfairly and falsely you allege that these are things which have been devised by us against the opinion of the Church.

Before descending to particulars, however, I have already cautioned you, and would have you again and again consider with what reason you can charge it upon our people, as a fault, that they have studied to explain the Scriptures. For you are aware, that by this study they have thrown such light on the Word of God, that, in this respect, even envy herself is ashamed to defraud them of all praise. You are just as uncandid when you aver that we have seduced the people by thorny and subtle questions, and so enticed them by that philosophy of which Paul bids Christians beware. What? Do you remember what kind of time it was when our Reformers appeared, and what kind of doctrine candidates for the ministry learned in the schools? You yourself know that it was mere sophistry, and sophistry so twisted, involved, tortuous, and puzzling, that scholastic theology might well be described as a species of secret magic. The denser the darkness in which any one shrouded a subject, the more he puzzled himself and others with preposterous riddles, the greater his fame for acumen and learning. And when those who had been formed in that forge wished to carry the fruit of their learning to the people, with what skill, I ask, did they edify the Church?

Not to go over every point, what sermons in Europe then exhibited that simplicity with which Paul wishes a Christian people to be always occupied? Nay, what one sermon was there from which old wives might not carry off more whimsies than they could devise at their own fireside in a month? For, as sermons were then usually divided, the first half was devoted to those misty questions of the schools which might astonish the rude populace, while the second contained sweet stories, or not unamusing speculations, by which the hearers might be kept on the alert. Only a few expressions were thrown in from the Word of God, that by their majesty they might procure credit for these frivolities. But as soon as our Reformers raised the standard, all these absurdities, in one moment, disappeared from amongst us. Your preachers, again, partly profited by our books, and partly compelled by shame and the general murmur, conformed to our example, though they still, with open throat, exhale the old absurdity. Hence, anyone who compares our method of procedure with the old method, or with that which is still in repute among you, will perceive that you have done us no small injustice. But had you continued your quotation from Paul a little farther, any boy would easily have perceived that the charge which you bring against us is undoubtedly applicable to yourselves. For Paul there interprets "vain philosophy" (Col. ii. 8) to mean that which preys upon pious souls, by means of the constitutions of men, and the elements of this world: and by these you have ruined the Church.

Even you yourself afterwards acquit us by your own testimony; for among those of our doctrines which you have thought proper to assail, you do not adduce one, the knowledge of which is not essentially necessary for the edification of the Church.

Justification by faith

You, in the first place, touch upon justification by faith, the first and keenest subject of controversy between us. Is this a knotty and useless question? Wherever the knowledge of it is taken away, the glory of Christ is extinguished, religion abolished, the Church destroyed, and the hope of salvation utterly overthrown. That doctrine, then, though of the highest moment, we maintain that you have nefariously effaced from the memory of men. Our books are filled with convincing proofs of this fact, and the gross ignorance of this doctrine, which even still continues in all your churches, declares that our complaint is by no means ill founded. But you very maliciously stir up prejudice against us, alleging that, by attributing everything to faith, we leave no room for works.

I will not now enter upon a full discussion, which would require a large volume; but if you would look into the Catechism which I myself drew up for the Genevans, when I held the office of Pastor among them, three words would silence you. Here, however, I will briefly explain to you how we speak on this subject.

First, We bid a man begin by examining himself, and this not in a superficial and perfunctory manner, but to sift his conscience before the tribunal of God, and when sufficiently convinced of his iniquity, to reflect on the strictness of the sentence pronounced upon all sinners. Thus confounded and amazed at his misery, he is prostrated and humbled before God; and, casting away all self-confidence, groans as if given up to final perdition. Then we show that the only haven of safety is in the mercy of God, as manifested in Christ, in whom every part of our salvation is complete. As all mankind are, in the sight of God, lost sinners, we hold that Christ is their only righteousness, since, by his obedience, he has wiped off our transgressions; by his sacrifice, appeased the divine anger; by his blood, washed away our stains; by his cross, borne our curse; and by his death, made satisfaction for us. We maintain that in this way man is reconciled in Christ to God the Father, by no merit of his own, by no value of works, but by gratuitous mercy. When we embrace Christ by faith, and come, as it were, into communion with him, this we term, after the manner of Scripture, the righteousness of faith.

What have you here, Sadolet, to bite or carp at? Is it that we leave no room for works? Assuredly we do deny that, in justifying a man, they are worth one single straw. For Scripture everywhere cries aloud, that all are lost; and every mans's own conscience bitterly accuses him. The same Scripture teaches, that no hope is left but in the mere goodness of God, by which sin is pardoned, and righteousness imputed to us. It declares both to be gratuitous, and finally concludes that a man is justified without works, (Rom. iv. 7.) But what notion, you ask, does the very term Righteousness suggest to us, if respect is not paid to good works? I answer, if you would attend to the true meaning of the term *justifying* in Scripture, you would have no difficulty. For it does not refer to a man's own righteousness, but to the mercy of God, which, contrary to the sinner's deserts, accepts of a righteousness for him, and that by not imputing his unrighteousness. Our righteousness, I say, is that which is described by Paul, (2 Cor. v. 19,) that God bath reconciled us to himself in Jesus Christ. The mode is afterwards subjoined—by not imputing sin. He demonstrates that it is by faith only we become partakers of that blessing, when he says that the ministry of reconciliation is contained in the gospel. But faith, you say, is a general term, and has a larger signification. I answer, that Paul, whenever he attributes to it the power of justifying, at the same time restricts it to a gratuitous promise of the divine favor, and keeps it far removed from all respect to works. Hence his familiar inference—if by faith, then not by works. On the other hand—if by works, then not by faith.

But, it seems, injury is done to Christ, if, under the pretence of his grace, good works are repudiated; he having come to prepare a people acceptable to God, zealous of good works, while, to the same effect, are many similar passages which prove that Christ came in order that we, doing good works, might, through him, be accepted by God. This calumny, which our opponents have ever in their mouths, viz., that we take away the desire of well-doing from the Christian life by recommending gratuitous righteousness, is too frivolous to give us much concern. We deny that good works have any share in justification, but we claim full authority for them in the lives of the righteous. For, if he who has obtained justification possesses Christ, and, at the same time, Christ never is where his Spirit in not, it is obvious that gratuitous righteousness is necessarily connected with regeneration. Therefore, if you would duly understand how inseparable faith and works are, look to Christ, who, as the Apostle teaches, (1 Cor. i. 30,) has been given to us for justification and for sanctification. Wherever, therefore, that righteousness of faith, which we maintain to be gratuitous, is, there too Christ is, and where Christ is, there too is the Spirit of holiness, who regenerates the soul to newness of life. On the contrary, where zeal for integrity and holiness is not in vigor, there neither is the Spirit of Christ nor Christ himself; and wherever Christ is not, there in no righteousness, nay, there is no faith; for faith cannot apprehend Christ for righteousness without the Spirit of sanctification.

Since, therefore, according to us, Christ regenerates to a blessed life those whom he justifies, and after rescuing them from the dominion of sin, hands them over to the dominion of righteousness, transforms them into the image of God, and so trains them by his Spirit into obedience to his will, there is no ground to complain that, by our doctrine, lust is left with loosened reins. The passages which you adduce have not a meaning at variance with our doctrine. But if you will pervert them in assailing gratuitous justification, see how unskilfully you argue. Paul elsewhere says (Eph. i. 4) that we were chosen in Christ, before the creation of the world, to be holy and unblameable in the sight of God through love. Who will venture thence to infer, either that election is not gratuitous, or that our love is its cause? Nay, rather, as the end of gratuitous election, so also that of gratuitous justification is, that we may lead pure and unpolluted lives before God. For the saying of Paul is true, (1 Thess. iv. 7,) we have not been called to impurity, but to holiness. This, meanwhile, we constantly maintain, that man is not only justified freely once for all, without any merit of works, but that on this gratuitous justification the salvation of man perpetually depends. Nor is it possible that any work of man can he accepted by God unless it be gratuitously approved. Wherefore, I was amazed when I read your assertion, that love is the first and chief cause of our salvation. O, Sadolet, who could ever have expected such a saying from you? Undoubtedly the very blind, while in darkness, feel the mercy of God too surely to dare to claim for their love the first cause of their salvation, while those who have merely one spark of divine light feel that their salvation consists in nothing else than their being adopted by God. For eternal salvation is the inheritance of the heavenly Father, and has been prepared solely for his children. Moreover, who can assign any other cause of our adoption than that which is uniformly announced in Scripture, viz., that we did not first love him, but were spontaneously received by him into favor and affection?

Your ignorance of this doctrine leads you on to the error of teaching that sins are expiated by penances and satisfactions. Where, then, will be that one expiatory victim, from which, if we depart, there remains, as Scripture testifies, no more sacrifice for sin? Search through all the divine oracles which we possess; if the blood of Christ alone is uniformly act forth as purchasing satisfaction, reconciliation, and ablution, how dare you presume to transfer so great an honor to your works? Nor have you any ground for ascribing this blasphemy to the Church of God. The ancient Church, I admit, had its satisfactions, not those, however, by which sinners might atone to God and ransom themselves from guilt, but by which they might prove that the repentance which they professed was not feigned, and efface the remembrance of that scandal which their sin had occasioned. For satisfactions were not regularly prescribed to all and sundry, but to those only who had fallen into some heinous wickedness.

[. . .]

 "As to the charge of forsaking the Church, which they were wont to bring against me, there is nothing of which my conscience accuses me, unless, indeed, he is to he considered a deserter, who, seeing the soldiers routed and scattered, and abandoning the ranks, raises the leaders standard, and recalls them to their posts. For thus, O Lord, were all thy servants dispersed, so that they could not, by any possibility, hear the command, but had almost forgotten their leader, and their service, and their military oath. In order to bring them together, when thus scattered, I raised not a foreign standard, but that noble banner of thine whom we must follow, if we would be classed among thy people.

[. . .]

Now, Sadolet, if you please, compare this pleading with that which you have put into the mouth of your plebeian. It will be strange if you hesitate which of the two you ought to prefer. For the safety of that man hangs by a thread whose defense turns wholly on this—that he has constantly adhered to the religion handed down to him from his forefathers. At this rate, Jews, and Turks, and Saracens, would escape the judgment of God. Away, then, with this vain quibbling at a tribunal which will be erected not to approve the authority of man, but to condemn all flesh of vanity and falsehood, and vindicate the truth of God only.

[. . .]

While, throughout your Letter, you treat us without mercy, towards its conclusion, you pour out the venom of your bitterness upon us with open mouth. But though your invectives by no means hurt us, and have already been partly answered, I would yet ask, what could make you think of accusing us of avarice? Think you our Reformers were so dull as not to perceive from the very outset, that they were entering on a course most adverse to gain and lucre? And, when they charged you with greediness, did they not see that they were necessarily binding themselves to temperance and frugality, if they were not to become ridiculous even to children? When they showed that the method of correcting that greediness was to disburden pastors of their excessive wealth, in order that they might be more at liberty to care for the Church, did they not spontaneously shut against themselves the avenue to wealth? For what riches now remained to which they might aspire? What! Would not the shortest road to riches and honors have been to have transacted with you at the very first, on the terms which were offered? How much would your Pontiff then have paid to many for their silence? How much would he pay for it, even at the present day? If they are actuated in the least degree by avarice, why do they cut off all hope of improving their fortune, and prefer to be thus perpetually wretched, rather than enrich themselves without difficulty, and in a twinkling? But ambition, forsooth, withholds them! What ground you had for other insinuation I see not, since those who first engaged in this cause could expect nothing else than to be spurned by the whole world, and those who afterwards adhered to it exposed themselves knowingly and willingly to endless insults and reviling from every quarter. But where is this fraud and inward malice? No suspicion of such things cleaves to us. Talk of them rather in your sacred Consistory, where they are in operation every day.

As I hasten to a conclusion, I am compelled to pass by your calumny, that, leaning entirely to our own judgment, we find not in the whole Church one individual to whom we think deference is due. That it is a calumny, I have already sufficiently demonstrated. For, although we hold that the Word of God alone lies beyond the sphere of our judgment, and that Fathers and Councils are of authority only in so far as they accord with the rule of the Word, we still give to Councils and Fathers such rank and honor as it is meet for them to hold, under Christ.

But the most serious charge of all is, that we have attempted to dismember the Spouse of Christ. Were that true, both you and the whole world might well regard us as desperate. But I will not admit the charge, unless you can make out that the Spouse of Christ is dismembered by those who desire to present her as a chaste virgin to Christ,—who are animated by a degree of holy zeal to preserve her spotless for Christ,—who, seeing her polluted by base seducers, recall her to conjugal fidelity,—who unhesitatingly wage war against all the adulterers whom they detect laying snares for her chastity. And what but this have we done? Had not your faction of a Church attempted nay, violated her chastity, by strange doctrines? Had she not been violently prostituted by your numberless superstitions? Had she not been defiled by that vilest species of adultery, the worship of images? And because, forsooth, we did not suffer you so to insult the sacred chamber of Christ, we are said to have lacerated his Spouse! But I tell you that that laceration, of which you falsely accuse us, is witnessed not obscurely among yourselves; a laceration not only of the Church, but of Christ himself, who is there beheld miserably mangled. How can the Church adhere to her Spouse, while she has him not in safety? For where is the safety of Christ, while the glory of his justice, and holiness, and wisdom, is transferred elsewhere?

But it seems, before we kindled the strife, all was tranquility and perfect peace! True! among pastors, and also among the common people, stupor and sloth had caused, that there were almost no controversies respecting religion. But in the schools, how lustily did sophists brawl? You cannot, therefore, take credit for a tranquil kingdom, when there was tranquility for no other reason than because Christ was silent. I admit, that, on the revival of the gospel, great disputes arose, where all was quietness before. But that is unjustly imputed to our Reformers, who, during the whole course of their proceedings, desired nothing wore than that religion being revived, the Churches, which discord had scattered and dispersed, might be gathered together into true unity. And not to go back upon old transactions, what sacrifices did they, on a late occasion, decline to make, merely that they might procure peace to the Churches? But all their efforts are rendered vain by your opposition. For, while they desire peace, that along with it the kingdom of Christ may flourish, and you, on the other hand, think that all which is gained to Christ is lost to you, it is not strange that you strenuously resist. And you have arts by which you can in one day overturn all that they accomplish for the glory of Christ in many months. I will not overwhelm you with words, because one word will make the matter clear. Our Reformers offered to render an account of their doctrine. If overcome in argument, they decline not to submit. To whom, then, is it owing that the Church enjoys not perfect peace, and the light of truth? Go now, and charge us as seditious, in not permitting the Church to be quiet!

But, (that you might not omit anything which might tend to prejudice our cause,) since, during these few years many sects have sprung up, you, with your usual candor, lay the blame upon us. See with what fairness, or even with what plausibility! If we deserve hatred on that account, the Christian name also must, in times of old, have deserved it from the ungodly. Therefore, either cease to molest us on this subject, or openly declare that the Christian religion, which begets so many tumults in the world, ought to be banished from the memory of man! It ought not to hurt our cause in the least, that Satan has tried in all ways to impede the work of Christ. It were more to the point to inquire which party has devotedly opposed itself to all the sects which have arisen. It is plain, that while you were idle and fast asleep, we alone bore all the brunt.

The Lord grant, Sadolet, that you and all your party may at length perceive, that the only true bond of Ecclesiastical unity would exist if Christ the Lord, who hath reconciled us to God the Father, were to gather us out of our present dispersion into the fellowship of his body, that so, through his one Word and Spirit, we might join together with one heart and one soul.

Basle, September 1, 1539.

John Knox

The History of the Reformation of Scotland

Glasgow: Blackie, Fullarton, & Co. and Edinburgh: A. Fullarton & Co., 1831

The reaction to his first sermon, preached on the theme that the Roman Church is a harlot, preached in St. Andrews, 1547

. . . Of this sermon, which was the first that ever John Knox made in public, were there divers bruits: Some said, others hewed the branches of papistry, but he striketh at the root, to destroy the whole. Others said, if the doctors, and *magistri nostri,* defend not now the pope and his authority, which in their own presence is so manifestly impugned, "The devil have my part of him, and his laws both." Others said, "Mr George Wishart spake never so plainly, and yet he was burnt, even so will he be." In the end, others said, "The tyranny of the cardinal made not his cause the better, neither yet the suffering of God's servant made his cause the worse. And therefore we would counsel you and them, to provide better defences than fire and sword, for it may be that else ye shall be disappointed; men now have other eyes than they had then." This answer gave the laird of Niddry, a man fervent and upright in religion. The bastard bishop, who was not yet execrated, consecrated they call it, wrote to the subprior of St Andrews, who, *sede vacante,* was vicar-general, "That he wondered that he suffered such heretical and schismatical doctrine to be taught, and not to oppose himself to the same." Upon this rebuke, was a convention of grey friars and black fiends appointed, with the said subprior dean John Winram, in St Leonard's Yards, whereunto was first called John Rough, and certain articles read unto him; and thereafter was John Knox called for. The cause of their convention, and why that they were called, is explained; and the articles were read, which were these :

I. No mortal can be the head of the church.

II. The pope is an antichrist, and so is no member of Christ's mystical body.

III. Man may neither make nor devise a religion that is acceptable to God, but roan is bound to observe and keep the religion that from God is received, without chopping or changing thereof.

IV. The sacraments of the New Testament, ought to be ministered as they were instituted by Christ Jesus, and practised by his apostles ; nothing ought to be added unto them, nothing ought to be diminished from them.

V. The mass is abominable idolatry, blasphemous to the death of Christ, and a profanation of the Lord's Supper.

VI. There is no purgatory, in the which the souls of men can neither be pained or purged after this life; but heaven rests to the faithful, and hell to the reprobate and unfaithful.

VII. Praying for the dead is vain, and to the dead is idolatry.

VIII. There are no bishops, except they preach even by themselves, without any substitute.

IX The teinds by God's law do not appertain of necessity to the kirkmen.

"The strangeness," said the subprior, "of these articles which are gathered forth of your doctrine have moved us to call for you, to hear your own answers." John Knox said, "I for my part praise my God, that I see so honourable, and apparently so modest and quiet an auditory ; but because it is long since that I have heard, that ye are one that is not ignorant of the truth, I must crave of you, in the name of God, yea, and I appeal your conscience before that supreme Judge, that if ye think any article there expressed, contrary unto the truth of God, that ye oppose yourself plainly unto it, and suffer not the people therewith to be deceived; but, and if in your conscience ye know the doctrine to be true, then will I crave your patrocinie [adherence] thereto ; that by your authority the people may be moved the rather to believe the truth, whereof many doubt by reason of our youth." The subprior answered, "I came not here as a judge, but only familiarly to talk, and, therefore, I will neither allow nor yet condemn ; but if ye list, I will reason. Why may not the kirk," said he, "for good causes devise ceremonies to decore the sacraments, and other God's service?"

John Knox—"Because the kirk ought to do nothing, but in faith, and ought not to go before, but is bound to follow the voice of the true pastor."

The Subprior.—"It is in faith that the ceremonies are commanded, and they have proper signification to help our faith, as the hards in baptism signify the roughness of the law, and the oil the softness of God's mercy ; and likewise every one of the ceremonies has a godly signification ; and therefore they both proceed from faith, and are done to faith."

John Knox.—"It is not enough that a man invent a ceremony, and then give a signification according to his pleasure. For so might the ceremonies of the gentiles, and this day the ceremonies of Mahomet be maintained. But if any thing proceed from faith, it must have the word of God for the assurance ; for ye are not ignorant, 'That faith comes by hearing, and hearing by the word of God.' Now, if ye will prove that your ceremonies proceed from faith, and do please God, ye must prove that God in express words has commanded them ; or else shall ye never prove that they proceed from faith, nor yet that they please God ; but that they are sin, and so displease him, according to the words of the apostle, 'Whatsoever is not of faith is sin.' "

The Subprior.—"Will ye bind us so strait, that we may do nothing without the express word of God? What, and I ask a drink ? think ye that I sin? and yet have I not God's word for me?" This answer gave be, as might appear, to shift over the argument upon the friar, as that he did.

John Knox.—"I would ye should not jest in so grave a matter, neither would I that ye should begin to elude the truth with sophistry ; and if ye do, I will defend me the best that I can. And, first, to your drinking, I say, that if ye either eat or drink without assurance of God's word, that in so doing ye displease God, and ye sin in your very eating and drinking ; for says not the apostle, speaking even of meat and drink, 'That the creatures are sanctified unto man, even by the word and by prayer.' The word is this, 'All things are clean to the clean.' Now, let me hear this much of your ceremonies, and I shall give you the argument; but I wonder that ye compare things profane and holy things so indiscreetly together; the question was not, nor is not of meat or drink, whereinto the kingdom of heaven consists not; but the question is of God's true worshipping-, without the which we can have no society with God. And, here it is doubted, if we may take the same freedom in the using of Christ's sacraments, that we may do in eating and drinking. One meat I may eat, another I may refuse, and that without scruple of conscience. I may change one with another, even as oft as I please. Whether may we do the same in matters of religion? May we cast away what we please, and retain what we please? If I be well remembered, Moses, in the name of God, says to the people of Israel, 'All that the Lord thy God commands thee to do, that do thou to the Lord thy God, add nothing to it, diminish nothing from it.' By this rule, think I, that the kirk of Christ will measure God's religion, and not by that which seemeth good in their own eyes."

The Subprior.—"Forgive me, I speak it but in jest, and I was dry. And now, father," said he to the friar, "follow the argument, ye have heard what I said, and what is answered to me again."

Arbuckle Grayfriar.—"I shall prove plainly that ceremonies are ordained by God."

John Knox.—"Such as God has ordained we allow, and with reverence we use them ; but the question is of those that God has not ordained, such as in baptism, are spittle, salt, candle, cap— except it be to keep the bairn from cold—hards, oil, and the rest of the papistical inventions."

Arbuckle.—"I will even prove these that ye damn to be ordained of God."

John Knox.—"The proof thereof I would gladly hear."

Arbuckle.—"Says not St Paul, 'that, any other foundation than Jesus Christ, may no man lay.' But upon this foundation some build gold, silver, and precious stones, some, hay, stubble, and wood. The gold, silver, and precious stones are the ceremonies of the church, which do abide the fire, and consume not away," &c. This place of scripture is most plain, says the foolish fiend.

John Knox.—"I praise my God, through Jesus Christ, for I find his promise sure, true, and stable. Christ Jesus bids us 'Not fear, when we shall be called before men, to give confession of his truth;' for he promises 'That it shall be given unto us in that hour what we shall speak. 'If I had sought the whole scriptures, I could not have produced a place more proper for my purpose, nor more potent to confound you. Now to your argument: the ceremonies of the kirk, say ye, are gold, silver, and precious stones, because they are able to abide the fire; but I would learn of you, what fire it is which your ceremonies does abide? And in the meantime, till that ye be advised to answer, I will show my mind, and make an argument against yours upon the same text. And, first, I say, that I have heard this text adduced for a proof of purgatory; but for defence of ceremonies I never heard, nor yet read it. But omitting whether ye understand the mind of the apostle or not, I make my argument, and say, that which may abide the fire, may abide the word of God; but your ceremonies may not abide the word of God. Ergo, they may not abide the fire; and if they may not abide the fire, then are they not gold, silver, nor precious stones. Now, if ye find any ambiguity in this term, fire, which I interpret to be the word, find ye me another tire, by the which things built upon Christ Jesus should be tried than God and his word, which both in the scriptures are called fire, and I shall correct my argument."

Arbuckle.—"I stand not thereupon; but I deny your minor premise, *to wit,* that our ceremonies may not abide the trial of God's word."

John Knox—"I prove that abides not the trial of God's word, which God's word condemneth ; but God's word condemns your ceremonies: therefore, they do not abide the trial thereof; but as a thief abideth the trial of the inquest, and thereby is condemned to be hanged; even so may your ceremonies abide the trial of God's word, but not else. And now, in few words to make plain that wherein ye may seem to doubt, *to wit,* that God's word damneth your ceremonies, it is evident, for the plain and strait commandment of God is, "Not that thing which appeareth good in thy eyes, shall thou do to the Lord thy God, but that the Lord thy God has commanded thee, that do you; add nothing to it, diminish nothing from it.' Now, unless ye be able to prove, that God has commanded your ceremonies, this his former commandment will damn both you and them."

The friar, somewhat abashed what first to answer, while he wanders about in the mist he falls in a foul mire ; for, alleging that we may not be so bound to the word, he affirmed, "That the apostles had not received the Holy Ghost when they did write their epistles; but after they received him, and then they did ordain the ceremonies." Few would have thought, that so learned a man would have given so foolish an answer; and yet it is even as true as he bore a grey cowl.

John Knox hearing the answer, started and said, "If that be true, I have long been in an error, and I think I shall die therein still."

The subprior said to him, "Father, what say ye? God forbid that ye affirm that, for then farewell the ground of our faith."

The friar, astonished, made the best shift that he could to correct his fault, but it would not be: John Knox brought him oft again to the ground of the argument, but he would never answer directly, but ever fled to the authority of the church; whereto the said John answered, oftener than once, "That the spouse of Christ had neither power nor authority against the word of God."

Then said the friar, "If so be, ye will leave us no kirk."

"Indeed," said the other, "in David I read, that there is a church of the malignante, for he says, ' *Odi ecclesiam malignantium;'* that church ye may have without the word, and doing many things directly fighting against the word of God; of that church if ye will be, I cannot impede you ; but as for me, I will be of none other church, except of that which hath Christ Jesus to be their pastor, which hears his voice, and will not hear a stranger."

In this disputation many other things were merrily scoffed over; for the friar after his fall could speak nothing to any purpose. For purgatory he had no better proof but the authority of Virgil, in the sixth of his Æneid; and the pains thereof to him was an evil wife. How John Knox answered that and many other things, himself did witness, in a treatise that he did write in the galleys, containing the sum of his doctrine, and the confession of his faith, and sent it to his familiars in Scotland, with his exhortation, that they should continue in the truth which they had professed, notwithstanding any worldly adversity that might ensue thereof. This much of that disputation have we inserted here, to the intent that men may see how that Satan ever travails to obscure the light; and yet how that God, by his power, working in his weak vessels, confounds his craft, and discloses his darkness.

Image Sources (all works in the public domain):

Petrarch from **Petrarch, His Life and Times** by H C. Hollway-Calthrop, New York : G. P. Putnam's Sons & London: Methuen & Co., 1907

Lorenzo de Medici from **Illustrations Historical and Critical of the Life of Lorenzo de' Medici** by William Roscoe, London: T. Cadell, Strand, 1822

Savonarola from **The Renaissance** by Arthur, Count Gobineau, New York: G.P. Putnam's Sons, 1913

Leonardo from **Leonardo Da Vinci** by Eugène Müntz, New York: Charles Scribner's Sons, 1898

Michelangelo from **Raphael and Michelangelo** by Charles C. Perkins, Boston: James R. Osgood and Company, 1878

Machiavelli from **The World's Best Essays**, David J. Brewer, editor, St. Louis, Ferd. P. Kaiser, 1900

Jan Hus from Wikimedia Commons

Luther by Cranach 1520 from **Life of Luther** by Julius Köstlin, London: Longmans, Green, and Co. 1895

Indulgence from **Thirty-five Years of Luther Research** By Johann Michael Reu, Chicago: Wartburg Publishing House, 1917

Title Page – Von der Freihiet from **Thirty-five Years of Luther Research** By Johann Michael Reu, Chicago: Wartburg Publishing House, 1917

Frederick the Wise from **German Masters of Art** by Helen A. Dickinson, New York: Frederick A. Stokes Company, 1914

Title Page of the Babylonian Captivity of the Church from **Martin Luther: The Hero of the Reformation** by Henry Eyster Jacobs, New York and London: G.P. Putnam's Son, 1898

Zwingli from **History of the Christian Church** by Philip Schaff, New York: Charles Scribner's Sons, 1892

Cromwell from **Ten Tudor Statesmen** by Arthur D. Innes, London: Eveleigh Nash, 1906

Calvin from **History of the Reformation: Volume II the Swiss Reformation** by Philip Schaff, New York: Charles Scribner's Sons, 1894

Made in the USA
San Bernardino, CA
10 July 2013